Savings and Investment Information for Teens

TEEN FINANCE SERIES

First Edition

Savings and Investment Information for Teens

Tips for a Successful Financial Life

*Including Facts about Making Money Grow,
with Information about the Economy,
Bank Accounts, Stocks, Bonds, Mutual Funds,
Online Investing, and More*

◆

Edited by Kathryn R. Deering

615 Griswold Street • Detroit, MI 48226

Bibliographic Note

Because this page cannot legibly accommodate all the copyright notices, the Bibliographic Note portion of the Preface constitutes an extension of the copyright notice.

Edited by Kathryn R. Deering

Teen Finance Series

Karen Bellenir, *Managing Editor*
Elizabeth Barbour, *Research and Permissions Coordinator*
Cherry Stockdale, *Permissions Assistant*
Laura Pleva Nielsen, *Index Editor*
EdIndex, Services for Publishers, *Indexers*

* * *

Omnigraphics, Inc.

Matthew P. Barbour, *Senior Vice President*
Kay Gill, *Vice President—Directories*
Kevin Hayes, *Operations Manager*
Leif Gruenberg, *Development Manager*
David P. Bianco, *Marketing Director*

* * *

Peter E. Ruffner, *Publisher*

Frederick G. Ruffner, Jr., *Chairman*

Copyright © 2005 Omnigraphics, Inc.

ISBN 0-7808-0781-2

Library of Congress Cataloging-in-Publication Data

Savings and investment information for teens : tips for a successful
financial life including facts about making money grow, with information
about the economy, bank accounts, stocks, bonds, mutual funds, online
investing, and more / edited by Kathryn R. Deering.
    p. cm. -- (Teen finance series)
    Summary: "Provides information for teens about saving and investing, the
monetary system, and the economy"--Provided by publisher.
    Includes bibliographical references and index.
    ISBN 0-7808-0781-2 (hardcover : alk. paper)
    1. Saving and investment. 2. Teenagers--Finance, Personal. I. Deering,
Kathryn R. II. Series.
    HG4521.S337 2005
    332.024'055--dc22
                                                            2005018743

$$\infty$$

Table Of Contents

Part V: Stocks, Bonds, And Mutual Funds

Part VI: Advanced Investing For Teens

Part VII: If You Need More Information

Preface

About This Book

According to national surveys of economic literacy, teens—like many of their parents—lack a working knowledge of the basics regarding saving and investing their money. They often don't understand how to make good decisions, how to stay ahead of inflation, and how to achieve personal financial success. Teens, however, possess a significant economic advantage that many overlook: time. While they are young, they can start growing their future fortunes. By saving even a few dollars a week, they can begin to build wealth that will multiply in the years ahead.

Savings and Investment Information for Teens encourages young people to establish healthy patterns of saving money. But because simply putting their savings into piggybanks will not keep them ahead of inflation, it also teaches teens how to grow their money by establishing bank accounts and how to invest some of their money to reap higher interest rates. This book presents information about how the economy works and explains the risks and rewards of such investments as stocks, bonds, and mutual funds. *Savings and Investment Information for Teens* can give teens a mastery of the world of investment that many adults never attain.

How To Use This Book

This book is divided into parts and chapters. Parts focus on broad areas of interest; chapters are devoted to single topics within a part.

Part I: Money Basics provides a brief history of money and discusses how coins and currency are manufactured. It introduces the Federal Reserve banking system and explains how "The Fed" controls money supply and interest rates.

Part II: The Economy demystifies the study of economics by explaining the components of an economic system, the influence of government regulation and deregulation, the differences between fiscal policy and monetary policy, and how the federal budget impacts personal finances.

Part III: How To Save And Grow Your Money underlines the importance of saving from a young age—how to make it happen; the comparative features of various kinds of accounts in terms of liquidity, risk, and return; understanding the importance of compound interest; and avoiding debt.

Part IV: Basic Investing For Teens introduces and explains foundational terminology such as "securities," "equity," and "portfolio diversification." It also spells out how teens can get good advice and choose wise investments.

Part V: Stocks, Bonds, And Mutual Funds provides more detail about capital markets and the specialized language of stocks, bonds, and mutual funds, including "load" vs. "no-load" funds.

Part VI: Advanced Investing For Teens describes how to choose a financial advisor; what to look for in investment research (including how to read financial statements and market reports); other forms of investing such as real estate, gold/tangible assets, and insurance/annuities; investment clubs; and online investing.

Part VII: If You Need More Information includes a directory of websites about saving and investing money, a directory of investment organizations, and a list of teen-friendly resources for additional reading.

Bibliographic Note

This volume contains documents and excerpts from publications issued by the following government agencies: Bureau of the Public Debt; Commerce Department, Bureau of Economic Analysis (BEA); Department of the Treasury; United States Securities and Exchange Commission (SEC); United States Government Accountability Office (GAO); and the United States State Department.

In addition, this volume contains copyrighted documents and articles produced by the following organizations: American Savings Education Council; Arizona Corporation Commission; CCH Incorporated; Consumer Action; Consumer Federation of America Foundation; Federal Reserve Bank of Dallas; Federal Reserve Bank of Minneapolis; Federal Reserve Bank of New York; Illinois Secretary of State Securities Department; Investopedia, Inc.; Kansas State University Agricultural Experiment Station and Cooperative Extension Service; Kiplinger Washington Editors, Inc.; Massachusetts Secretary of the Commonwealth Securities Division; Missouri Secretary of State Securities Division; Moneypaper, Inc.; National Association of Securities Dealers (NASD); New York State Attorney General; TeenAnalyst.com; and Visa, U.S.A.

Full citation information is provided on the first page of each chapter. Every effort has been made to secure all necessary rights to reprint the copyrighted material. If any omissions have been made, please contact Omnigraphics to make corrections for future editions.

Acknowledgements

In addition to the organizations listed above, special thanks are due to research and permissions coordinator Elizabeth Barbour and to managing editor Karen Bellenir.

Part One

Money Basics

Chapter 1

What Is Money, Anyway?

The History Of Money

Consider this problem: You catch fish for your food supply, but you're tired of eating it every day. Instead you want to eat some bread. Fortunately, a baker lives next door. Trading the baker some fish for bread is an example of barter, the direct exchange of one good for another.

However, barter is difficult when you try to obtain a good from a producer that doesn't want what you have. For example, how do you get shoes if the shoemaker doesn't like fish? The series of trades required to obtain shoes could be complicated and time-consuming.

Early societies faced these problems. The solution was money. Money is an item, or commodity, that is agreed to be accepted in trade. Over the years, people have used a wide variety of items for money, such as seashells, beads, tea, fish hooks, fur, cattle and even tobacco.

About This Chapter: "The History of Money" is excerpted from *Our Money*, a curriculum unit produced by the Federal Reserve Bank of Minneapolis, n.d. The complete text of this publication is available on the Federal Reserve Bank of Minneapolis website, http://minneapolisfed.org. Reprinted with permission. "What Is Money?" and "The Fight Against Inflation" are excerpted and reprinted from "Everyday Economics: Money, Banking and Monetary Policy," August 2003, a publication of the Federal Reserve Bank of Dallas, http://www.dallasfed.org.

Coins

Most early cultures traded precious metals. In 2500 B.C. the Egyptians produced metal rings for use as money. By 700 B.C., a group of seafaring people called the Lydians became the first in the Western world to make coins. The Lydians used coins to expand their vast trading empire. The Greeks and Romans continued the coining tradition and passed it on to later Western civilizations. Coins were appealing since they were durable, easy to carry, and contained valuable metals.

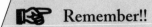 **Remember!!**

Money serves three purposes:

1. *Medium of Exchange:* People accept money in trade for goods and services.

2. *Standard of Value:* The value of a good or service can be measured with money. For example, a car with a price of $2,000 is worth twice as much as a car with a price of $1,000.

3. *Store of Value:* Money can be saved and used in the future.

Source: Federal Reserve Bank of Minneapolis, n.d.

During the 18th century, coins became popular throughout Europe as trading grew. One of the most widely used coins was the Spanish 8-reale. It was often split into pieces or bits to make change. Half a coin was 4 bits, a quarter was 2 bits, a term still used today.

Coins containing precious metals are an example of "commodity money." The item was traded because it held value. For example, the value of the coin depended upon the amount of gold and silver it contained.

Paper Currency

The Chinese were the first to use paper money, beginning in the T'ang Dynasty (618–907 A.D.). During the Ming Dynasty in 1300 A.D., the Chinese placed the emperor's seal and signatures of the treasurers on a crude paper made from mulberry bark.

"Representative money" is tokens or pieces of paper that are not intrinsically valuable themselves, but can be exchanged for a specific commodity, such as gold or silver. In 1715 Maryland, North Carolina, and Virginia issued a "tobacco note" which could be converted to a certain amount of tobacco. This type of money was easier to make large payments and carry than coin or tobacco leaves.

In the late 1800s, the U.S. government issued gold and silver certificates.

"Fiat" money is similar to representative money except it can't be redeemed for a commodity, such as gold or silver. The Federal Reserve notes we use today are an example of fiat money. In 1967 Congress authorized the U.S. Treasury to stop redeeming silver certificates in silver dollars or bullion beginning the following year. By 1970, silver was removed from the production of coins. The old coins were gradually removed from circulation and replaced with new copper-cored coins that were faced or "clad" with layers of an alloy of 75 percent copper and 25 percent nickel—the same alloy used in nickels.

People are willing to accept fiat money in exchange for the goods and services they sell only because they are confident it will be honored when they buy goods and services. The Federal Reserve is responsible for maintaining the integrity of U.S. currency by setting monetary policy—controlling the amount of money in circulation—to keep prices stable. If prices remain stable, people have confidence that the dollar they use to buy goods and services today will buy a similar amount in the future.

What Is Money?

Suppose money as we know it didn't exist. How would you pay for the things you want to buy?

That was the situation in the early days of the American colonies. British money was scarce, so colonists substituted basic products of their local economies that were always in demand—things like tobacco, grain, and fish. For small change, they often received nails and bullets.

♣ It's A Fact!!

Of the over $400 billion issued by the U.S. government currently in circulation, about 95% is in the form of Federal Reserve notes and the remainder is coin.

Source: Federal Reserve Bank of Minneapolis, n.d.

But their barter system had many shortcomings. How many fish would it take to buy a bag of flour or an oil lamp, for example? Suppose the merchant didn't want fish, or they spoiled before he could trade them to someone else. Later, as trade developed with other colonies and countries, colonists used various foreign coins, such as the gold Spanish reales. That's when money as we know it finally gained a foothold in the U.S. economy.

Money is a medium of exchange accepted by the community, meaning it's what people buy things with and sell things for. Money provides a standard for measuring value, so that the worth of different goods and services can be compared. And lastly, money is a store of value that can be saved for later purchases.

The young United States experimented with a variety of monetary mechanisms for well over a century before settling on today's system, which is based on coins, paper currency and money in bank checking accounts. The early government tried unsuccessfully several times to make paper money work, but people relied mostly on gold, silver, and copper coins because they were made of precious metals that had intrinsic value.

Today, though, our coins don't contain any gold or silver. You can see this for yourself by looking at the edge of a dime or quarter; you'll see a copper core, sandwiched between silvery nickel. The metal value of modern American coins is much less than its worth as money. American currency no longer is backed by gold or silver either, but it no longer really matters.

That's because what gives money real value is its purchasing power, not what it's made of. In fact, any economy's health can be measured not by how much money people earn, but by how much their money buys. The overall assortment and quantity of goods and services your money lets you buy reflects your standard of living.

Like diamonds, money is relatively scarce—on purpose—and that's just what makes it valuable. You as an individual want to earn as much as you can, of course. But the national economy can actually have too much money. When the amount of money circulating grows faster than the rate at which goods and services are produced, the result is inflation.

✎ What's It Mean?

Money Supply: The amount of money (coins, paper currency, and checking accounts) that is in circulation in the economy.

Source: U.S. State Department, 2001.

The Fight Against Inflation

The goal of the complex U.S. monetary system [see chapter 3] is simple: to keep the economy stable and growing at a pace that can be sustained without inflation. Economic security underlies nearly every hope and dream people have. It enables businesses to know they can afford to hire more workers, and it lets people plan for the future. If you are saving for college now, for instance, you want to know how much you need altogether and how much you must set aside each month. An inflationary economy can wreck your plans—what you've saved isn't nearly enough anymore, and you don't know how much more will be needed.

A healthy monetary policy, sensitive to changing economic conditions, helps prevent such worries.

Chapter 2

How Is Money Made?

The United States Mint produces more than 28 billion coins for general circulation each year. These are made in the United States Mints at Philadelphia and Denver. While most of the coins the United States Mint produces are for general circulation, the United States Mint also produces bullion coins and limited editions of coins sold to collectors as numismatic items [for collectors]. The United States Mint facilities in Philadelphia, Pennsylvania; Denver, Colorado; San Francisco, California; and West Point, New York produce numismatic items. Bullion coins are produced at the Mint facilities in San Francisco and West Point.

The Treasury Department prints paper currency at the Bureau of Engraving and Printing headquarters, located in Washington, D.C. The Bureau of Engraving and Printing is responsible for designing and printing our paper currency. There is also a satellite production facility located in Fort Worth, Texas, which began operations in January 1991. The Bureau of Engraving and Printing produces approximately 37 million currency notes each day with a face value of about $696 million, and 45% of these notes are the $1 denomination. About 95% of the currency notes printed each year are used to replace notes that are already in circulation.

About This Chapter: Excerpted from undated Fact Sheets and FAQs from the U.S. Treasury Department, as follows: "Coins: Production and Circulation," "Currency: Production and Circulation," "Coins: Buying, Selling, and Redeeming," "Manufacturing Process for U.S. Coins," "Mint and Other Coin Production Facilities," and "Distribution of Currency and Coins;" accessed on March 4, 2005.

How Coins Are Made

The one-cent coin is made of copper-plated zinc. (This is a major alteration that was made in 1982, when it was changed from the standard alloy of 95% copper and 5% zinc.) The five-cent coin is composed of a homogeneous alloy containing 75% copper and 25% nickel. The ten-cent coin, quarter-dollar coin, half-dollar coin and one-dollar coin are all "clad" coins, produced from three coin strips that are bonded together and rolled to the required thickness. The face of these coins is 75% copper and 25% nickel, and the core, which is visible along the edges of the coins, is composed of pure copper.

All of the materials used for producing coins are purchased from commercial manufacturers. The United States Mint obtains one-cent coin blanks already made, but produces the blanks for five-cent coins and the cupronickel [copper nickel alloy] clad coins from strip. Coin strip is fed into high-speed automatic presses which cut the coin blanks, known as *planchets.*

The planchets are softened by annealing in a special furnace, then they are cleaned in large rotating barrels which contain a chemical solution that washes and polishes them, and then they are dried.

Next, the planchets are put through an edge-rolling operation in the *upsetting machine.* This gives them the familiar thickened edge found on the one-cent coins and five-cent coins. It also serves two other purposes. The edge hardens during the upsetting process, thereby preventing soft metal from squirting between the collar and the dies during stamping. It also removes any burrs and smoothes the edge, making it easier to automatically feed them into the high-speed coin presses.

Finally, the upset planchets go to the coinage presses, where with a single stroke, they are stamped with the designs and inscriptions that make them into coins. Most of the presses are equipped to strike four coins simultaneously, while others simultaneously strike two coins.

Generally, the manufacturing process is the same for all denominations, except that the edges of dimes, quarters, half-dollars and dollars are marked

♣ It's A Fact!!
Coin Production Process

There are six stages to the manufacture of a U.S. coin. Every coin is blanked, annealed, upset, struck, inspected, and finally, counted and bagged.

Step 1—Blanking: The U.S. Mint buys strips of metal approximately 13 inches wide and 1,500 feet long to manufacture the nickel, dime, quarter, half-dollar, and dollar. The strips come rolled in a coil. Each coil is fed through a blanking press, which punches out round discs called blanks. The leftover strip, called webbing, is shredded and recycled. To manufacture pennies, the Mint buys ready-made planchets after supplying fabricators with copper and zinc.

Step 2—Annealing, Washing and Drying: The blanks are heated in an annealing furnace to soften them. Then they are run through a washer and dryer.

Step 3—Upsetting: The blanks go through an upsetting mill. This raises a rim around their edges, turning the blanks into planchets.

Step 4—Striking: Finally, the planchets go to the coining press. Here, they are stamped with the designs and inscriptions that make them genuine United States legal tender coins.

Step 5—Inspection: A press operator uses a magnifying glass to spot-check each batch of new coins.

Step 6—Counting and Bagging: An automatic counting machine counts the coins and drops them into bags. The bags are sealed, loaded on pallets, and taken by forklifts to be stored. New coins are shipped by truck to Federal Reserve banks. From there, the coins go to your local bank.

with tiny ridges. This process is known as *reeding*. It is done by a collar, which is a part of the stamping operation. More than just a decoration, reeding was originally intended as a preventative measure to discourage the illegal shaving or clipping of the precious metal in the gold and silver coins. It has been retained on today's cupronickel-clad coins not only in deference to a long-standing practice dating back to colonial days, but also as a distinct aid to the visually handicapped.

After striking, each coin is inspected. The coins are then counted and bagged. Each bag is weighed before shipment to ensure that it contains the correct number of coins. One-dollar coin bags contain $2,000; bags of ten-cent coins, quarter-dollar coins and half-dollar coins contain $1,000; five-cent coin bags contain $200; and one-cent coin bags contain $50. The canvas bags used to ship coins are purchased from commercial suppliers.

The final step in the manufacturing process is when the United States Mint ships the newly made coins to the Federal Reserve banks for distribution into the economy through the banking system.

About Paper Currency

The paper that the Bureau of Engraving and Printing uses to produce our currency is distinctive. A paper manufacturer produces it according to Bureau of Engraving and Printing specifications. It is composed of 75% cotton and 25% linen. The paper also contains red and blue fibers of various lengths that are evenly distributed throughout the paper.

All denominations of paper currency notes printed since 1929 are the same size, measuring approximately 2.61 inches (6.63 centimeters) by

♣ It's A Fact!!

• The present denominations of currency in production are $1, $2, $5, $10, $20, $50 and $100. U. S. Bureau of Engraving and Printing has no plans to change the denominations in use today.

• The largest denomination of currency ever printed was the $100,000 Series 1934 Gold Certificate featuring the portrait of President Wilson. The notes were used only for official transactions between Federal Reserve Banks and were not circulated among the general public.

• The Treasury Department is no longer printing currency in denominations of $500, $1,000, $5,000 and $10,000. Production of these denominations stopped during World War II. Their main purpose was for bank transfer payments. With the arrival of more secure transfer technologies, however, they were no longer needed for that purpose. While these notes are legal tender and may still be found in circulation today, the Federal Reserve Banks remove them from circulation and destroy them as they are received.

6.14 inches (15.60 centimeters). Each note is 0.0043 inches thick, and a stack of currency notes one mile high would contain over 14.5 million notes. If all of the currency notes printed were laid end to end, they would stretch around the earth's equator approximately 24 times. Each currency note, regardless of its denomination, weighs about one gram. There are 454 grams in one U.S. pound, so there should be 454 notes in a pound.

> ♣ **It's A Fact!!**
>
> *Why are U. S. paper currency notes printed using green ink?*
>
> When the currency notes in use today were first introduced in 1929, pigment of that color was readily available in large quantity. Also, the color is high in its resistance to chemical and physical changes. Besides, the public psychologically identified the color green with the strong and stable credit of the government. There is no definite reason that green was chosen originally for our currency notes, except that it made counterfeiting more difficult.

Both the United States Mint (coins) and the Bureau of Engraving and Printing (currency), both of which are branches of the Treasury Department, must produce coins and currency in quantities sufficient to fill the needs of the public.

Distribution Of Currency And Coins

After production, the Treasury ships the coins and currency notes directly to Federal Reserve banks and branches. The Federal Reserve then releases them as required by the commercial banking system. The demand for money by the public varies from day to day and from week to week. There are even differences from season to season. Banks are usually first to feel the impact of the public's demand for cash. To meet the needs of the public, banks turn to their regional Federal Reserve bank for coins and currency when their supplies are low.

Coin Distribution

The Federal Reserve banks, which are responsible for putting coins and paper money into circulation and also for withdrawing them from circulation when they are worn out.

♣ It's A Fact!!

Federal Reserve banks store the coins until they need to fill orders from the commercial banks in their district. The Federal Reserve banks fill these orders from their vault stocks of both new and circulated coins. They fill the orders without regard to date or mint mark. Coin shipments leave the Federal Reserve banks by armored car, registered mail, or express.

When a private bank needs coins to provide to you and its other customers, it purchases them from a Federal Reserve bank. Banks have checking accounts at the Federal Reserve banks, just as you do at your bank. To buy cash for you, your bank uses special checkbook money called a "reserve balance." The coins make their way back to the Federal Reserve bank at some point because banks often accumulate more cash than they need for day-to-day transactions. They deposit the excess cash into their checking account at a local branch of the Federal Reserve bank until their customers need it. Coins circulate from the Federal Reserve bank to the private banks to you and back again until they are worn out, unfit for circulation. The Federal Reserve replaces those coins by ordering new ones from the U.S. Mint—and once those coins are minted, a new circulation cycle begins. A circulating coin generally lasts thirty years or longer.

To assure smooth and sufficient flow of coins, the United States Mint continually revises its techniques for estimating coinage demands. In planning production and scheduling coin shipments, the United States Mint uses long-range economic indicators and historic seasonal trends such as Christmas to decide how many coins to manufacture. Experience has shown that forecasting coin demand cannot be done with absolute accuracy. This means that estimates must also include an amount sufficient to provide an inventory that would absorb any deviation that might occur. Armored carriers usually transport ten-cent coins, quarter-dollar coins and half-dollar coins, while tractor-trailer trucks transport one-cent coins and five-cent coins.

Federal Reserve banks arrange in advance to received new coin shipments for the coming year. They do this in amounts and on a time schedule to maintain their inventories at the required levels. Under this arrangement, the United States Mint can schedule its production schedule efficiently. Even with advance planning, there are occasions when coin shortages arise. The Federal Reserve banks must follow the advance shipping schedules. Except in an emergency, there are no provisions for obtaining additional coins.

If a commercial bank has excess coins on hand, they may return the coins to the Federal Reserve bank. It then sorts the coins for fitness. They return badly worn or bent coins to the United States Mint, which melts them down and makes them into new coins. Also, the banks remove foreign and counterfeit coins from circulation. According to Federal Reserve sources, over 20 billion coins valued at well over $2 billion pass through their coin processing units each year.

Currency Distribution

Every summer, the currency departments at each of the 12 Federal Reserve banks make recommendations about future currency needs. The banks then place orders with the Comptroller of the Currency. After reviewing the requests, the Comptroller forwards them to the Bureau of Engraving and Printing. It then produces the appropriate denominations of currency notes bearing the seal of the Federal Reserve bank placing the order. The Federal Reserve bank pays only the cost of producing the notes. These Federal Reserve notes are claims on the assets of the issuing Federal Reserve bank and liabilities of the United States government.

♣ It's A Fact!! Shredded Currency

The Federal Reserve System destroys worn currency notes at some of its various banks located throughout the country. Certain Federal Reserve banks sell it only under contract to buyers who will purchase all of the residue for at least a one year period. (It is not readily available for distribution nor for sale in small quantities to individuals.)

Shredded currency may only be used under certain circumstances. One permitted use is recycling it (mixing it with other materials) to form a useful manufactured product such as roofing shingles or insulation. In addition, the shredded currency may be placed in firmly sealed containers as novelty items like pens, ornaments and jewelry.

The law requires that each Federal Reserve bank hold collateral that equals at least 100% of the value of the currency it issues. Most of that collateral is in U.S. government securities owned by the Federal Reserve System. It also includes gold certificates, special drawing rights or other "eligible" paper. Eligible paper can be bills of exchange or promissory notes, and some foreign government or agency securities obtained by the Federal Reserve.

You can read more about the Federal Reserve system of banks in the next chapter.

Chapter 3

The Federal Reserve System And Money

Money, Banking, And Monetary Policy

Money, the banking system, and monetary policy must work together smoothly for the economy to run well. Money makes it possible for people to exchange goods and services without having to rely on a system of bartering. Banking provides a means for savers to lend their money to borrowers and earn interest in the process, and it gives borrowers a place to go for loans. The aim of monetary policy is to ensure that there is sufficient money in the economy to keep it growing, but not so much that the economy overheats. When the economy overheats, the result is inflation. Inflation—too much money chasing too few goods—creates an inefficient price system. It also distorts decision-making, reduces productivity and lowers the economy's long-term rate of growth. This results in lower living standards for everyone.

About This Chapter: This chapter begins with text excerpted and reprinted from "Everyday Economics: Money, Banking and Monetary Policy," August 2003, a publication of the Federal Reserve Bank of Dallas, http://www.dallasfed.org; "An Independent Agency," is excerpted from *Outline of the U.S. Economy*, a publication of the Bureau of International Information Programs, U. S. State Department, February 2001; "Goals Of The Fed" is excerpted and reprinted from "Interest Rates: An Introduction," an online financial education publication of the Federal Reserve Bank of New York, http://www.newyorkfed.org, April 2004.

The Fed's Role

Keeping prices stable is part of the job of the Federal Reserve ("The Fed"), which was created by Congress in 1913. There had been two attempts at establishing a central bank in the United States in the 19th century, but politics killed them even though they were successful. Back then, state-chartered banks issued their own paper money backed only by their individual gold and silver reserves. As a result, there were once more than 10,000 different kinds of bank notes in circulation.

Suppose you owned a store in those days. How would you know which banks had enough gold reserves to make their currency worth its face value? Should you decrease the value of bills from a weaker bank? And how would you keep track of all those bank notes? You can imagine the shopkeeper's dilemma. If a bank went broke, its currency was instantly worthless, and those who held its notes could lose everything.

Naturally, people hurried to withdraw their money at the first hint of trouble in the economy. The result was periodic financial panics that could devastate the national economy for years. Finally, after a particularly bad panic in 1907, Congress decided to solve the problem with the creation of the Federal Reserve System. The Fed was established to provide for a safer and more flexible banking and monetary system.

With the Fed as a safeguard, banks can perform their proper role of bringing savers and borrowers together for the benefit of both. For any economy to be successful, a country first needs political stability so its citizens feel safe; then it needs a stable financial system that includes both trustworthy money and reliable financial institutions. Healthy, profitable banks, therefore, are a vital part of the nation's economic welfare.

Banks provide many services, but for most people, banking consists of depositing their salaries into checking accounts and writing checks on that account to buy things that cost more money than they want to carry in their wallets. People also commonly have savings accounts in which they deposit money they don't need right away or they are saving for a particular purpose. The bank pays interest, or a price paid for use of the money, on savings accounts and often on checking accounts, too.

> ### ✎ What's It Mean?
>
> <u>Depression</u>: A severe decline in general economic activity in terms of magnitude and/or length.
>
> <u>Economic Growth</u>: An increase in a nation's capacity to produce goods and services.
>
> <u>Panic</u>: A series of unexpected cash withdrawals from a bank caused by a sudden decline in depositor confidence or fear that the bank will be closed by the chartering agency, i.e. many depositors withdraw cash almost simultaneously. Since the cash reserve a bank keeps on hand is only a small fraction of its deposits, a large number of withdrawals in a short period of time can deplete available cash and force the bank to close and possibly go out of business.
>
> Source: U.S. State Department, 2001.

Very little of this money is kept in the bank's vault, however. While the Federal Reserve requires banks to keep a specified percentage of customer deposits on hand to meet routine withdrawals, they lend the excess. Banks, like any other business, must make a profit to stay in business. Their profit comes from interest people pay on the money they borrow.

How Banks Create Money

Banks actually create money when they lend it. Here's how it works: Most of a bank's loans are made to its own customers and are deposited in their checking accounts. Because the loan becomes a new deposit, just like a paycheck does, the bank once again holds a small percentage of that new amount in reserve and again lends the remainder to someone else, repeating the money-creation process many times.

The tricky part of monetary policy is making sure there is enough money in the economy, but not too much. When people have the money to demand more products than the economy can supply, prices go up and the resulting inflation hurts everyone. While in the United States we get concerned when inflation climbs above 3 percent a year, we've been more fortunate than some other countries. Just imagine trying to survive in post-World War II Hungary, for instance, where inflation for a while averaged nearly 20,000 percent per month.

Monetary Policy And The Economy

Controlling the money supply to help the economy grow steadily without inflation is the Federal Reserve's job. Called setting monetary policy, the Fed does this primarily by buying and selling Treasury securities on the open market. Buying securities on the open market can make it easier for banks to loan money and can give the economy a boost, while selling securities can restrict lending and can help cool down an overheated economy. When the Fed buys securities, the Fed pays for them by crediting the reserve accounts of the sellers' banks. With more money in their reserves, banks can lend more. By contrast, when the Fed sells securities, the Fed collects for the sale by debiting the reserve accounts of the buyers' banks. With less money in their reserves, banks can't lend as much.

Conducting monetary policy is a tremendous responsibility, for the nation's economic health is at stake. You can see why politicians might want to control the money supply for short-term interests. For that reason, the Fed, by law, is not government controlled or funded by Congress. While it is a centralized banking system comprised of 12 regional banks, it is independent in operation.

Besides conducting monetary policy, the Fed also acts as the bankers' bank. As people withdraw more currency to buy things when the economy is booming, the banks in turn pull additional currency from their own reserve accounts with the Fed. When the economy slows down and people increase their savings, banks return the surplus to their reserve accounts. The Fed handles check processing for banks as well, to make sure the billions and billions of dollars in checks written each year move smoothly from one bank to another.

The Fed has other functions also. It helps regulate and supervise banks to keep them financially sound, and it serves as the government's banker by maintaining the U.S. Treasury's "checking account."

An Independent Agency

The Federal Reserve System is an independent U.S. government agency. The Fed includes 12 regional Federal Reserve banks and 25 Federal Reserve bank branches. All nationally chartered commercial banks are required by law to be members of the Federal Reserve system; membership is optional for state-chartered banks. In general, a bank that is a member of the Federal

Reserve System uses the Reserve Bank in its region in the same way that a person uses a bank in his or her community.

The Federal Reserve Board of Governors administers the Federal Reserve system. It has seven members who are appointed by the president to serve overlapping 14-year terms. Its most important monetary policy decisions are made by the Federal Open Market Committee (FOMC), which consists of the seven governors, the president of the Federal Reserve Bank of New York, and presidents of four other Federal Reserve banks who serve on a rotating basis. Although the Federal Reserve system periodically must report on its actions to Congress, the governors are, by law, independent from Congress and the president. Reinforcing this independence, the Fed conducts its most important policy discussions in private and often discloses them only after a period of time has passed. It also raises all of its own operating expenses from investment income and fees for its own services.

✎ What's It Mean?

Central Bank: A country's principal monetary authority, responsible for such key functions as issuing currency and regulating the supply of credit in the economy.

Commercial Bank: A bank that offers a broad range of deposit accounts, including checking, savings, and time deposits, and extends loans to individuals and businesses—in contrast to investment banking firms such as brokerage firms, which generally are involved in arranging for the sale of corporate or municipal securities.

Discount Rate: The interest rate paid by commercial banks to borrow funds from Federal Reserve Banks.

Federal Reserve Bank: One of the 12 operating arms of the Federal Reserve system, located throughout the United States, that together with their 25 branches carry out various functions of the U.S. central bank system.

Federal Reserve System: The principal monetary authority (central bank) of the United States, which issues currency and regulates the supply of credit in the economy. It is made up of a seven-member Board of Governors in Washington, D.C., 12 regional Federal Reserve banks, and their 25 branches.

Source: U.S. State Department, 2001.

The Federal Reserve has three main tools for maintaining control over the supply of money and credit in the economy, as follows:

- The most important is known as *open market operations*, or the buying and selling of government securities. To increase the supply of money, the Federal Reserve buys government securities from banks, other businesses, or individuals, paying for them with a check (a new source of money that it prints); when the Fed's checks are deposited in banks, they create new reserves—a portion of which banks can lend or invest, thereby increasing the amount of money in circulation. On the other hand, if the Fed wishes to reduce the money supply, it sells government securities to banks, collecting reserves from them. Because they have lower reserves, banks must reduce their lending, and the money supply drops accordingly.

- The Fed also can control the money supply by specifying what reserves deposit-taking institutions must set aside either as currency in their vaults or as deposits at their regional Reserve banks. Raising *reserve requirements* forces banks to withhold a larger portion of their funds, thereby reducing the money supply, while lowering requirements works the opposite way to increase the money supply. Banks often lend each other money over night to meet their reserve requirements. The rate on such loans, known as the "federal funds rate," is a key gauge of how "tight" or "loose" monetary policy is at a given moment.

- The Fed's third tool is the *discount rate*, or the interest rate that commercial banks pay to borrow funds from Reserve Banks. By raising or lowering the discount rate, the Fed can promote or discourage borrowing and thus alter the amount of revenue available to banks for making loans.

✎ What's It Mean?

Open Trading System: A trading system in which countries allow fair and nondiscriminatory access to each other's markets.

Securities: Paper certificates or electronic records showing ownership of stocks or bonds.

Source: U.S. State Department, 2001.

These tools allow the Federal Reserve to expand or contract the amount of money and credit in the U.S. economy. If the money supply rises, credit is said to be loose. In this situation, interest rates tend to drop, business spending and consumer spending tend to rise, and employment increases; if the economy already is operating near its full capacity, too much money can lead to inflation, or a decline in the value of the dollar. When the money supply contracts, on the other hand, credit is tight. In this situation, interest rates tend to rise, spending levels off or declines, and inflation abates; if the economy is operating below its capacity, tight money can lead to rising unemployment.

Many factors complicate the ability of the Federal Reserve to use monetary policy to promote specific goals, however. For one thing, money takes many different forms, and it often is unclear which one to target. In its most basic form, money consists of coins and paper currency. A more important component of the money supply consists of checking deposits, or bookkeeping entries held in banks and other financial institutions. Individuals can make payments by writing checks, which essentially instruct their banks to pay given sums to the checks' recipients. Money also includes money market funds, which are shares in pools of short-term securities, as well as a variety of other assets that can be converted easily into currency on short notice.

The amount of money held in different forms can change from time to time, depending on preferences and other factors that may or may not have any importance to the overall economy. Further complicating the Fed's task, changes in the money supply affect the economy only after a lag of uncertain duration.

Goals Of The Fed

So we see that monetary policy consists of the efforts of the Fed to influence money and credit conditions in the economy in order to achieve the country's macroeconomic goals.

Those goals include stable prices, high employment, and maximum sustainable growth in the economy. Prices are considered stable when they change slowly enough so that people pay little attention to price changes in making economic decisions.

Growth can be measured by the rate of change of real gross domestic product (GDP)—that is, the output of the economy adjusted for changes in prices. The level of sustainable growth, the rate at which the economy can grow without causing the inflation rate to accelerate, is determined by how fast the hours worked by the U.S. labor force and output per worker grow.

The Fed formulates monetary policy by setting a target for the federal funds rate, the interest rate that banks change one another for very short-term loans.

✔ **Quick Tip**

For a diagram with a thorough explanation of how the decisions of the Federal Open Market Committee (the part of the Fed that makes monetary policy) affect the economy, click on www.newyorkfed.org/research/econ_pol/2002/502indx.html and then on "The Monetary Transmission Mechanism: Some Answers and Further Questions," and go to the second page of the article.

Source: Federal Reserve Bank of New York, 2004.

Because the fed funds rate is what banks pay when they borrow, it affects the rates they charge when they lend. Those rates, in turn, influence other short-term interest rates in the economy, and, with a lag, economic activity and the rate of inflation.

The Fed implements monetary policy by using open market operations, the sale or purchase of previously issued U.S. government securities, to influence the amounts that banks can lend, thereby raising or lowering the federal funds rate. When the Fed buys securities, it injects funds into the banking system, giving banks more to lend and putting downward pressure on the fed funds rate; when it sells securities, it does the opposite.

The results of the Fed's monetary policy actions cannot be predicted with precision. The Federal Reserve's influence over short-term interest rates can create conditions conducive to economic growth, but ever-changing market and political conditions, here and abroad, also heavily influence the millions of economic and financial decisions of households and businesses.

What Is The Discount Rate?

The Federal Reserve sets the discount rate, which is the interest rate that banks pay on short-term loans from the Fed. The Fed often makes identical changes in its target for the federal funds rate and in the discount rate. Thus, discount rate cuts typically reflect the Fed's desire to stimulate the economy, and increases in the discount rate often reflect the Fed's concern over the threat of inflation.

For monetary policy purposes, the discount rate is not as important as the federal funds rate, because banks don't borrow very much from the Fed.

The Federal Reserve stresses that it is a "lender of last resort." That means the banks have to try to borrow elsewhere before they come to borrow from the Fed, and it means also that a bank should not ask to borrow from the Fed too often.

✔ Quick Tip

To learn more about monetary policy, click on http://www.kc.frb.org/fed101html/Monetary/basics.htm.

When was the most recent change in monetary policy? What did the Fed do on that occasion? Find the answers at www.federal reserve.gov/fomc/fundsrate.htm.

Source: Federal Reserve Bank of New York, 2004.

Part Two

The Economy

Chapter 4

What Does "The Economy" Mean?

In every economic system, entrepreneurs and managers bring together natural resources, labor, and technology to produce and distribute goods and services. But the way these different elements are organized and used also reflects a nation's political ideals and its culture.

The United States is often described as a "capitalist" economy, a term coined by 19th-century German economist and social theorist Karl Marx to describe a system in which a small group of people who control large amounts of money, or capital, make the most important economic decisions. Marx contrasted capitalist economies to "socialist" ones, which vest more power in the political system.

While those categories, though oversimplified, have elements of truth to them, they are far less relevant today. If the pure capitalism described by Marx ever existed, it has long since disappeared, as governments in the United States and many other countries have intervened in their economies to limit concentrations of power and address many of the social problems associated with unchecked private commercial interests. As a result, the American economy is perhaps better described as a "mixed" economy, with government playing an important role along with private enterprise.

About This Chapter: This chapter is excerpted and adapted from "Chapter 2: How the U.S. Economy Works" and "Glossary of Economic Terms" in *Outline of the U.S. Economy*, a publication of the Bureau of International Information Programs, U. S. State Department, February 2001.

Although Americans often disagree about exactly where to draw the line between their beliefs in both free enterprise and government management, the mixed economy they have developed has been remarkably successful.

✎ What's It Mean?

Capitalism: An economic system in which the means of production are privately owned and controlled and which is characterized by competition and the profit motive.

Mixed Economy: An economic system in which both the government and private enterprise play important roles with regard to production, consumption, investment, and savings.

Socialism: An economic system in which the basic means of production are primarily owned and controlled collectively, usually by government under some system of central planning.

Basic Ingredients Of The U.S. Economy

Natural Resources. The first ingredient of a nation's economic system is its *natural resources*. The United States is rich in mineral resources and fertile farm soil, and it is blessed with a moderate climate. It also has extensive coastlines and waterways, which have helped shape the country's economic growth over the years and have helped bind America's 50 individual states together in a single economic unit.

Labor. The second ingredient is *labor*, which converts natural resources into goods. The number of available workers and, more importantly, their productivity, help determine the health of an economy.

Although the United States has experienced some periods of high unemployment and other times when labor was in short supply, immigrants have tended to come when jobs were plentiful. Often willing to work for somewhat lower wages than acculturated workers, they generally prospered, earning far more than they would have in their native lands. The nation prospered as well, so that the economy grew fast enough to absorb even more newcomers.

The state of the nation's economy hinges on various aspects of labor:

- The *quality* of available labor—how hard people are willing to work and how skilled they are—is at least as important to a country's economic success as the number of workers. In the early days of the United States, frontier life required hard work. A strong emphasis on education, including technical and vocational training, also contributed to America's economic success, as did a willingness to experiment and to change.

- Labor *mobility* has likewise been important to the capacity of the American economy to adapt to changing conditions. When immigrants flooded labor markets on the East Coast, many workers moved inland, often to farmland waiting to be tilled. Similarly, economic opportunities in industrial, northern cities attracted black Americans from southern farms in the first half of the 20th century.

Labor-force quality continues to be an important issue. Today, Americans consider "human capital" a key to success in numerous modern, high-technology industries. As a result, government leaders and business officials increasingly stress the importance of education and training to develop workers with the kind of nimble minds and adaptable skills needed in new industries such as computers and telecommunications.

Business Management. But natural resources and labor account for only part of an economic system. These resources must be organized and directed as efficiently as possible.

The traditional managerial structure in America is based on a top-down chain of command; authority flows from the chief executive in the boardroom, who makes sure that the entire business runs smoothly and efficiently, through various lower levels of management responsible for coordinating different parts of the enterprise, down to the foreman on the shop floor. Numerous tasks are divided among different divisions and workers.

Many enterprises continue to operate with this traditional structure, but others have taken changing views on management. Facing heightened global competition, American businesses are seeking more flexible organization structures, especially in high-technology industries that employ skilled workers and must develop, modify, and even customize products rapidly. Excessive hierarchy and division of labor increasingly are thought to inhibit creativity. As a result, many companies have "flattened" their organizational structures, reduced the number of managers, and delegated more authority to interdisciplinary teams of workers.

Corporations

> ### ✎ What's It Mean?
>
> Human Capital: The health, strength, education, training, and skills that people bring to their jobs.
>
> Industrial Revolution: The emergence of the factory system of production, particularly from about 1770 to 1830, in which workers were brought together in one plant and supplied with tools, machines, and materials with which they worked in return for wages. More broadly, the term applies to continuing structural economic change in the world economy.
>
> Labor Force: As measured in the United States, the total number of people employed or looking for work.

Before managers or teams of workers can produce anything, of course, they must be organized into business ventures. In the United States, the corporation has proved to be an effective device for accumulating the funds needed to launch a new business or to expand an existing one. The corporation is a voluntary association of owners, known as stockholders, who form a business enterprise governed by a complex set of rules and customs.

Corporations must have financial resources to acquire the resources they need to produce goods or services. They raise the necessary capital largely by selling stock (ownership shares in their assets) or bonds (long-term loans of money) to insurance companies, banks, pension funds, individuals, and other investors. Some institutions, especially banks, also lend money directly to corporations or other business enterprises. Federal and state governments have developed detailed rules and regulations to ensure the safety and soundness of this financial system and to foster the free flow of information so investors can make well-informed decisions.

A Mixed Economy: The Role Of The Market

The United States is said to have a *mixed economy* because privately owned businesses and government both play important roles. Indeed, some of the most enduring debates of American economic history focus on the relative roles of the public and private sectors.

The American free enterprise system emphasizes private ownership of businesses. The nation is sometimes characterized as having a "consumer economy."

This emphasis on private ownership arises, in part, from American beliefs about personal freedom. From the time the nation was created, Americans have feared excessive government power, and they have sought to limit government's authority over individuals.

Americans believe that with unfettered economic forces, supply and demand will determine the prices of goods and services. Prices, in turn, tell businesses what to produce; if people want more of a particular good than the economy is producing, the price of the good rises. That catches the attention of new or other companies that, sensing an opportunity to earn profits, start producing more of that good. On the other hand, if people want less of the good, prices fall and less competitive producers either go out of business or start producing different goods. Such a system is called a market economy.

A socialist economy, in contrast, is characterized by more government ownership and central planning. Most Americans are convinced that social-ist economies are inherently less efficient because government, which relies on tax revenues, is far less likely than private businesses to heed price signals or to feel the discipline imposed by market forces.

The U.S. economy has changed. The population and the labor force have shifted dramatically away from farms to cities, from fields to factories, and, above all, to service industries. In today's economy, the providers of personal and public services far outnumber producers of agricultural and manufac-tured goods. As the economy has grown more complex, statistics also reveal over the last century a sharp long-term trend away from self-employment toward working for others.

✎ **What's It Mean?**

Free Enterprise System: An economic system characterized by private ownership of property and productive resources, the profit motive to stimulate production, competition to ensure efficiency, and the forces of supply and demand to direct the production and distribution of goods and services.

Market Economy: The national economy of a country that relies on market forces to determine levels of production, consumption, investment, and savings without government intervention.

Government's Role In The Economy

Americans have always believed that some services are better performed by public rather than private enterprise.

Government often is asked to intervene in the economy to correct situations in which the price system does not work. It regulates monopolies and it uses antitrust laws to control or break up other business combinations that become so powerful that they can surmount market forces. [See chapter 5 for a more complete explanation of government regulation.]

Government also addresses issues beyond the reach of market forces. It provides *welfare* and *unemployment* benefits to people who cannot support themselves, either because they encounter problems in their personal lives or lose their jobs as a result of economic upheaval; it pays much of the cost of *medical care* for the aged and those who live in poverty; it regulates private industry to limit air and water *pollution*; it provides low-cost *loans* to people who suffer losses as a result of natural disasters; and it has played the leading role in the *exploration of space*, which is too expensive for any private enterprise to handle.

While consumers and producers make most decisions that mold the economy, government activities have a powerful effect on the U.S. economy in at least four areas.

Stabilization And Growth

The federal government guides the overall pace of economic activity, attempting to maintain steady growth, high levels of employment, and price stability. By adjusting spending and tax rates (fiscal policy) or managing the money supply and controlling the use of credit (monetary policy) [see chapter 6], it can slow down or speed up the economy's rate of growth—in the process, affecting the level of prices and employment.

Until the 1960s, government had great faith in fiscal policy—manipulation of government revenues to influence the economy. Since then, a period of high inflation, high unemployment, and huge government deficits has weakened confidence in fiscal policy as a tool for regulating the overall pace of economic activity. Instead, monetary policy—controlling the nation's money supply through such devices as interest rates—has assumed growing prominence. Monetary policy is directed by the nation's central bank, known as the Federal Reserve Board [see chapter 3], with considerable independence from the president and the Congress.

Direct Services

Each level of government provides many direct services. The federal government is responsible for national defense, backs research that often leads to the development of new products, conducts space exploration, and runs programs designed to help workers develop workplace skills and find jobs.

State governments are responsible for the construction and maintenance of most highways. State, county, or city governments play the leading role in financing and operating public schools. Local governments are primarily responsible for police and fire protection.

❖ It's A Fact!!

In a mixed economy, individuals help guide the economy not only through the choices they make as consumers but through the votes they cast for officials who shape economic policy. Consumers voice concerns about product safety, environmental threats posed by certain industrial practices, and potential health risks; government responds by creating agencies to protect consumer interests and promote the general public welfare.

Direct Assistance

Government also provides many kinds of help to businesses and individuals. It offers low-interest loans and technical assistance to small businesses, and it provides loans to help students attend college. Government-sponsored enterprises encourage lending for home mortgages. Government also actively promotes exports and seeks to prevent foreign countries from maintaining trade barriers that restrict imports.

Government supports individuals who cannot adequately care for themselves. Social Security, which is financed by a tax on employers and employees, accounts for the largest portion of Americans' retirement income. The Medicare program pays for many of the medical costs of the elderly. The Medicaid program finances medical care for low-income families. In many states, government maintains institutions for the mentally ill or people with severe disabilities. The federal government provides food stamps to help poor families obtain food, and the federal and state governments jointly provide welfare grants to support low-income parents with children.

♣ **It's A Fact!!**

In the United States, government is primarily responsible for the following areas:

- the administration of justice

- education (although there are many private schools and training centers)

- the road system

- social statistical reporting

- national defense

♣ **It's A Fact!!**

The gross domestic product (GDP) measures the total output of goods and services in a given year. But while these figures help measure the economy's health, they do not gauge every aspect of national well-being. GDP shows the market value of the goods and services an economy produces, but it does not weigh a nation's quality of life. And some important variables—personal happiness and security, for instance, or a clean environment and good health—are entirely beyond its scope.

You And The Economy

All of us are citizens—of a village, a city, a county or similar region, a state or province, and a nation. As such, we live together as neighbors, workers, and consumers. Therefore, "the economy" is part of the fabric of our human life, whether we realize it or not. (This would be true even if we still lived in a primitive, barter-based society.) Although the subject may seem to be hard to understand, it can be examined in its smaller aspects and is important for us to grasp.

Chapter 5

How Government Regulations Affect The Economy

The success of America's free enterprise system seems to validate the view that the economy operates best when government leaves businesses and individuals to succeed—or fail—on their own merits in open, competitive markets. But exactly how "free" is business in America's free enterprise system? The answer is, "not completely." A complex web of government regulations shape many aspects of business operations. Every year, the government produces thousands of pages of new regulations, often spelling out in painstaking detail exactly what businesses can and cannot do.

Laissez-Faire Versus Government Intervention

Historically, the U.S. government policy toward business was summed up by the French term *laissez-faire*—"leave it alone." The concept came from the economic theories of Adam Smith, the 18th-century Scot whose writings greatly influenced the growth of American capitalism. Smith believed that private interests should have a free rein. As long as markets were free and competitive, he said, the actions of private individuals, motivated by

About This Chapter: This chapter is comprised of text excerpted from "Chapter 6: The Role of Government in the Economy" and "Glossary of Economic Terms" in *Outline of the U.S. Economy*, a publication of the Bureau of International Information Programs, U. S. State Department, February 2001.

self-interest, would work together for the greater good of society. Laissez-faire practices appealed to Americans, whose country was built on faith in the individual and distrust of authority.

Laissez-faire practices have not prevented private interests from turning to the government for help on numerous occasions, however. Railroad companies accepted grants of land and public subsidies in the 19th century. Industries facing strong competition from abroad have long appealed for protections through trade policy. American agriculture, almost totally in private hands, has benefited from government assistance. Many other industries also have sought and received aid ranging from tax breaks to outright subsidies from the government.

> ✎ **What's It Mean?**
>
> <u>Laissez-Faire</u>: (from the French) "Leave it alone"—An economic policy under which private individuals and businesses are not over-regulated.
>
> <u>Regulation</u>: Government rules or laws that control or structure a certain industry or activity.

Categories Of Regulation

Government regulation of private industry can be divided into two categories—economic regulation and social regulation.

Economic regulation seeks, primarily, to control prices. Designed in theory to protect consumers and certain companies (usually small businesses) from more powerful companies, it often is justified on the grounds that fully competitive market conditions do not exist and therefore cannot provide such protections themselves.

Social regulation, on the other hand, promotes objectives that are not economic—such as safer workplaces or a cleaner environment. The government controls smokestack emissions from factories, for instance, and it provides tax breaks to companies that offer their employees health and retirement benefits that meet certain standards.

American history has seen the pendulum swing repeatedly between laissez-faire principles and demands for government regulation of both types.

Growth Of Government Intervention

In the early days of the United States, government leaders largely refrained from regulating business. As the 20th century approached, however, the consolidation of U.S. industry into increasingly powerful corporations spurred government intervention to protect small businesses and consumers. In 1890, Congress enacted the Sherman Antitrust Act, a law designed to restore competition and free enterprise by breaking up monopolies. In 1906, it passed laws to ensure that food and drugs were correctly labeled and that meat was inspected before being sold. In 1913, the government established the Federal Reserve to regulate the nation's money supply and to place some controls on banking activities.

The largest changes in the government's role occurred during the "New Deal," President Franklin D. Roosevelt's response to the Great Depression. During this period in the 1930s, the United States endured the worst business crisis and the highest rate of unemployment in its history. Many Americans concluded that unfettered capitalism had failed. So they looked to government to ease hardships and reduce what appeared to be self-destructive competition. Roosevelt and the Congress enacted a host of new laws that gave government the power to intervene in the economy. Among other things, these laws regulated sales of stock, recognized the right of workers to form unions, set rules for wages and hours, provided cash benefits to the unemployed and retirement income for the elderly, established farm subsidies, and insured bank deposits.

✎ What's It Mean?

Industry Regulation: Government regulation of an entire industry such as airline, railroad, trucking, banking, or television broadcasting. [See *Economic regulation* in text.]

Social Regulation: Government-imposed restrictions designed to discourage or prohibit harmful corporate behavior (such as polluting the environment or putting workers in dangerous work situations) or to encourage behavior deemed socially desirable. U.S. government regulatory agencies include the Equal Employment Opportunity Commission, the Environmental Protection Agency, the National Highway Traffic Safety Administration, the Occupational Safety and Health Administration, and the Consumer Product Safety Commission.

By the early 1990s, Congress had created more than one hundred federal regulatory agencies in fields ranging from trade to communications, from nuclear energy to product safety, and from medicines to employment opportunity. Many regulatory agencies are structured so as to be insulated from the president and, in theory, from political pressures. They are run by independent boards whose members are appointed by the president and must be confirmed by the Senate. By law, these boards must include commissioners from both political parties who serve for fixed terms, usually of five to seven years. Each agency has a staff, often more than 1,000 persons. Congress appropriates funds to the agencies and oversees their operations. In some ways, regulatory agencies work like courts. They hold hearings that resemble court trials, and their rulings are subject to review by federal courts.

Federal Efforts To Control Monopoly

Monopolies were among the first business entities the U.S. government attempted to regulate in the public interest. Consolidation of smaller companies into bigger ones enabled some very large corporations to escape market discipline by "fixing" prices or undercutting competitors. The Sherman Antitrust Act, passed in 1890, declared that no person or business could monopolize trade or could combine or conspire with someone else to restrict trade.

In 1914, Congress passed two more laws designed to bolster the Sherman Antitrust Act: the Clayton Antitrust Act and the Federal Trade Commission Act. The Clayton Antitrust Act defined more clearly what constituted illegal restraint of trade. The Federal Trade Commission Act established a government commission aimed at preventing unfair and anti-competitive business practices.

Deregulating Transportation

While antitrust law may have been intended to increase competition, much other regulation had the opposite effect. As Americans grew more concerned about inflation in the 1970s, regulation that reduced price competition came under renewed scrutiny. In a number of cases, government decided to ease controls in cases where regulation shielded companies from market pressures. This is called deregulation.

Transportation was the first target of deregulation. From 1977 to 1981, Congress enacted a series of laws that removed most of the regulatory shields around aviation, trucking, and railroads, in the process eventually abolishing two major economic regulators: the Interstate Commerce Commission and the Civil Aeronautics Board.

After government controls were lifted on the airline industry, new competitors emerged, often employing lower-wage nonunion pilots and workers and offering cheap, "no-frills" services. Some large companies failed.

What's It Mean?

Deregulation: Lifting of government controls over an industry.

Antitrust Law: A law passed by the U.S. government that seeks to curtail monopolistic powers within a market by imposing restrictions on business ownership, control, mergers, pricing, and mutual cooperation. The first antitrust law was the Sherman Antitrust Act, passed in 1890.

Most transportation companies initially opposed deregulation, but they later came to accept, if not favor, it. Analysts generally agree that air fares are lower than they would have been had regulation continued.

Telecommunications

Until the 1980s, the term "telephone company" was synonymous with American Telephone & Telegraph. AT&T controlled nearly all aspects of the telephone business. Its regional subsidiaries, known as "Baby Bells," were regulated monopolies, holding exclusive rights to operate in specific areas. The Federal Communications Commission regulated rates on long-distance calls between states, while state regulators had to approve rates for local and in-state long-distance calls.

> ## ♣ It's A Fact!!
> Have you noticed an official-looking sticker on the door of your bank? It reads, "Each depositor insured to $100,000—FDIC—Federal Deposit Insurance Corporation." This means that if that bank fails, the U.S. government will pay back every person's losses up to $100,000.
>
> —KRD

Beginning around the 1970s, sweeping technological developments promised rapid advances in telecommunications. Telecommunications deregulation ended AT&T's telephone monopoly. MCI Communications and Sprint Communications won some of the long-distance business. Then new technologies, including cable television, cellular (wireless) service, the Internet, and others, offered alternatives to local telephone companies, and Congress passed the Telecommunications Act of 1996. The law allowed long-distance telephone companies such as AT&T, as well as cable television and other start-up companies, to begin entering the local telephone business.

The Special Case Of Banking

Banks are a special case when it comes to regulation. On one hand, they are private businesses just like toy manufacturers and steel companies. But they also play a central role in the economy and therefore affect the well-being of everybody, not just their own consumers. Since the 1930s, Americans have devised regulations designed to recognize the unique position banks hold.

One of the most important of these regulations is deposit insurance. During the Great Depression, America's economic decline was seriously aggravated when vast numbers of depositors, concerned that the banks where they had deposited their savings would fail, sought to withdraw their funds all at the same time. In the resulting "runs" on banks, depositors often lined up on the streets in a panicky attempt to get their money. Many banks, including ones that were operated prudently, collapsed because they could not convert all their assets to cash quickly enough to satisfy depositors. As a result, the supply of funds banks could lend to business and industrial enterprise shrank, contributing to the economy's decline.

Deposit insurance was designed to prevent such runs on banks. The government said it would stand behind deposits up to a certain level—$100,000 currently. Now, if a bank appears to be in financial trouble, depositors no longer have to worry. The government's bank-insurance agency, known as the Federal Deposit Insurance Corporation, pays off the depositors, using funds collected as insurance premiums from the banks themselves. If necessary, the government also will use general tax revenues to protect depositors from losses. Regulators supervise banks and order corrective action if the banks are found to be taking undue risks. [For more information about the FDIC, see chapter 10.]

Other government regulation (and deregulation) concerns the types of financial services that banks—and savings and loans—may offer consumers, as well as interest rate regulations. While banks generally should be allowed to fail when they become insolvent, Americans believe that the government has a continuing responsibility to supervise them and prevent them from engaging in unnecessarily risky lending that could damage the entire economy.

☞ **Remember!!**

Lessons learned from banking regulation include the following:

- Government deposit insurance protects small savers and helps maintain the stability of the banking system.

- Interest rate controls do not work.

- Government should not direct what investments banks should make; rather, investments should be determined on the basis of market forces and economic merit.

- Bank lending to insiders or to companies affiliated with insiders should be closely watched and limited.

- When banks do fail, they should be closed as quickly as possible, their depositors paid off, and their loans transferred to other, healthier lenders.

Protecting The Environment

The regulation of practices that affect the environment is a good example of government intervention in the economy for a social purpose. For instance, air pollution represents what economists call an "externality"—a cost the responsible entity can escape but that society as a whole must bear. With market forces unable to address such problems, environmentalists say that government has a moral obligation to protect the earth's fragile ecosystems, even if doing so requires that some economic growth be sacrificed.

The U.S. Environmental Protection Agency (EPA) brings together in a single agency many federal programs charged with protecting the environment. The EPA sets and enforces tolerable limits of pollution, and it establishes timetables to bring polluters into line with standards. The EPA also has the authority

♣ **It's A Fact!!**
Laws enacted to control pollution include the Clean Air Act, the Clean Water Act, and the Safe Drinking Water Act.

to coordinate and support research and anti-pollution efforts of state and local governments, private and public groups, and educational institutions. Regional EPA offices develop, propose, and implement approved regional programs for comprehensive environmental protection activities.

Other Regulation

The role of government in the American economy extends far beyond its activities as a regulator of specific industries. The government also manages the overall pace of economic activity, seeking to maintain high levels of employment and stable prices. It has two main tools for achieving these objectives: *fiscal policy*, through which it determines the appropriate level of taxes and spending; and *monetary policy*, through which it manages the supply of money. See the next chapter for a discussion of what these terms mean.

Chapter 6

How The Federal Budget Affects You

Monetary And Fiscal Policy

Much of the history of economic policy in the United States since the Great Depression of the 1930s has involved a continuing effort by the government to find a mix of fiscal and monetary policies that will allow sustained growth and stable prices. That is no easy task, and there have been notable failures along the way.

The government has gotten better at promoting sustainable growth. From 1854 through 1919, the American economy spent almost as much time contracting as it did growing, but expansion has far outstripped recession since 1919.

Inflation, however, has proven more intractable. In part, the government's relatively poor record on inflation reflects the fact that it has put more stress on fighting recessions (and resulting increases in unemployment), only shifting

About This Chapter: This chapter begins with text excerpted from "Chapter 7: Monetary and Fiscal Policy" and includes excerpts from "Glossary of Economic Terms" in *Outline of the U.S. Economy,* a publication of the Bureau of International Information Programs, U.S. State Department, February 2001. Text under the heading "Revenue Sources" is excerpted and adapted from the following undated Fact Sheets from the U.S. Treasury Department: "Budget of the U.S. Government," "Economics of Taxation," "FAQs: National Debt," and "FAQs: Taxes and the Economy. Additional text is excerpted and reprinted from "Understanding the Federal Budget" by Ed Steinberg, Federal Reserve Bank of New York, http://www.newyorkfed.org, 2000.

its attention to inflation in the late 1970s. In recent years, the nation has experienced a gratifying combination of strong growth, low unemployment, and slow inflation.

Fiscal Policy: Budget And Taxes

The growth of government since the 1930s has been accompanied by steady increases in government spending. Fiscal decision-making is an elaborate process. Each year, the president proposes a budget, or spending plan, to Congress. Lawmakers consider the president's proposals in several steps. First, they decide on the overall level of spending and taxes. Next, they divide that overall figure into separate categories—for national defense, health and human services, and transportation, for instance. Finally, Congress considers individual appropriations bills spelling out exactly how the money in each category will be spent. Each appropriations bill ultimately must be signed by the president in order to take effect. This budget process often takes an entire session of Congress; the president presents his proposals in early February, and Congress often does not finish its work on appropriations bills until September (and sometimes even later).

> ✤ **It's A Fact!!**
>
> Prices were remarkably stable prior to World War II; the consumer price level in 1940, for instance, was no higher than the price level in 1778. But 40 years later, in 1980, the price level was 400% above the 1940 level.
>
> Source: U.S. State Department, 2001.

The federal government's chief source of funds to cover its expenses is the income tax on individuals, which bring just under half of total federal revenues. Payroll taxes, which finance the Social Security and Medicare programs, have become increasingly important as those programs have grown. The federal government raises another 10% of its revenue from a tax on corporate profits, while miscellaneous other taxes account for the remainder of its income. (Local governments, in contrast, generally collect most of their tax revenues from property taxes. State governments traditionally have depended on sales and excise taxes, although state income taxes have grown more important.)

The overall level of taxation is decided through budget negotiations. From the outset, the income tax has been a progressive levy, meaning that rates are higher for people with more income. Over the years, lawmakers have carved out various exemptions and deductions from the income tax to encourage specific kinds of economic activity. Most notably, taxpayers are allowed to subtract from their taxable income any interest they must pay on loans used to buy homes. Similarly, the government allows lower- and middle-income taxpayers to shelter from taxation certain amounts of money that they save in special Individual Retirement Accounts (IRAs) to meet their retirement expenses and to pay for their children's college education.

Revenue Sources

To meet their expenses, governments need income, called "revenue," which it raises through taxes. In our country, governments levy several different types of taxes on individuals and businesses. The federal government relies mainly on income taxes for its revenue. State governments depend on both income and sales taxes. Most county and city governments use property taxes to raise their revenue.

Government Services

Oliver Wendell Holmes, former Justice of the United States Supreme Court, once said, "Taxes are what we pay for a civilized society." People cannot purchase some things for themselves, such as police and fire protection, national defense, highways, or public assistance. People who live together in a society must bear the cost of providing such services. Thus, we pay taxes.

✎ What's It Mean?

Economic Expansion: An increase in output of goods and services.

Fiscal Policy: The federal government's decisions about the amount of money it spends and collects in taxes to achieve full employment and non-inflationary economy.

Monetary Policy: Federal Reserve System actions to influence the availability and cost of money and credit as a means of helping to promote high employment, economic growth, price stability, and a sustainable pattern of international transactions.

Recession: A significant decline in general economic activity extending over a period of time.

Source: U.S. State Department, 2001.

♣ It's A Fact!!
What are the ways that the federal
government receives the revenue it uses
to fund programs?

The major source of revenue is from individual income taxes. Other revenue is received through social insurance taxes and contributions, excise taxes, trust funds, estate and gift taxes, and customs duties. Finally, the government receives earnings from the Federal Reserve System's lending to financial institutions, fees for permits and regulatory and judicial services, and from gifts and contributions.

Source: U.S. Treasury Department, n.d.

Since the free enterprise system cannot produce all the services needed by society, some services are more efficiently provided when government agencies plan and administer them. Two good examples are national defense and state or local police protection. Everyone benefits from these services, and the most practical way to pay for them is through taxes instead of a system of service fees. Other examples are the management of our natural resources, such as our water supply or publicly owned land, and the construction of hospitals or highways. Taxes are collected to pay for planning these services and to finance construction or maintenance. Revenue is also collected through user fees, such as at the entrances to national parks or at toll booths on highways and bridges.

Children receive their education mainly at public expense. City and county governments have the primary responsibility for elementary and secondary education. Most states support colleges and universities. The federal government supports education through grants to states for elementary, secondary, and vocational education. Federal grants used for conducting research are an important source of money for colleges and universities.

Since the 1930s, the federal government has been providing income or services, often called a "safety net," for those in need. Major programs include health services for the elderly and financial aid for the disabled and unemployed. Other major programs include financial aid to families with dependent children, and social services for low-income individuals and families.

Taxes In The United States

Governments pay for these services through revenue obtained by taxing three economic bases: income, consumption, and wealth. The federal government taxes income as its main source of revenue. State governments use taxes on income and consumption, while local governments rely almost entirely on taxing property and wealth.

Taxes On Income. The earnings of both individuals and corporations are subject to income taxes. Most of the federal government's revenue comes from income taxes. The personal income tax produces about five times as much revenue as the corporate income tax.

Not all income tax taxed in the same way. For example, taxpayers owning stock in a corporation and then selling it at a gain or loss must report it; this item and any other gains or losses get calculated separately before they get added to other income. By comparison, the interest they earn on money in a regular savings account gets included with wages, salaries and other "ordinary" income. There are also many types of tax-exempt and tax-deferred savings plans available that have an impact on people's taxes.

Payroll taxes are an important source of revenue for the federal government. Employers are responsible for paying these taxes, which include Social Security insurance and unemployment compensation. Employees also pay into the Social Security program through money withheld from their paychecks. Some state governments also use payroll taxes to pay for the state's unemployment compensation programs.

Over the years, the amount paid in Social Security taxes has greatly increased. This is because there are fewer workers paying into the system for each retired person now receiving benefits. Today, some workers pay more Social Security tax than income tax.

Taxes On Consumption. The most important taxes on consumption are sales and excise taxes. Sales taxes usually get paid on such things as cars, clothing, and movie tickets. Sales taxes are an important source of revenue for most states and some large cities and counties. The tax rate varies from state to state, and the list of taxable goods or services also varies from one state to the next.

Excise taxes, sometimes called "luxury taxes," are used by both state and federal governments. Examples of items subject to federal excise taxes are heavy tires, fishing equipment, airplane tickets, gasoline, beer and liquor, firearms, and cigarettes. The objective of excise taxation is to place the burden of paying the tax on the consumer. A good example of this use of excise taxes is the gasoline excise tax. Governments use the revenue from this tax to build and maintain highways, bridges, and mass transit systems. Only people who purchase gasoline—who use the highways—pay the tax.

Some items get taxed to discourage their use. This applies to excise taxes on alcohol and tobacco. Excise taxes are also used during a war or national emergency. By raising the cost of scarce items, the government can reduce the demand for these items.

Taxes On Property And Wealth. The property tax is local government's main source of revenue. Most localities tax private homes, land, and business property based on the property's value. Some state and local governments also impose taxes on the value of certain types of personal property. Examples of personal property often taxed are cars, boats, recreational vehicles, and livestock.

☞ Remember!!

Many young people believe that, because they are not old enough to vote, they have no representation in government and, therefore, should not be required to pay taxes. Remember:

- The members of Congress, who establish the tax laws, speak and vote as representatives of all the people, including those who did not vote.

- It would be unfair to provide an exemption from tax for the income of a young person who cannot vote, while imposing the tax on the same amount earned by an older person.

- Every citizen or resident of the United States must pay any tax due if his or her gross income for the tax year exceeds a specified amount. The law does not excuse anyone from tax because of age.

Source: U.S. Treasury Department, n.d.

Property taxes account for more than three-fourths of the revenue raised through taxes on wealth. Other taxes imposed on wealth include inheritance, estate, and gift taxes.

The Federal Income Tax

A basic principle underlying the income tax laws of the United States is that people should be taxed according to their "ability to pay." Taxpayers with the same total income may not have the same ability to pay. Those with high medical bills, mortgage interest payments, or other allowable expenses can subtract these amounts as "itemized deductions" to reduce their taxable incomes. Similarly, taxpayers may subtract a certain amount on their tax returns for each allowable "exemption." By lowering one's taxable income, these exemptions and deductions support the basic principle of taxing according to ability to pay.

Those with high taxable incomes pay a larger percentage of their income in taxes. This percentage is the "tax rate." Since those with higher taxable incomes pay a higher percentage, the federal income tax is a "progressive" tax.

Sales and excise taxes, by comparison, are considered "regressive." Since the goods get taxed at the same percentage, those with lower incomes pay a larger percentage of their income in sales and excise taxes. Federal income taxes are collected on a "pay-as-you-go" withholding system. Most employers must withhold taxes from their employees' paychecks and send the money for deposit into the General Fund of the Treasury. Self-employed individuals and businesses must pay their taxes in regular installments, known as estimated tax payments. Paying taxes through withholding or estimated taxes during the year helps reduce the government's expense for borrowing money. It also provides an easier method for taxpayers to pay their taxes.

What are my tax dollars spent on every year?

The federal government operates on a fiscal year that begins on October 1 and ends on September 30. The tax money the government collects is placed into the General Fund of the Treasury to pay for essential government services.

There are many categories of services provided by the federal government:

- Social Security and Medicare benefits.

- National defense (salaries and pensions for members of the armed services and to provide equipment and supplies for our armed forces).

- Net interest (payments of interest on the public debt, less interest received by trust funds and other interest received).

- Income security programs (unemployment compensation, retirement and disability programs, food stamps and housing subsidies)

- Health care programs (Medicaid, training for health care professionals, medical research activities).

- Education, training, and social services (grants to elementary, secondary, and vocational schools and assistance to colleges and universities).

- Grants to state and local governments for social services programs.

- Benefits and services to veterans and their dependents (pensions, medical services, education training, and life insurance programs).

- Transportation (grants to states and local governments for constructing highways, mass transit systems, and airports).

- Miscellaneous functions of the federal government.

A detailed breakdown of the specific uses of federal tax dollars is available in *The Budget of the United States Government.* This book can be found in most large public libraries.

To keep collection costs down, the Internal Revenue Service expects all taxpayers to comply with the law voluntarily. Most taxpayers figure out how much tax they are supposed to pay and file their income tax return by the date it is due. Without this voluntary compliance, it would cost the Internal Revenue Service a great deal more to collect the same amount of revenue.

Understanding The Federal Budget

If you receive an allowance from your family, or if you have a part-time job, you know that you have to operate within a budget—that is, the amount you can spend is limited by the size of your income. Similarly, your family has to live within a budget—that is, the amounts it can spend on food, clothing, housing, entertainment, and other items are limited by the size of your family's income. Of course, for a limited time, you or your family can spend more than your income—by borrowing or by dipping into your savings—but you can't do that on a permanent basis.

The federal government, too, has to operate within a budget. Decisions have to be made as to how much the government will spend on each of many items, such as national defense, Social Security, the FBI, and space exploration.

A budget usually applies to a certain period of time. Your family may have a monthly budget, deciding how much to spend each month on food, clothing, housing, etc.; or perhaps it has a yearly budget that includes items such as a summer vacation. The federal government prepares its budget for each fiscal year. The fiscal year, the 12-month period used for budgetary purposes, runs from October 1 to September 30.

Spending

Your family's budget and the government's budget are alike in that both include some items on which spending is discretionary, or controllable, and some items on which spending is mandatory, or not controllable.

For example, if your family rents its house or apartment, it has to pay the rent each month, and if you live in your own home and have a mortgage, you have to pay the mortgage each month. Such payments are mandatory (they have to be made); they are not discretionary. On the other hand, the amounts that your family chooses to spend on items such as food and entertainment are discretionary. In any particular month, for example, you may decide to eat out more or less often.

Similarly, the federal government's budget contains both mandatory and discretionary elements. Consider, for example, Social Security, which accounts

✎ What's It Mean?

Budget Deficit: The amount each year by which government spending is greater than government income.

Budget Surplus: The amount each year by which government income exceeds government spending.

Source: U.S. State Department, 2001.

for more than 20% of total federal expenditures. (Social Security is a program that taxes people when they are working, and then provides them with income when they retire; it also provides income for workers who become disabled and for the dependents of workers who die.) By law, the government has to pay Social Security benefits to anyone who qualifies for them.

Other examples of mandatory spending are Medicare, Medicaid, benefits to retired civil servants, and interest on the debt that the government has accumulated over the years. (Medicare is a program that pays for health care for the elderly and certain disabled persons, while Medicaid is a joint federal-state program that provides medical assistance to low-income persons.) In contrast, spending on items such as national defense, space exploration, and the FBI is discretionary; the government can do more or less of it, as it decides.

Spending Priorities Change Over Time

Thirty-five years ago, for example, defense accounted for more than two-thirds of all discretionary spending, and discretionary spending exceeded mandatory spending, because many of today's social programs were much smaller. For example, the number of retired workers receiving Social Security benefits was only about one-third as large as it is today, and Medicare, which today accounts for more than one-tenth of the budget, was not yet in effect. Also, because the federal debt was much smaller, interest payments were a smaller share of the budget. Today, mandatory spending accounts for the majority of the federal budget. The largest single discretionary item is national defense, which accounts for almost half of the discretionary share of the budget.

Your family's income probably consists largely of wages and salaries, or perhaps the profits of a family business. In contrast, the federal government's income, or revenues, consists predominantly of taxes.

Individual income taxes make up about one-half of federal revenues, Social Security payroll taxes and related revenues (such as unemployment insurance taxes) provide another one-third, and corporate income taxes another 10%. Something the federal government has in common with many U.S. families is that income is higher in good economic times than in bad economic times, such as in a recession. When times are good, family incomes are larger because it is easier to find work, overtime work may be more available, and business profits are higher. Similarly, the government's revenues are higher in good times because more people are working and they pay more taxes on their larger incomes, and corporations pay more taxes on their higher profits.

✦ It's A Fact!!

In 2002 the United States was in the middle of a group of seven major industrialized nations when comparing net general government debt—which includes the consolidated debt of all levels of government (national, state or regional, and local)—as a share of the economy.

Source: U.S. Government Accountability Office (GAO), August 12, 2004.

Government Borrowing

The difference between the government's revenues and spending in a fiscal year is the government's annual surplus or deficit. If the government's revenues exceed its spending in a particular year, there is a surplus. If outlays exceed revenues, there is a deficit.

✦ It's A Fact!!

What caused the debt of the United States government? The total debt is largely a legacy of war, economic recession, and inflation. It represents the accumulated deficits in the government's budgets over the years. Through the sale of Treasury bills, notes, bonds, and United States Savings Bonds to the public, the Treasury Department borrows money.

Source: U.S. Treasury Department, n.d.

If your family spends more than its income, it may borrow to make up the difference, perhaps by taking on some credit card debt or by taking out a loan from a bank or credit union. The government borrows mainly by issuing Treasury bills, notes, and bonds. Bills are loans that the government repays in a year or less, notes have maturities of from two to ten years, and bonds mature in more than ten years.

When someone buys a U.S. Savings Bond, for example, the person is lending to the federal government. While Savings Bonds exist in paper form, the other government IOUs exist only as electronic accounting entries on computers. That allows the large IOUs to be bought and sold easily, and it reduces their vulnerability to theft and loss.

Interestingly, the government has to borrow even when it doesn't have a deficit. The reason is that the government is constantly paying off old debt. Suppose, for example, that the government is running a balanced budget—revenues are precisely equal to spending—and you cash in a Savings Bond. Because the government's spending is already equal to its revenues, the government has to borrow the funds it needs to pay off your Savings Bond. People are constantly cashing in government IOUs, so the government has to do new borrowing to offset that, and it actually does some borrowing every week.

♣ It's A Fact!!

The United States first got into debt in 1790 when it assumed the Revolutionary war debts of the Continental Congress; it was approximately $75 million. For a brief period in the mid-1830s the public debt was virtually zero. At the start of World War I in 1916, the public debt was $1 billion. It then rose to $26 billion in 1919 to finance the war. The debt declined for the next decade. During the Great Depression of the 1930s, the debt increased from $16 billion to $42 billion. During the Second World War the public debt rose sharply to a peak of $279 billion in 1946. From its postwar low in 1949, the outstanding public debt grew gradually for nearly the next two decades. Then, beginning at the time of the Vietnam War in the mid-1960s, the rate of increase accelerated sharply.

To find out the current level of the debt—to the penny—go to http://www.publicdebt.treas.gov/opd/opdpenny.htm.

Source: U.S. Treasury Department, n.d.

Paying Back With Interest

What determines how much inter-est the government has to pay when it borrows? The answer is that in-terest is the price of credit, and, as in any competitive market, price is determined by demand and supply. Thus, the interest rates that the government has to pay are deter-mined by the interaction of the government's demand for credit and the supply of credit to the government by lenders, including banks, corporations, private citizens, U.S. government agencies, and foreign individuals and institu-tions. That supply, in turn, is determined by such factors as the willing-ness of the U.S. consumer to save, the borrowing needs of U.S. business to invest in new equipment and buildings, and the total budget surplus or deficit of state and local governments.

♣ It's A Fact!!

The U.S. government has never defaulted on the principal or declared an interest payment moratorium on any of its obligations. Consequently, U.S. Treasury securities are considered the safest financial in-vestment in the world.

Source: U.S. Treasury Department, n.d.

You should remember two major points about the interest that the federal government pays. First, the government can borrow at lower in-terest rates than private parties (such as your family), because lenders are less worried about not being repaid when they lend to the government than they are when they lend to private parties; people are sure the gov-ernment will pay its debts. Second, rates generally are higher on longer maturities than on shorter maturities, because people who lend for longer periods have to be compensated for the risk that inflation might acceler-ate during the longer periods. If inflation accelerates, the lenders will be repaid with dollars that cannot buy as much as could the dollars that they originally lent to the government.

The Federal Debt: A Growing Problem

While the deficit is the amount by which government spending exceeds revenues in a particular year, the federal debt is the total amount of funds that the government has borrowed over the years, but has not yet repaid.

Is the debt too large? To answer that question, economists sometimes compare the size of the debt with that of the country's Gross Domestic Product (GDP), the dollar value of all the goods and services produced in the economy each year. Just as your family can put the debt it owes into perspective by measuring it against your family's income, so, too, we can gain some perspective on the size of the federal debt by measuring it against GDP, the total income from which the government can derive its revenue.

Why worry at all about the size of the federal debt? After all, doesn't the government simply owe the debt mainly to U.S. residents and to U.S. business firms? In a sense, don't we (through the government) simply owe the debt to ourselves?

To a large extent, the answer is yes, but many economists have at least two worries about a large federal debt. The first is that if the government does a lot of borrowing, the increased demand for credit may push interest rates up. The higher interest rates, in turn, make investment more expensive, and thus may discourage some investment in the buildings and equipment that help our economy grow. In that way, a large federal debt could lead to slower economic growth for the United States.

Second, there has been an increase in the proportion of the debt that is owed to foreigners. A large foreign-held debt can be a concern, because it is something we don't owe to ourselves. In order to pay it off, we will have to transfer some of our purchasing power to foreigners, and that means that in the future, the ability of U.S. households to consume goods and services will be diminished.

Budget deficits force the government to borrow money in the private capital markets. That borrowing competes with (1) borrowing by businesses that want to build factories and machines that make workers more productive and raise incomes, and (2) borrowing by families

> ### ✎ What's It Mean?
> Gross Domestic Product (GDP): The total value of a nation's output, income, or expenditure produced within its physical boundaries.
>
> Revenue: Payments received.
>
> Source: U.S. State Department, 2001.

who hope to buy new homes, cars, and other goods. The competition for funds tends to produce higher interest rates.

Deficits increase the federal debt and, with it, the government's obligation to pay interest. The more it must pay in interest, the less it has available to spend on education, law enforcement, and other important services, or the more it must collect in taxes—forever after.

We can provide a solid foundation for future generations, just as parents try to do within a family. For a nation, this means a strong economy and low interest rates and debt. Alternatively, we can generate large deficits and debt for those who come after us.

♣ **It's A Fact!!**
Reducing The
Federal Debt

The Treasury Department is concerned about the need to reduce the federal debt. Debt reduction can occur only when Federal outlays do not exceed federal receipts. The power to appropriate lies with the legislative, not the executive, branch of the government. While the arithmetic of reducing the outstanding debt is simple, the policy choices to achieve a budget surplus are not.

Source: U.S. Treasury Department, n.d.

Part Three

How To Save And Grow Your Money

Chapter 7

Saving Money: Not Always An Easy Thing To Do

Generations ago, Americans routinely put their money in savings accounts and generally did not consider alternative savings mechanisms. If they thought about or discussed it at all, Americans viewed the stock market as a pastime of the idle rich—"playing" the market, an elite version of playing the lottery.

Today, however, there is little "play" involved—investing in the market is serious business, a necessity for accumulating the funds essential for retirement or other financial goals. Now, more than ever before, Americans of all income levels are investing in the securities markets, both directly through the purchase and sale of stocks and bonds and indirectly through investment in mutual funds. Americans today have more of their money in the stock market than ever before—more than one-quarter of all U.S. household assets.

Knowing how to secure your financial well-being is one of the most important things you'll ever need in life. You don't have to be a genius to do it. You just need to know a few basics, form a plan, and be ready to stick to it.

About This Chapter: This chapter is excerpted and adapted from *The Facts on Saving and Investing*, U.S. Securities and Exchange Commission, April 1999; and *The SEC's Roadmap to Saving and Investing*, Office of the Investor Education and Assistance, U.S. Securities and Exchange Commission, October 8, 2004.

No matter how much or little money you have, the important thing is to educate yourself about your opportunities.

There is no guarantee that you'll make money from investments you make. But if you get the facts about saving and investing and follow through with an intelligent plan, you should be able to gain financial security over the years and enjoy the benefits of managing your money.

No one is born knowing how to save or to invest. Every successful investor starts with the basics. A few people may stumble into financial security— a wealthy relative may die, or a business may take off. But for most people, the only way to attain financial security is to save and invest over a long period of time. Time after time, people of even modest means who begin the journey reach financial security and all that it promises.

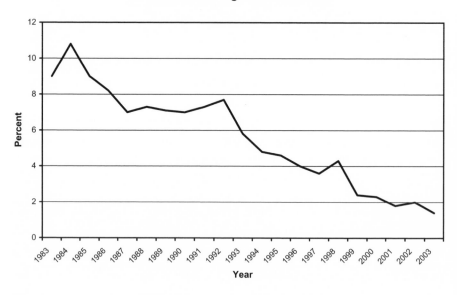

U.S. Personal Savings Rate 1983–2003

Figure 7.1. Source: From "Table 2.1. Personal Income and It's Disposition, line 34 (Personal saving as a percentage of disposable personal income), 1983–2003," Bureau of Economic Statistics, Commerce Department, 2004.

"Saving Is So Hard..."

The U.S. personal saving rate is plunging. In September 1998, "the personal saving rate turned negative for the first time since the 1930s."[1] According to U.S. Department of Commerce statistics, "the amount saved by American consumers as a proportion of their after-tax income dipped to minus 0.2 percent in September as overall spending grew robustly... For every $100 that consumers earned net of taxes in wages, salaries, and interest income, they spent $100.20."[2]

The idea that one must save to have the financial resources necessary for retirement seems so simple. But saving is often given a low priority or overlooked altogether. And many individuals who do attempt to plan for their future retirement needs find that their savings fall far short of the minimum necessary.

The reasons for this shortfall vary. A 1994 study identified six key barriers that many Americans confront in trying to save for retirement. Excerpted below is a discussion of each:

- *Retirement is not a priority for most people.* Most people feel too overwhelmed by daily concerns (monthly bills, work, healthcare costs) to give much attention to retirement.

- *Many Americans simply do not earn enough.* About one-third (34%) of Americans are convinced that they cannot save more for their retirement because they do not have the money to do so.

- *Many Americans lack knowledge.* Seven in ten Americans do not know how much money they need for retirement. Thirty-seven percent substantially underestimate the percentage of their yearly income they will need in retirement.

- *Many Americans expect the new "essentials" of middle-class life.* Some Americans are clearly struggling to make ends meet, and have extreme difficulty saving money for any purpose, including retirement. But even more comfortable middle-class Americans strongly resist cutting back on luxuries or nonessentials to save for their retirement. About two-thirds of respondents (68%) say they could cut back on their spending by eating out less often to save more for retirement. But of those, only 18% say they are very likely to actually cut back.

- *Personality matters.* Distinct personality patterns influence how individuals approach financial planning and retirement. "Planners" (about 21% of Americans) are in control of their financial affairs. "Strugglers" (about 25% of Americans) clearly have trouble keeping their heads above rough financial waters. "Deniers" (about 19% of Americans) are almost deliberate in their refusal to deal with retirement. "Impulsives" (about 15% of Americans) are driven to seek immediate gratification—spending today and letting tomorrow take care of itself.

> ✔ **Quick Tip**
> **Why save?**
>
> - In case of an emergency
>
> - To have the option of taking advantage of unforeseen opportunities
>
> - To reach financial goals
>
> Source: From *Practical Money Skills for Life*, a financial literacy education program from Visa, http://www.practicalmoneyskills.com. © 2005 Visa U.S.A. All rights reserved. Reprinted with permission.

- *The public has a "play it safe" approach to investment.* People seem so concerned with avoiding investment disasters that they make do with overly conservative investments. Much of the public is intimidated by the stock market and frightened of its volatility.[3]

"But Credit Is So Easy"

The obvious companion to a lack of savings is a potentially dangerous dependence on credit. The rate of bankruptcies is rising. According to the FDIC, the rise in the personal bankruptcy rate "has coincided with a marked increase in consumer loan charge-offs at FDIC-insured institutions" and "continues a steady upward trend in personal bankruptcies nationwide that goes back to the late 1970s."[4] Credit has become an easy way for Americans to spend money they do not have and to maintain lifestyles that they could not otherwise afford.[5] This has even become the case for young people. According to an analysis in *Consumer Reports*, "college students make up 10 to 15% of those seeking money-management help."[6]

Too Many Americans Fail "Finance 101"

Nothing is simple anymore. The days of standard pensions and straightforward savings accounts are over. Americans are left to plan their financial futures on their own and must figure out how to build a diversified portfolio of stocks, bonds, and cash or cash equivalents. In theory, this presents Americans with an opportunity to take charge of their financial destinies, but in practice, more often than not, Americans find themselves floundering because they do not know what to do.

The National Association of Securities Dealers, Inc. (NASD) released the findings of a survey it conducted to assess investors' financial literacy.[7] Quoted below are two of the NASD's key findings:

- While 63% of Americans know the difference between a halfback and a quarterback, only 14% can tell the difference between a growth stock and an income stock.

- While 78% of Americans can name a character on a television sitcom, only 12% know the difference between a "load" and "no-load" fund.

✔ Quick Tip
Pay Yourself First

Why?

- To make a habit of saving money to reach your financial goals

What it takes:

- Commitment

- Discipline

- Delayed gratification

Ways to do it:

- From each paycheck or allowance, deposit a set amount or percentage into your savings account before spending money on anything else.

- At the end of the day, put all your change in a savings container. Once a month, deposit the money in a savings account.

- Whenever you get unexpected money, put a portion of it into savings.

Remember: Amount saved isn't as important as getting into the habit.

Source: From *Practical Money Skills for Life*, a financial literacy education program from Visa, http://www.practicalmoneyskills .com. © 2005 Visa U.S.A. All rights reserved. Reprinted with permission.

Navigating Without A Road Map

Many have described a "financial plan" as a road map that helps the traveler get to where he or she is going. Yet, a surprising number of people have never prepared one.

A report prepared for the Consumer Federation of America, reinforces the importance of having a financial plan, regardless of income level. Key findings of the report excerpted below include:[8]

- An estimated 65 million American households will probably fail to realize one or more of their major life goals because they have failed to develop a comprehensive financial plan.

- One in five American households describe themselves as "nonsavers" who have not yet put aside any money for any of their financial goals.

- Only one-third of Americans who describe themselves as "savers" have developed a comprehensive financial plan.

- In households with annual incomes of less than $100,000, savers who say they have financial plans report having twice as much in saving and investments as do savers who do not have plans.

The next chapter is all about the road map—a personal financial plan.

References

1. "Saving Disgrace," *The Economist,* 80 (November 14, 1998).

2. Caren Bohen, *U.S. Savings Rate Falls to Depression-Era Low,* Reuters News Service (November 2, 1998).

3. Promises to Keep, study done by Public Agenda in collaboration with EBRI, 1994.

4. FDIC, *Bank Trends: Analysis of Emerging Risks in Banking* (undated) (available on the Internet at www.fdic.gov/publish/bktrnds/bt_9801.pdf) ("Bank Trends Homepage").

5. Steve Farkas and Jean Johnson, *Miles to Go: A Status Report of American's Plans for Retirement, A Report From Public Agenda,* 17 (1997).

6. "Future Debtors of America," *Consumer Reports,* 16 (December 1997).

7. NASD, *NASD Launches Major Public Disclosure, Investor Education Initiative,* Press Release (February 19, 1997).

8. *Planning for the Future: Are Americans Prepared to Meet Their Financial Goals? A Summary of Key Findings,* prepared for the Consumer Federation of America and NationsBank by Princeton Survey Research Associates (1997).

Chapter 8

What Are Your Financial Goals?

Saving Versus Investing

Most, if not all, individuals and families have some financial goals. However, setting aside enough money for savings and investments to accomplish these goals, as well as choosing the appropriate financial products, can be difficult. Making a firm commitment to saving and investing is probably the most important step in achieving these goals.

You may think of saving as a form of investing—and with deregulation of financial markets, there has been some "blurring" of the lines between financial products traditionally considered for investment purposes and those more feasible for savings. However, there are differences between saving and investing.

Savings provide funds for emergencies and for making specific purchases in the relatively near future (generally within two years). The primary goal is to store funds and keep them safe. This is why savings are generally placed in

About This Chapter: This chapter begins with "Saving Versus Investing" excerpted from *Investment Basics: Getting Started Saving and Investing,* by Joyce Jones, Ph.D., reprinted with permission of the Kansas State University Agricultural Experiment Station and Cooperative Extension Service, Manhattan, Kansas, http://www.oznet.ksu.edu/. Copyright © 1995. All rights reserved. "How Many Risks Are You Willing To Take?" is excerpted and reprinted with permission from "Savings and Investment," published by the Office of the New York State Attorney General, n.d.

interest-bearing accounts that are safe (such as those insured or guaranteed by the federal government) and liquid (those in the form of cash or easily changed into cash on short notice with minimal or no loss). However, these generally have low yields. Because of the opportunities for earning a higher return with a relatively small pool of funds, some financial experts suggest that savers consider slightly higher-risk (but liquid) alternatives for at least part of their savings.

The goal of investing is generally to increase net worth and work toward long-term goals. Investing involves risk. For example, earnings generally are not guaranteed and you could lose some of your original investment (principal).

Before you invest, consider getting your general financial situation under control first, such as by having:

• An emergency fund

• Some savings for short-term goals

• Adequate insurance

• Control over credit use

• A retirement plan

• And possibly, equity in a home

An Emergency Fund. Financial experts tend to agree that everyone needs an emergency fund equal to three to six months of living expenses. The exact amount needed depends on such factors as the stability of your income; family size; the amount of your basic expenses; whether you are covered by unemployment compensation or other income loss plans; disability and other insurance benefits available to you in an emergency; other savings and investments that could be accessed; and the employment or earning skills of other family members.

Why do you need an emergency fund before you start to invest? Households that fail to maintain an adequate emergency fund are financially vulnerable to unexpected occurrences.

An emergency fund can help meet these unexpected financial needs and, at the same time, prevent having to sell or liquidate investments to cover the emergency. Further, it may not be the best time to liquidate these investments or you may have to pay a penalty to get your funds.

✤ It's A Fact!!
Where To Get Funds To Save And Invest

Here are some ideas for setting aside funds to save and invest. Some may involve relatively small amounts of money, but, in combination with other techniques, the total can be substantial.

- Pay yourself first. Make savings and investments a regular, fixed expense (like your rent or mortgage payments).

- Make savings and investments automatically happen. Use payroll deductions, automatic bill payment systems, and other ways to have funds transferred directly from your paycheck or checking account. Have distributed capital gains, dividends, and interest automatically reinvested.

- Save windfall income. Put bonuses, cash gifts, tax refunds, and overtime pay into savings and investments.

- Pay installments to yourself. Once you have paid off an installment loan, continue to budget for the payment but put it into savings and investments.

- Be frugal. Substitute the local library, public parks, and other free or low-cost services for higher-cost services. Cut back or cut out something (such as eating out). Sometimes it is easier to cut back in increments—reducing your spending by 5%; then by another 5%—rather than all at once. Or, every month or two, try doing without all but the essentials for one week. Save or invest the amount by which you have reduced your spending.

- Don't spend your next raise. Save or invest at least 50% of it. The remainder can be used to offset higher costs of living.

- Break a habit. Put aside the amount you would have spent.

- Check your wallet. At the end of each day, empty your wallet or pocket of loose coins and place them in a container. Or, take $1 out of your wallet each day and place in the container. Periodically, put the funds into savings and investment vehicles.

Source: Kansas State University, 1995.

Savings For Short-Term Goals. Funds often need to be set aside for irregular expenses (those that do not occur every month, such as real estate and personal property taxes, insurance premiums, and back-to-school clothing) and to meet other specific short-term goals (such as for a new refrigerator or a vacation). These expenses and goals usually do not extend beyond one or two years, so, like an emergency fund, safety and liquidity are of primary concern.

Unlike short-term goals, intermediate- and long-term goals involve a longer period of time, ranging from a few years to many years. Because of this, you can commit your funds for a longer time and consider a range of investment alternatives. While you may risk not having your money available immediately, you gain the opportunity for greater earnings and protection from inflation.

✔ Quick Tip

Set and prioritize your financial goals.
The goal-setting process:

- Short-term goals (1–4 weeks)
- Medium-term goals (2–12 months)
- Long-range goals (1 year or longer)

Source: From *Practical Money Skills for Life*, a financial literacy education program from Visa, http:// www.practicalmoneyskills .com. © 2005 Visa U.S.A. All rights reserved. Reprinted with permission.

Adequate Insurance. Having adequate insurance for your family is also important. This generally includes health insurance (with major medical and catastrophic coverage), life insurance as protection for dependents, disability income insurance for major income earners, and property and liability insurance (homeowner's or renter's insurance, automobile insurance, and business insurance where appropriate).

Control Over Credit. A general rule of thumb for most families is not to commit more than 16 to 20% of spendable income to consumer credit obligations (excluding mortgage payments). Families with higher percentages of debt should consider increasing credit payments to reduce debt before taking risks with their money, especially if consumer credit interest rates are high and returns on most investments are low.

A Retirement Plan. Providing for a secure retirement (either through an employer plan, on your own, or both) requires careful planning and regular contributions. Before investing, it's important to have at least begun planning how to fund your retirement and making contributions toward that plan. Adequate retirement funds—such as replacing at least 65 to 75% of preretirement income—will probably be one of your investment goals, also.

Equity In A Home. This prerequisite depends upon your values. If home ownership is important, some equity in a home is a good idea before starting to invest. If home ownership is not important, or if a down payment on a home is a goal that you plan to work toward simultaneously, meeting this requirement may not be necessary before starting an investment plan.

Table 8.1. Monthly Income and Expenses

Income:	_____
Expenses:	_____
Savings	_____
Investments	_____
Housing:	
rent or mortgage	_____
electricity	_____
gas/oil	_____
telephone	_____
water/sewer	_____
property tax	_____
furniture	_____
Food	_____
Transportation	_____
Loans	_____
Insurance	_____
Education	_____
Recreation	_____
Health care	_____
Gifts	_____
Other	_____
Total	_____

Source: From *The SEC's Roadmap to Saving and Investing*, Office of the Investor Education and Assistance, U.S. Securities and Exchange Commission, October 8, 2004.

Investment Considerations

There are many things to consider when beginning an investment plan. Some are personal, requiring you to carefully evaluate yourself (knowledge, attitudes, skills, goals, and personality) and your financial situation. Others involve using selection criteria to evaluate specific investments (and specific types of investments).

The interplay of these two sets of considerations is crucial to wise investment decision-making. It's also important to note that, while the remainder of this publication addresses investment considerations, similar considerations need to be taken into account when choosing where to put savings dollars.

Personal Considerations. When beginning an investment plan, careful consideration needs to be given to:

• Your investment goals

• Time available for working with investments

• Knowledge of investments

• Available funds for investing

• Ability to handle a loss

• Present financial situation

• Risk tolerance

Investment Goals. What do you and your family hope to achieve through investments? Do you want a secure and comfortable retirement, funds for your children's college educations, or to build an estate? How much money will you need to reach your goals? How long do you have to reach these goals? Because these goals are long-term, it is important that you make them specific, realistic, measurable, and in writing. This may involve working with a variety of financial advisers. You also need to prioritize these goals, since working toward one goal can sometimes hinder progress toward another goal.

Gathering a large sum of money may be overwhelming when you think of the amount as a lump sum. However, when you look at the amounts month by month and year by year, they can be both possible and manageable. The chart below may help you determine a monthly target amount to invest in order to reach a goal.

Table 8.2. Monthly Amount Needed To Reach A Goal

Total dollars needed	Years to achieve goal				
	3	5	10	15	20
6% rate of return (after taxes)					
$5,000	$126	$71	$30	$17	$11
10,000	253	143	61	34	22
15,000	379	214	91	51	32
20,000	506	285	121	68	43
30,000	759	428	182	103	65
9% rate of return (after taxes)					
$5,000	$121	$66	$26	$13	$7
10,000	241	132	51	26	15
15,000	362	197	77	39	22
20,000	482	263	103	52	30
30,000	724	395	154	79	45

Source: Kansas State University, 1995.

Time Available For Working With Investments. Different investments take different amounts of time to study, evaluate, and manage. How much time are you willing to devote to researching, studying, and monitoring your current (as well as potential) investments?

Knowledge Of Investment Alternatives. This consideration is tied to the "time available" one above. Investment advisers recommend investing in what you know about or are willing to learn about. If you don't have that knowledge already, are you willing to invest the time to learn about and evaluate investment alternatives? Even if you work with an investment adviser, you will need a certain amount of knowledge about investments in order to ask the right questions and, perhaps even more important, understand the answers and the consequences of the decisions.

Amount To Invest. Realistically, how much money do you have to invest? Is money available from a one-time occurrence (such as an inheritance), or do you expect to have a certain continuing amount from current cash flow? Do you have (or can you acquire) the ability to consistently and regularly contribute to an investment plan? Recommendations for regular contributions to savings and investments vary from 5 to 20% or more of your take-home income, depending on your financial situation, your family size, and the number of years until you retire.

Amount To Lose. What amount, if any, can you afford to lose? Be realistic. The amount of loss you can accept will influence the types of and specific investments you choose. For example, if that figure is nothing or next to nothing, you probably should not even consider investing, but rather stick to savings. Because of relatively low yields on savings products, however, inflation will create some loss of purchasing power.

Present Financial Situation. What is your present financial situation? What is your income? What do you own (assets)? What do you owe (liabilities)? Do your assets match your investment goals? There are some financial factors also relating to risk. In general, the larger your investment portfolio, the more financially secure you are, the farther off your retirement, and the more optimistic about the economy you are, the more risk you may comfortably assume. But your situation may involve conflicting risk factors. For example, as you near retirement, you probably have a larger investment portfolio (i.e., can assume more risk), but you have fewer years of future earnings coupled with fewer years before retirement income is needed (i.e., can assume less risk).

How Many Risks Are You Willing To Take?

Another important consideration in your financial plan is how much you are willing to risk your money, this decision will affect both how much and where your put your money. Generally, the higher the return on an investment the riskier that investment is. When you put your money into an insured bank or credit union account, you don't get as much in interest as you could by investing in the stock market. But in a bank account, if something goes wrong the government has promised to pay you back every cent (up to $100,000 per account). On the other hand if the company you invested in goes bankrupt and the stock loses all of its value you could lose your entire investment.

Diversification Of Risk. Is it a good idea to keep your entire 1,000-page novel on your computer with no back up copies and no printed version? Not if you are worried about keeping it. The same idea is true with money, investors put money to work for them in a number of different ways in order to meet different goals and in order to minimize the chance of losing all their money. People put money into savings accounts and savings bonds, they buy houses and other assets, and they invest in different markets to diversify where their risk lies. If the house burns down, or the stock market declines, not all off your money is lost.

How Quickly Can You Get To Your Money?

Liquidity. Another difference between savings and other kinds of investment is how quickly you can get your money. With a savings account you can go to the bank and withdraw your money. Some kinds of accounts will charge you a fee if you take out the money before the specified time. Still other kinds of assets you cannot sell quickly or easily when you need cash. What kinds of goals you have set will help you determine how quickly you may need your money.

How Much Will The Government Get?

Taxes. One last consideration for your financial plan is taxes—both how much you pay now and how much you will pay in the future. Some investments are tax-free for a number of years (usually until you take the money out) and so they can accrue more money in interest. It is important to compare tax-free and taxable accounts, because a 6% return on a tax exempt investment is the same as a 7% return in the 15% income tax bracket. (It is the same as an 8.3% in the 28% tax bracket and 9% in the 33% tax bracket.)

Chapter 9
Where Should You Keep Your Money?

Save And Invest

You have budgeted and identified an amount to save monthly. Where are you going to put your savings? By investing, you put the money you save to work making more money and increasing your wealth. An investment is anything you acquire for future income or benefit. Investments increase by generating income (interest or dividends) or by growing (appreciating) in value. Income earned from your investments and any appreciation in the value of your investments increase your wealth.

Get Guidance

There is an art to choosing ways to invest your savings. Good investments will make money; bad investments will cost money. Do your homework.

About This Chapter: "Save And Invest," is excerpted from "Building Wealth: A Beginner's Guide to Securing Your Financial Future," 2002, a financial education publication of the Federal Reserve Bank of Dallas, http://www.dallasfed.org. "A Financial Plan" is reprinted with permission from "Savings and Investment," published by the Office of the New York State Attorney General (n.d.); "Successful Saving And Investing" reprinted with permission from *Successful Saving and Investing*, a brochure created by Consumer Action with funding from the Bank of America Consumer Education Fund. © 2000 Consumer Action. All rights reserved; "Investment Selection Criteria" is excerpted from *Investment Basics: Getting Started Saving and Investing*, by Joyce Jones, Ph.D., reprinted with permission of the Kansas State University Agricultural Experiment Station and Cooperative Extension Service, Manhattan, Kansas, http://www.oznet.ksu.edu/. Copyright © 1995. All rights reserved.

Gather as much information as you can. Seek advice from personnel at your bank or other trained financial experts. Read newspapers, magazines and other publications. Identify credible information sources on the Internet. Join an investment club. Check out the information resources listed in the back pocket of this publication.

Understand The Risk-Expected Return Relationship

When you are saving and investing, the amount of expected return is based on the amount of risk you take with your money. Generally, the higher the risk of losing money, the higher the expected return. For less risk, an investor will expect a smaller return.

For example, a savings account at a financial institution is fully insured by the Federal Deposit Insurance Corp. up to $100,000. The return—or interest paid on your savings—will generally be less than the expected return on other types of investments.

On the other hand, an investment in a stock or bond is not insured. The money you invest may be lost or the value reduced if the investment doesn't perform as expected.

How much risk do you want to take? Here are some things to think about when determining the amount of risk that best suits you.

- **Financial goals.** How much money do you want to accumulate over a certain period of time? Your investment decisions should reflect your wealth-creation goals.

- **Time horizon.** How long can you leave your money invested? If you will need your money in one year, you may want to take less risk than you would if you won't need your money for 20 years.

> **✔ Quick Tip**
> Know yourself. How would you complete the following sentences?
>
> My financial goals are ...
>
> My time horizon is ...
>
> My financial risk tolerance is ...
> - small
> - moderate
> - significant
>
> Source: Federal Reserve Bank of Dallas, 2002.

- **Financial risk tolerance.** Are you in a financial position to invest in riskier alternatives? You should take less risk if you cannot afford to lose your investment or have its value fall.

- **Inflation risk.** This reflects savings' and investments' sensitivity to the inflation rate. For example, while some investments such as a savings account have no risk of default, there is the risk that inflation will rise above the interest rate on the account. If the account earns 5% interest, inflation must remain lower than 5% a year for you to realize a profit.

Tools For Saving

The simplest way to begin earning money on your savings is to open a savings account at a financial institution. You can take advantage of compound interest, with no risk.

Financial institutions offer a variety of savings accounts, each of which pays a different interest rate. The box below describes the different accounts. You can choose to use these typical accounts to save for the near future or for years down the road.

A Financial Plan

With a good financial plan, you can set aside some of today's income for the things you will want and need in the future. It takes more than luck to get what you want out of life, you have to know what you want and have a plan to meet your goals, otherwise it is unlikely that you will get the things that you want for the future.

Financial independence is an important goal, but people sometimes miss the opportunity to become financially independent because they avoid making decisions and taking action to influence their financial well-being.

A financial plan is a tool to help you reach your goals, it is not a straightjacket to keep you from enjoying life. Think of a financial plan as a road map to help you get where you want to go. People use a road map when they begin a trip where they have not traveled before, yet many will take a financial journey through life without a road map. As a sage once said, "If you don't know where you are going, you may end up somewhere else."

A financial plan works best if you keep it simple, use realistic income and expense estimates, and periodically review and adjust the plan to reflect changing conditions and goals. The first step is to carefully consider your present financial situation. How much money do you need for routine expenses, such as food, shelter, clothing, health care, transportation and entertainment? How much have you set aside for emergencies? Any money left over is the amount you can afford to invest.

Emergency Funds

An important goal of a financial plan is to protect against financial risk. Two ways people prepare for unexpected expenses or a decline in income are with emergency savings funds and with insurance. Everyone should have savings to meet financial emergencies that are not covered by insurance. Financial advisors suggest that you have money to cover at least three months living expenses in readily available funds. These funds should be placed in insured bank or credit union where money can be withdrawn easily when needed.

♣ It's A Fact!!
Types Of Savings Accounts

Savings Account (in general)

- Access your money at any time.

- Earn interest.

- Move money easily from one account to another.

- Have your savings insured by the FDIC up to $100,000.

Money Market Savings Account

- Earn interest.

- Pay no fees if you maintain a minimum balance.

- May offer check-writing services.

- Have your savings insured by the FDIC up to $100,000.

Certificate Of Deposit (CD)

- Earn interest during the term (three months, six months, etc.).

- Must leave the deposit in the account for the entire term to avoid an early-withdrawal penalty.

- Receive the principal and interest at the end of the term.

- Have your savings insured by the FDIC up to $100,000.

Source: Federal Reserve Bank of Dallas, 2002.

Making Money Work For You

If you have worked hard to save up some extra cash, you'd probably like a safe place to store it. For some people the inside of a mattress seems like the perfect spot. But hiding your money doesn't necessarily make it safe. It could get lost, stolen, or damaged. Also, your money would not be "working" to make you more money, in fact, when you consider factors such as the increasing cost of living, the money hidden in your mattress would be worth less in the future.

A better way to keep your money secure—and productive—is to invest it. An investment is anything you spend money on with the intention of making more money. Investments can be almost anything, from land, to precious metals, to stocks and savings bonds. To help decide what investment is best for you, you should determine your investment objectives. Do you want your investments to grow slowly but steadily over several decades? Or would you rather earn money right away? How much risk are you willing to take to get these results?

Not only are you making money, but you are keeping up with the future. Everything costs more in the future, due to inflation. If you keep your money in a mattress, the $100 that could buy something big in 1950 can only buy something small today. By saving or investing you will be able to afford the things you need in the future.

The Sooner The Better

The sooner you start to save money the more it can increase over time. If a 25-year-old invests $2000 a year for 10 years and then lets the money sit until he or she retires, that person will have $545,344 for the $20,000 investment. By comparison, if a 35-year-old invests the same

♣ **It's A Fact!!**

Money works for you by making more money. When you invest your money in a company or in a bank account someone is paying you to use that money. That payment is the return on the investment or the interest rate on the account. When you put money in a bank account you know what they will pay you, when you invest in the stock market, you get paid depending on how well the company uses your money to make itself better.

Source: New York State Attorney General, n.d.

$2000 for 30 years until he or she is ready to retire, that person will have only $352,427 for the $60,000 investment.

Planning for your future and determining your goals early will make it easier to achieve those goals. Let's look at how different deposits amounts can grow over time: for example, let's say you are saving for your children's or your own college tuition. $100 a month in a medium return account (8%) will yield $59,295 in 20 years.

Setting Financial Goals

Saving and investing will be more successful if you have specific goals in mind. Short-term goals are those to be reached within a year or less. Some short-term goals are to build an emergency fund, to buy a new stereo, to pay off a credit card, or to go on vacation. Long-term goals are those to be achieved in more than a year, sometimes over a lifetime. Some long-term goals are to buy a house, to go to college, to start a retirement fund, or to start a business.

Short-term goals can often help to reach a long term goal, for example you may want to save $100 a month in order to make the down payment on a new car. After you have identified your goals you must figure out how much each goal will cost, which goals are most important, and how much money you need to save to achieve these goals. The amount of money you need to set aside each month may depend on how quickly you want to reach the goal and what you do with the money you set aside.

Debt

Credit allows people to have and enjoy things now and pay for them later. It can be a cushion in emergencies and it is convenient. But credit costs money and tempts us to overspend. People who cannot pay their debts will soon have an unfavorable credit report—which can influence their ability to obtain new credit for years to come.

Paying cash is almost always less expensive than using credit (unless you can pay off your credit card every month.) When you do use credit, it is best to borrow as little as possible, seek the lowest finance charge, and pay off the loan as soon as possible.

It is important when you think of saving and investing to remember that *you can make money in interest payments or you can be paying interest payments.* It may be better to pay off your credit cards or mortgage than to invest or save money in accounts with low returns.

Successful Saving And Investing

Savings accounts are designed to keep your money safe and to help it grow. When you deposit your money in a savings account, the bank pays you interest.

♣ It's A Fact!!

You buy a pair of new shoes for $50 using your credit card. If your credit card charges 15% each month that the balance is not paid, and you take five months to pay for the shoes, they will have cost you over $100. On the other hand, if your credit card only charges you 6% every month that you do not pay off the balance the shoes will have cost you $67 in five months.

Source: New York State Attorney General, n.d.

Interest is the cost of using money; your bank pays you when you leave your money on deposit. Interest is usually expressed as an annual percentage rate (APR)—the amount your money would earn if left on deposit for one year.

Money in your bank account is safe from fire, loss or theft. Each account is insured by the federal government for up to $100,000. When you have a bank account, you don't have to carry large amounts of cash around. You can make deposits into your account and withdraw money when you need it.

Many financial planners say that money for short term goals should be kept in a savings account, where there is little risk of losing the money and where it is easily available when you need it.

After your savings start to grow, you may want to invest some of the money for long-term goals in a money market account, stocks, bonds or mutual funds. Such goals might include college for yourself or your children, a car, a home, a vacation or extra cash for holiday gifts.

Everyone should have a "nest egg" set aside for emergencies or achieving goals. (However, if you are on public assistance, there may be limits to how much you are allowed to have in savings. For example, some programs set a limit of several thousand dollars on all your cash "assets" such as savings, stocks and bonds and life insurance. Before you start a savings program, check with your benefits counselor.)

Opening A Savings Account

Most banks require two pieces of ID, one with a picture on it. You will usually need a Social Security number to open a bank account. You must have some money to open an account. Some banks require only $1 to open an account—others ask for $50, $100 or $500. You may use cash or a check to open an account.

When you have chosen the financial institution, visit a branch so that you can sit down with a bank officer and open your account. At this point, the bank may verify your banking history with an account screening company, such as ChexSystems. If you've ever had a problem with an account, such as closing your checking account without enough money to cover all outstanding checks, you may be denied an account. (Such information is kept on file for five years.) If you are told you cannot open an account because of the information, you have rights. If you believe the information that the denial is based on is incorrect, ask the bank officer how to contact the account screening company. If the company has incorrect information on file about you, you have a right to dispute it.

If one bank won't open an account for you, try another bank—different banks have different requirements.

Places To Save

Banks. Today banks offer a wide range of financial services to help you save. These include savings accounts, Certificates of Deposit (CDs), money market deposit accounts, Individual Retirement Accounts (IRAs), consumer, business and real estate loans and trust and investment services. Accounts in Federal Deposit Insurance Corporation (FDIC) member banks are federally insured up to $100,000.

Credit Unions. These are nonprofit savings and lending organizations that provide services to members who have a common bond, such as working for the same company, living in the same community or belonging to the same church or union. Just like banks, credit unions offer savings accounts and investment services. Deposits in federal and state chartered credit unions are insured for up to $100,000 through the National Credit Union Administration (NCUA).

Brokerage Houses And Mutual Fund Companies. These may offer a wide range of financial services, including savings and investment plans. Some accounts are insured, others are not. Many mutual fund companies waive the minimum deposit requirement if you agree to have a monthly amount (as little as $50) automatically transferred from your checking account each month.

Types Of Accounts

Regular savings accounts are sometimes called passbook accounts and usually have low opening deposit requirements. There may be limitations on the number of withdrawals.

Certificates of deposit (CDs) also are known as time deposit accounts because you agree to leave your money in the account for a specified period in return for a higher rate of interest. The times vary from six months to ten years. Some CDs do not allow additional deposits. Typically the funds are reinvested after the term is reached, unless you specify otherwise. There usually are penalties for early withdrawal. CDs pay from 4%–7% interest, depending on length and the institution.

Money market accounts usually have high minimum deposit requirements ($1,000 or more) and allow access to your money. Some but not all money market accounts are federally insured—don't forget to ask. You may be limited to a specific number of withdrawals per month.

U.S. Savings Bonds allow you ready access to your funds and they are not subject to federal or state income tax. You buy the bonds at a discount (a percentage of their value at maturity). Interest varies, but you are always guaranteed a minimum return.

Some companies offer to match employees contributions to a retirement fund. After a specified number of months or years with the company you will be "fully vested" and will own the company's contribution to your retirement fund. You may be allowed to invest up to 10% of your pre-tax income in a company retirement plan.

Individual Retirement Accounts (IRAs) and Keoghs are retirement accounts that are tax-deferred until withdrawal, usually after you are 59½. Contributions are tax deductible up to a specific amount each year, usually $2,000. There are tax penalties for early withdrawal. Roth IRAs are not tax deferred—they allow you to invest after-tax income and all returns are tax-free. Some retirement plans allow you to choose your own investments. If you are self-employed, you can also set up a Simplified Employee Pension (SEP) plan or a Keogh account, which allows you to deposit up to a specified percentage of your income and deduct that amount from taxes.

Investment Selection Criteria

Commonly accepted criteria for evaluating types of investments, as well as specific investments, include:

- Risk
- Return
- Liquidity and marketability
- Cost

- Diversification
- Taxes
- Effort and expertise

Risk. Risk refers to the uncertainty that the actual rate of return on an investment will differ from what is expected. There are many sources of risk to the investor. They can act together or separately and can impact your investments' principal, growth, and income.

Some risks are associated with the securities market and the economy as a whole. Generally, these risks cannot be reduced by individual investor decisions.

Other risks are related to characteristics of specific investments, companies, or industries. Individual investor decisions (such as diversifying investments) may help reduce this type of risk.

Return. The gain or profit you receive from investing is referred to as the return. This may include the receipt of income (interest, dividends, or rent) or capital gains (where the investment has increased or appreciated in value).

> ## ☞ Remember!!
>
> An investment is the use of money to create more money. Investments include stocks and mutual funds, bonds and annuities (a form of investment sold by insurance companies). The money you have to invest is sometimes called "capital." Successful saving and investing depend on balancing several factors:
>
> - *Return.* What interest rate will your money earn?
>
> - *Security.* Is your money insured by the Federal Deposit Insurance Corporation (FDIC)?
>
> - *Risk.* When you invest in stocks and bonds, your money is not covered by federal bank insurance. How much loss from investments could you live with? If the answer is none or very little, consider avoiding securities investments, such as stocks and bonds, which can lose some—or all—of their value.
>
> - *Liquidity.* How easy is it for you to withdraw your money or use it for other investments?
>
> It is unlikely that you will find a single investment that gives you the best of all three: high return, low risk and ease of access. For example, your savings account at a local bank is easy to access and very secure but fairly low in return (interest). Stocks offer a higher return but are also riskier and less accessible.
>
> Source: Consumer Action, 2000

The combination of income and capital gains is the total return from an investment.

Obviously, if the value of the investment has fallen, a negative rate of return may result (depending upon whether income received from the investment exceeds the loss in value). However, if an investor doesn't actually sell or liquidate the investment (but rather holds it) and the value of the investment goes up, the loss may only be a "paper" one.

Most investors measure return on a yield or rate of return basis—that is, as a percentage of the amount invested on an annualized basis—rather than in dollars. That way, you can compare the yields on different investments and find out how much you earned per dollar invested. Remember that the rate of inflation and your tax bracket reduce your actual rate of return on any investment.

♣ It's A Fact!!
Minimum Rate Of Return (RR)

You can estimate the minimum rate of return (RR) you need to break even with inflation and federal taxes. Divide the inflation rate by 100 minus your marginal tax bracket (the tax rate you would pay on the next dollar of income earned). For example, imagine that the inflation rate is 4% and you are in the 15% marginal tax bracket.

$$RR = \frac{4}{100-15} = .047 \text{ or } 4.7\%$$

The minimum rate of return needed to break even is 4.7%. In the 28% bracket, the rate needed with a 4% inflation rate is 5.6%.

Source: Kansas State University, 1995.

Liquidity And Marketability. Liquidity is the ability to turn an investment into cash without significant loss when you need it. Savings accounts and money market accounts are among the most liquid places to keep funds. Real estate and collectibles (such as coins, antiques, and art) are among the least liquid because of the likelihood of taking a loss should they have to be sold to obtain quick cash.

Liquidity is important when there is an emergency and money is needed right away. Overall, collective liquidity is important to the management of a general investment portfolio. Liquidity allows you to change your strategy as the investment climate changes. For example, when interest rates were at historic highs, some investors were not able to move long-term investments into those earning the higher rates of return.

Marketability, on the other hand, is the ability to find a buyer when you want to sell, regardless of the potential gain or loss involved. For example, homeowners may discover that their homes do not sell as quickly as they would like (i.e., are less marketable than desired).

Cost. Costs include that of the particular security, as well as any fees for purchasing or selling the investment, maintenance, or other services. Further, there may be a minimum required to invest in a particular security.

Diversification. Diversification is a technique for managing risk. In the simplest terms, it means that not all of your funds are placed in any one type of investment. When purchasing stocks, diversification may mean that you own stock in several companies within an industry or stock in companies that represent several different industries.

Similarly, when buying bonds, it may mean you have bonds from different companies within an industry or bonds from companies that represent different industries. Bonds or certificates of deposit (CDs) may also have staggered maturities.

As a result, if one investment fails to meet your expectations (or if interest rates, the economy, or other investment conditions change), the impact on overall returns may be less severe. It might be easier for you to remember diversification in terms of a simple rule: *Do not put all of your eggs in one basket.*

Taxes. Your personal tax status is related to your marginal tax bracket. When your marginal tax rate is high, you send more tax dollars to the government. This lowers the amount you have to save, spend, or invest, as well as the amount you earn from savings and investments.

Of course, there are some investments where contributions are tax-deductible, where interest earned is tax-free, or where taxes on earnings or capital gains can be deferred until some point in the future.

Effort And Expertise. This is a factor that cannot be overlooked. Certain types of investments require little or no time commitment or special knowledge. Others may require constant management and a great deal of specialized expertise.

Consider carefully the amount of effort and expertise necessary for a particular investment, in light of the personal considerations mentioned earlier. Further, the amount of effort and expertise necessary may determine whether, and to what extent, you rely on an investment adviser.

For example, if you have the time, energy, ability, and interest in studying, researching, and monitoring investments, you may want to consider stocks and bonds. If you lack this time, energy, ability, and interest, you may want to consider investments such as mutual funds.

Chapter 10

Types Of Savings Accounts

Financial Institution Deposits

Financial institutions (banks, savings and loan associations, and credit unions) offer a variety of ways to save, such as interest-bearing checking, savings or share accounts, and certificates of deposit (CDs) or share certificates.

Deposited funds are safe. Banks and savings and loan associations are insured by the Federal Deposit Insurance Corporation and credit unions are insured by the National Credit Union Association, up to a maximum of $100,000 for each depositor.

Funds are liquid (although CDs are subject to early withdrawal penalties) and they earn interest. Interest is subject to federal, state, and local income taxes as it is earned and credited to your account.

Interest-Bearing Checking

Checking accounts give individuals a safe, convenient way to pay financial obligations and to have a record of payments. The opportunity to earn interest

About This Chapter: This chapter begins with "Financial Institution Deposits" excerpted from *Investment Basics: Financial Institution Deposits and U.S. Government Securities*, by Joyce Jones, Ph.D., reprinted with permission of the Kansas State University Agricultural Experiment Station and Cooperative Extension Service, Manhattan, Kansas, http://www.oznet.ksu.edu/. Copyright © 1995. All rights reserved. "Callable CDs" is excerpted from "Certificates of Deposit: Tips for Investors," published by the U.S. Securities and Exchange Commission, November 1, 2004.

on checking accounts was a feature first added in the mid-1970s at credit unions and in the early 1980s at banks and savings and loan associations.

Typically, banks and savings and loan associations refer to interest-bearing checking accounts as NOW (negotiable orders of withdrawal) accounts, SuperNOW accounts, and money market deposit accounts. Credit unions refer to interest-bearing checking accounts as share draft accounts.

The specifics of NOW and share draft accounts are established by the financial institution, so services, fees, and interest rates vary. SuperNOW and money market deposit accounts are similar to NOW accounts, except that they earn variable market rates, tend to have higher minimum required balances, and charge higher fees when minimum balances are not maintained. (It should be noted that some banks and savings and loans are combining SuperNOW and NOW accounts into one "interest-bearing checking" account with higher interest rates paid on higher balances.)

Money market deposit accounts have limited check-writing or electronic fund transfer (EFT) privileges (up to six indirect transactions per month, although the maximum number can be lower). In-person transactions, such as cash withdrawals, are generally not limited.

Some factors to consider when comparing interest-bearing checking accounts include:

- What is the minimum deposit required to open an account? Is there a minimum required to maintain an account?

- What is the interest rate? Is the rate fixed or does it vary with market rates? Is the interest rate lower if you fail to maintain a specific minimum balance?

- What is the annual percentage yield (APY)? This takes into account the interest rate, as well as the frequency of compounding (that is, how often earnings are computed). The more frequent the compounding, the higher the annual percentage yield.

- Is there a monthly service charge? What is it? Does it change if your account drops below a certain minimum balance?

- If you close the account during the month, is interest paid during that month?

- What is the overdraft charge? How much is the returned check fee?

- Is there a charge for stop payment orders? How much is it?

- What conditions do you need to meet in order to qualify for free check-writing?

- What is the cost for printed, personalized checks? Are they available free for first accounts, those keeping a large minimum balance, students, senior citizens, or other groups? Where else can you purchase checks?

- What other services are provided by the financial institution for this type of account (such as automatic bill-payment services or deposit, withdrawal, transfer, and loan payment via cash machines)? What are the fees associated with these services?

Savings Accounts

Savings accounts are available at banks and savings and loan associations, and share accounts are available at credit unions.

Some factors to consider when selecting a savings account (or share account) include:

- What is the interest rate?

- How often is interest compounded (and thus, what is the annual percentage yield or APY)? The more frequently the interest is compounded, the higher the APY.

- When is interest actually paid to the account? What happens if the account is closed before that date?

- Are there any penalties or fees, such as those associated with withdrawals above a specified number?

- Is there a minimum balance required before interest is earned?

- Are there any fees (or is no interest earned) on inactive accounts (and what is considered an inactive account)?

- What other terms or conditions could affect earnings?

- What other services are offered by the financial institution? What are the fees for these other services?

Certificates Of Deposit

An alternative to a regular savings account is a certificate of deposit (CD) from banks or savings and loan associations, or a share certificate from a credit union. Besides paying a higher interest rate, CDs and share certificates differ from savings accounts in two basic ways. First, you agree to leave your money with the financial institution for a specified period of time (that is why they are called "time" deposits). If you withdraw the funds prior to that date, you pay an interest penalty for early withdrawal. Second, the financial institution usually requires a minimum deposit. Generally, the larger the dollar value placed in the CD or share certificate and the longer you agree to leave your money with the financial institution, the higher the rate of return.

Interest rates may be fixed or variable. Deregulation has led to more competition among financial institutions, with interest rates and other specifics of the CD or share certificate now established by each financial institution.

☞ Remember!!
Savings Accounts

- Passbook and statement accounts

- NOW accounts

Advantage: Simplest way to earn interest on small amount of money while keeping money readily accessible.

Other Saving Methods

- Money-market deposit accounts

- Time deposits (certificates of deposit)

Source: Excerpted from *Practical Money Skills for Life*, a financial literacy education program from Visa, http://www.practical moneyskills .com. © 2005 Visa U.S.A. All rights reserved. Reprinted with permission.

♣ It's A Fact!!
Money Market Deposit Accounts: What They Are And How They Work

- Checking/savings account.

- Interest rate paid built on a complex structure that varies with size of balance and current level of market interest rates.

- Can access money from an ATM, a teller, or by writing up to three checks a month.

Benefits

- Immediate access to your money.

Trade-Offs

- Usually requires a minimum balance of $1,000 to $2,500.

- A limited number of checks can be written each month.

- Average yield (rate of return) higher than regular savings accounts.

Source: Excerpted from *Practical Money Skills for Life*, a financial literacy education program from Visa, http://www.practicalmoney skills.com. © 2005 Visa U.S.A. All rights reserved. Reprinted with permission.

Some factors to consider when selecting a certificate of deposit include:

- What is the minimum deposit amount required? Typical minimum deposits are $500 and $1,000, but the minimum can be more or less.

- What is the length of maturity? Typical maturities are seven to thirty-one days, three months, six months, and one, two, three, or more years. Some financial institutions allow flexible maturities, so savers can select the length of maturity that meets their specific needs.

- What is the interest rate? Is the rate fixed or does it vary with the economy (and what is the variable market rate tied to)?

- How often is the interest compounded? What is the annual percentage yield (APY)?

- How is interest paid? Typically, interest can be left in the certificate account and added to the balance (so that you are earning interest on interest, as well as principal), mailed to you quarterly or monthly, or credited to your regular checking or savings account.

- What happens when the certificate matures? If you do nothing, is the money rolled over automatically into a new certificate with the same

Table 10.1. Savings Products

The following savings products are most appropriate for those saving one to five years for a wealth-building goal such as an emergency fund, the down payment on a mortgage, or school tuition.

Type of Product	Savings Account (bank); Share Account (credit union)
Minimum Initial Deposit	Usually $25–100 but make certain monthly fees are not charged for small balances
Yield	Usually 1–2%
Safety	Government-insured*
Access to Funds	Immediate
Where to Purchase	At any bank, thrift, or credit union
How to Purchase	In person
How to Make Deposits	Through tellers, ATMs, or automatic monthly transfer from checking account
Other Features	At many institutions, minimum balance of $100–500 to avoid monthly fees

Type of Product	Certificate of Deposit (bank); Share Certificate (credit union)
Minimum Initial Deposit	At most institutions, at least $500
Yield	Usually 2–4%
Safety	Government-insured*
Access to Funds	Immediate but interest penalty
Where to Purchase	At any bank, thrift, or credit union
How to Purchase	In person or by mail
Other Features	Make certain financial institution will notify you when CD matures

*Accounts at some credit unions are privately insured

Type of Product	U.S. Savings Bond, Series EE
Minimum Initial Deposit	As low as $25 ($50 for payroll deduction)
Yield	About 3%
Safety	Government-guaranteed
Access to Funds	After first 12 months, immediate access but loss of 3 months interest

Where to Purchase	At any bank, thrift, or credit union or from the U.S. Treasury
How to Purchase	In person at financial institutions or by mail from U.S. Treasury
How to Make Deposits	Easy Saver program allows periodic payroll deposit or checking account deductions to purchase bonds
Other Features	Must cash in after 30 years or no more interest earned; face value of bond twice the purchase price ($50 bond costs $25)

Type of Product	**U.S. Savings Bond, Series I (with inflation protection)**
Minimum Initial Deposit	As low as $50
Yield	About 4%
Safety	Government-guaranteed
Access to Funds	After first 12 months, immediate access but loss of 3 months interest
Where to Purchase	From any bank, thrift, or credit union or from the U.S. Treasury
How to Purchase	In person at financial institutions or by mail from U.S. Treasury
How to Make Deposits	Easy Saver program allows periodic payroll deposit or checking account deductions to purchase bonds
Other Features	Must cash in after 30 years or no more interest earned

Type of Product	**Money Market Fund**
Minimum Initial Deposit	As low as $250 at some institutions
Yield	About 1.2%
Safety	Not government-insured
Access to Funds	Immediate
Where to Purchase	at Money market fund
How to Purchase	By phone with mailed check or wire transfer of funds from checking account
How to Make Deposits	By check or wire transfer of funds from checking account
Other Features	Many funds allow a few checks to be written each month

interest rate (or a newer, current interest rate)? Are funds transferred into a checking or savings account? Does the financial institution notify you of upcoming maturity dates?

- Does the financial institution offer other services that may influence your decision to save with them (such as monthly interest statements or preference for loan approval)?

It should be noted that some brokerage firms also offer certificates of deposit. They may pay higher rates of return. Some of these CDs may not have an early withdrawal penalty. However, they are not insured.

Callable CDs

At one time, most CDs paid a fixed interest rate until they reached maturity. But, like many other products in today's markets, CDs have become more complicated. Investors may now choose among variable rate CDs, long-term CDs, and CDs with other special features.

Some long-term, high-yield CDs have "call" features, meaning that the issuing bank may choose to terminate—or call—the CD after only one year or some other fixed period of time. Only the issuing bank may call a CD, not the investor. For example, a bank might decide to call its high-yield CDs if interest rates fall. But if you've invested in a long-term CD and interest rates subsequently rise, you'll be locked in at the lower rate.

☞ **Remember!!**

Certificates of Deposit: What They Are And How They Work

The bank pays a fixed amount of interest for a fixed amount of money during a fixed amount of time.

Benefits

- No risk
- Simple
- No fees
- Offers higher interest rates than savings or money market accounts

Trade-Offs

- Restricted access to your money
- Withdrawal penalty if cashed before expiration date (penalty might be higher than the interest earned)

Source: Excerpted from *Practical Money Skills for Life*, a financial literacy education program from Visa, http://www.practicalmoneyskills.com. © 2005 Visa U.S.A. All rights reserved. Reprinted with permission.

Callable CDs give the issuing bank the right to terminate—or "call"—the CD after a set period of time. But they do not give you that same right. If interest rates fall, the issuing bank might call the CD. In that case, you should receive the full amount of your original deposit plus any unpaid accrued interest. But you'll have to shop for a new one with a lower rate of return. Unlike the bank, you can never "call" the CD and get your principal back. So if interest rates rise, you'll be stuck in a long-term CD paying below-market rates. In that case, if you want to cash out, you will lose some of your principal. That's because your broker will have to sell your CD at a discount to attract a buyer. Few buyers would be willing to pay full price for a CD with a below-market interest rate.

♣ It's A Fact!!
Types Of Certificates Of Deposit

1. **Rising-rate CDs** with higher rates at various intervals, such as every six months.

2. **Stock-indexed CDs** with earnings based on the stock market.

3. **Callable CDs** with higher rates and long-term maturities, as high as 10–15 years. However, the bank may "call" the account after a stipulated period, such as one or two years, if interest rates drop.

4. **Global CDs** combine higher interest with a hedge on future changes in the dollar compared to other currencies.

5. **Promotional CDs** attempt to attract savers with gifts or special rates.

Source: Excerpted from *Practical Money Skills for Life*, a financial literacy education program from Visa, http://www.practicalmoneyskills .com. © 2005 Visa U.S.A. All rights reserved. Reprinted with permission.

Don't assume that a "federally insured one-year non-callable" CD matures in one year. It doesn't. These words mean the bank cannot redeem the CD during the first year, but they have nothing to do with the CD's maturity date. A "one-year non-callable" CD may still have a maturity date 15 or 20 years in the future. If you have any doubt, ask the sales representative at your bank or brokerage firm to explain the CD's call features and to confirm when it matures.

Chapter 11

What Is Your "Risk Tolerance"?

Determine Your Risk Tolerance

Let's review some key concepts:

Savings. Your "savings" are usually put into the safest places or products that allow you access to your money at any time. Examples include savings accounts, checking accounts, and certificates of deposit. At some banks and savings and loan associations your deposits may be insured by the Federal Deposit Insurance Corporation (FDIC). But there's a tradeoff for security and ready availability. Your money is paid a low wage as it works for you.

Most smart investors put enough money in savings to cover an emergency, such as sudden unemployment. Some make sure they have up to six months of their income in savings so that they know it will be there for them if they need it.

About This Chapter: "Determine Your Risk Tolerance" is excerpted from *The SEC's Roadmap to Saving and Investing*, Office of Investor Education and Assistance, U.S. Securities and Exchange Commission, October 8, 2004. "Risk Tolerance" is excerpted from *Investment Basics: Getting Started Saving and Investing*, by Joyce Jones, Ph.D., reprinted with permission of the Kansas State University Agricultural Experiment Station and Cooperative Extension Service, Manhattan, Kansas, http://www.oznet.ksu.edu/ . Copyright © 1995. All rights reserved. "What Every Investor Needs To Know: Risk And Suitability" is © 2003 Arizona Corporation Commission. All rights reserved. Reprinted with permission.

But how "safe" is a savings account if you leave all your money there for a long time, and the interest it earns doesn't keep up with inflation? Let's say you save a dollar when it can buy a loaf of bread. But years later when you withdraw that dollar plus the interest you earned, it might only be able to buy half a loaf. That is why many people put some of their money in savings, but look to investing so they can earn more over long periods of time, say three years or longer.

Investing. When you "invest," you have a greater chance of losing your money than when you "save." Unlike FDIC-insured deposits, the money you invest in securities, mutual funds, and other similar investments are not federally insured. You could lose your "principal," which is the amount you've invested. That's true even if you purchase your investments through a bank. But when you invest, you also have the opportunity to earn more money than when you save.

But what about risk? All investments involve taking on risk. It's important that you go into any investment in stocks, bonds or mutual funds with a full understanding that you could lose some or all of your money in any one investment. While over the long term the stock market has historically provided around 10% annual returns (closer to 6% or 7% "real" returns when you subtract for the effects of inflation), the long term does sometimes take a rather long, long time to play out. Those who invested all of their money in the stock market at its peak in 1929 (before the stock market crash) would wait over 20 years to see the stock market return to the same level. However, those that kept adding money to the market throughout that time would have done very well for themselves, as the lower cost of stocks in the 1930s made for some hefty gains for those who bought and held over the course of the next twenty years or more.

Diversification. It is true that the greater the risk, the greater the potential rewards in investing, but taking on unnecessary risk is often avoidable. Investors best protect themselves against risk by spreading their money among various investments, hoping that if one investment loses money, the other investments will more than make up for those losses. This strategy, called "diversification," can be neatly summed up as, "Don't put all your eggs in one basket." Investors also protect themselves from the risk of investing all their money at the wrong time (think 1929) by following a consistent pattern of adding new money to their investments over long periods of time.

Once you've saved money for investing, consider carefully all your options and think about what diversification strategy makes sense for you. A vast array of investment products exists—including stocks and stock mutual funds, corporate and municipal bonds, bond mutual funds, certificates of deposit, money market funds, and U.S. Treasury securities. Diversification can't guarantee that your investments won't suffer if the market drops. But it can improve the chances that you won't lose money, or that if you do, it won't be as much as if you weren't diversified. [See chapter 14 for more information about portfolio diversification.]

Risk Tolerance

How comfortable are you with risk? We all have different temperaments and tolerance levels when it comes to risk. If an investment causes you to lose sleep or not eat, it is a good indication that the investment has a higher risk level than your personal "risk-comfort zone."

Another element involved with risk tolerance is the emotional attachment you feel for a particular investment. Financial experts generally caution people not to become emotionally

---

☞ Remember!!
Analyze Your "Risk-Comfort Zone"

These questions may help you analyze your "risk-comfort zone":

- Do you prefer to work by yourself, make your own decisions, and be your own boss?

- If you received an unexpected "windfall," would you prefer to invest in a somewhat speculative investment (where the potential return could be great, but the potential loss could also be great)?

- When you lose something, do you spend little time searching for it?

- When you make decisions, is knowing immediately what the outcome will be not that important to you?

- Do you feel other people do a worse job of handling their finances than you do?

- Does the thought of traveling to a foreign country by yourself exhilarate you?

- Do you believe in yourself, have confidence in your decisions, and feel good about who you are most of the time?

The more "yes" answers, the more of a risk taker you probably are. However, only you can decide your tolerance for risk.

Source: Kansas State University, 1995.

involved with investments—to keep them on a business basis. Emotional attachment may prevent you from being objective. For this reason, your home is probably better seen as "housing," rather than a true investment.

What Every Investor Needs To Know: Risk And Suitability

Choosing an investment vehicle is complicated. Should you invest in stocks, bonds, mutual funds, CDs, commodities, options, futures contracts, mortgage-backed securities, or a myriad of other types of securities? And once you have chosen a type of investment, such as mutual funds, then you need to decide in which areas of the economy—such as technology or health care—you want to invest. Before you make any investment choices, however, you and your financial professional need to consider two factors that should influence all of your choices: your risk tolerance and what investments suit you.

Risk can be simply defined as the possibility of suffering a loss. One very important principle to always remember about risk is that the higher the return on your investment, the greater the risk you are taking. If the risk of loss is high, a higher interest rate is used to entice investment. This is why U.S. Treasury securities, often referred to as T-bills, T-notes, and T-bonds, have a lower rate of return as opposed to bonds issued by financially shaky companies that offer a higher rate of return.

You can minimize your investment risk through diversification, which may enable you to invest in a mixture of low-risk/high-risk investments. The old saying, "Don't put all your eggs in one basket," holds true with investing. Many people who invested solely in the "dot-com" emerging companies of the 1990s learned a hard lesson about securities diversification. Likewise, those who invest in only a few companies or even a few areas of the economy are assuming significant risk and should consider diversifying.

Now that you have thought about risk, what about suitability? Suitability means that the investment is in line with your investment objectives and financial situation. Your financial professional (securities salesman, stockbroker, or investment adviser) should not recommend an investment that exposes you to risk beyond what you can afford to lose. So, is buying a bond in a financially shaky company suitable for you? If you cannot afford to risk the money you invest, then absolutely not. If you are capable of and willing to accept the risk of losing all or part of your investment, then buying a bond in a financial shaky company may be suitable for you.

To determine if an investment is suitable, you must also consider how soon you need to have the money back out of the investment. Even if you can afford to lose your investment, putting your money into a real estate limited partnership when you want the money to send your child to college next year would not be suitable.

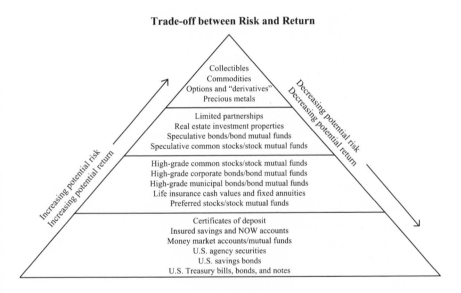

Trade-off between Risk and Return

Collectibles
Commodities
Options and "derivatives"
Precious metals

Limited partnerships
Real estate investment properties
Speculative bonds/bond mutual funds
Speculative common stocks/stock mutual funds

High-grade common stocks/stock mutual funds
High-grade corporate bonds/bond mutual funds
High-grade municipal bonds/bond mutual funds
Life insurance cash values and fixed annuities
Preferred stocks/stock mutual funds

Certificates of deposit
Insured savings and NOW accounts
Money market accounts/mutual funds
U.S. agency securities
U.S. savings bonds
U.S. Treasury bills, bonds, and notes

Increasing potential risk
Increasing potential return

Decreasing potential risk
Decreasing potential return

Figure 11.1. There is a trade-off between risk and return. The risk of an investment is related to its expected return. In general, if you want higher returns, you must be willing to accept greater risk. This relationship may not hold exactly true over short periods of time, but over a long investment period, increased return means increased risk.

While there are no hard and fast distinctions (since a particular investment may be more or less risky than others of a similar type, depending upon the specific characteristics of the individual investment), the graph below may provide an overall guide to types of savings and investments and their relative risk and return. Note that within each group, the savings and investments are listed alphabetically.

Source: Kansas State University, 1995.

If you work with a financial professional, he or she is required to have enough information about you to determine before even recommending a security to you whether that security matches your investment objectives and financial situation. The only way for financial professionals to determine if investments are suitable for you is for them to ask you questions to find out how risk tolerant you are, what your investment objectives are, and the status of your financial situation.

When you open your securities account, your financial professional should ask you questions about your income, net worth, liquid assets, tax bracket, prior investment experience, retirement goals, plans for major expenditures, and other similar relevant facts. Your financial professional should also discuss with you what your investment objectives are—for example, income, aggressive income, capital appreciation, or speculation. Your financial information and objectives typically are recorded on forms required to open a securities account. In many instances, the stockbroker or investment adviser completes these forms and has you sign them. But never, ever sign a blank form.

You must make sure that the information your financial professional has about you is accurate. Request a copy of any forms prepared by your financial professional to review for accuracy. Your financial professional should periodically review this information with you to keep it up to date. This way you and your financial professional can make sure he or she only recommends investments to you that are suitable for your specific situation.

Chapter 12

How Quickly Can You Get Rich?

Interest Rates: An Introduction

Interest rates receive a lot of attention in the media, but what are they, anyway? How are they determined? What do they do? This introduction provides some basic answers to these questions.

What Is Interest?

Interest is the compensation that someone receives for temporarily giving up the ability to spend money. Without interest, lenders wouldn't be willing to lend, or to temporarily give up the ability to spend, and savers would be less willing to defer spending.

Interest rates are expressed as percents per year. If the interest rate is 10% per year, and you borrow $100 for one year, you have to repay the $100 plus $10 in interest.

About This Chapter: This chapter begins with excerpts reprinted from "Interest Rates: An Introduction," an online financial education publication of the Federal Reserve Bank of New York, http://www.newyorkfed.org, April 2004. "The Magic of Compounding" is reprinted with permission from the American Savings Education Council, http://www.asec.org, © 2000. All rights reserved. "Take Advantage of Compound Interest" is excerpted from the brochure, "Building Wealth: A Beginner's Guide to Securing Your Financial Future," 2002, a financial education publication of the Federal Reserve Bank of Dallas, http://www.dallasfed.org.

Because interest rates are expressed simply as percents per year, we can compare interest rates on different kinds of loans, and even interest rates in different countries that use different currencies (yen, dollar, etc.).

What Are "APR" And "APY"?

The APR includes, as a percent of the principal, not only the interest that has to be paid on a loan, but also some other costs, particularly "points" on a mortgage loan.

Points (a point equals one percent of the mortgage loan amount) are fees that the mortgage lender charges for making the loan. In a sense, points are prepaid interest, or interest that is due when the loan is taken out.

Some lenders charge lower interest rates but more points than other lenders. The APR therefore provides a useful gauge for comparing the total cost of mortgage loans.

> ✎ **What's It Mean?**
>
> Interest: The price that someone pays for the temporary use of someone else's funds. To repay a loan, a borrower has to pay interest, a percentage of the principal.
>
> Principal: The amount of money borrowed originally; upon which amount interest is figured.
>
> Source: Federal Reserve Bank of New York, 2004.

APY is the effective interest rate from the standpoint of a person receiving interest. If you have $1,000 in each of two bank accounts, each paying the same interest rate, but the interest is credited more often (let's say, every month, rather than once a year) on one of the accounts, that account will have a higher APY, because the interest will build up more rapidly than on the other account.

Why Does Interest Exist?

From the lender's point of view—interest compensates lenders for the effects of inflation, or rising prices. Prices go up every year, so lenders are repaid with dollars that can't buy as much as the dollars they lent; the lenders must be compensated for that loss of purchasing power.

Interest also compensates lenders for the risks they take. One risk is that nobody knows for certain how much prices will go up during the time that the borrower has the lender's money. Other risks are that the borrower won't repay the loan fully, on time, or at all.

For a lender such as a bank, interest covers the costs of staying in business, including the cost of processing loans, and interest also provides the profit that a lender needs to stay in business.

✎ What's It Mean?

APR: APR stands for "Annual Percentage Rate."

APY: APY stands for "Annual Percentage Yield."

Source: Federal Reserve Bank of New York, 2004.

From the borrower's point of view—individuals are willing to pay interest to borrow money in order to be able to spend now, rather than later, on cars and many other items. They are willing to pay interest in order to be able to afford a large purchase, such as a home, for which they don't have enough funds of their own. People are willing to pay interest on loans to pay for education, which can increase their earning ability.

Businesses are willing to pay interest in order to borrow to invest in equipment, buildings, and inventories that will increase their profits.

✔ Quick Tip

To get an idea of how volatile the rate of inflation can be, click on www.newyorkfed.org/research/dirchrts/I-bcd_15.pdf.

Source: Federal Reserve Bank of New York, 2004.

Banks are willing to pay interest on their customers' deposits because they can lend the funds at higher interest rates and make a profit.

Some borrowers are willing to pay interest on certain loans because of the associated tax advantages. Mortgage interest, for example, is tax deductible. That means that in calculating how much income tax you have to pay, you can subtract the mortgage interest that you pay from your income.

Interest: Cost To Some, Income To Others

Interest is income to people willing to give up the temporary use of their money. When you put money into a bank account, or when you buy a U.S. Savings Bond, for example, you receive interest income.

Interest is a cost to borrowers. You pay interest, for example, if you don't pay your entire credit card bill at the end of the month, if you take out a mortgage loan to buy a house, or if you own a business that borrows in order to invest in machinery.

Interest is a signal that directs funds to where they can earn the highest rates, or to where loans can do the most for the economy.

Interest is a measure of the cost of holding money. The rate of interest that you could earn by lending your money is the cost to you of holding your money in a way (such as in cash) that doesn't earn any interest. Economists use the term "opportunity cost" to refer to what you give up by choosing a certain course of action. By holding money, you give up the interest that you could have earned, so the interest rate measures the opportunity cost of holding money.

The Level Of Interest Rates

What determines the overall level of interest rates—that is, why are rates higher at some times than at others?

Interest is the price of a loan, so it is determined to a large extent by the supply of, and demand for, credit, or loanable funds. Many different parties contribute to the supply and demand for credit.

✔ Quick Tip
To see how the level of interest rates varies over time, click on www.newyorkfed.org/research/dirchrts/I-page19.pdf.
Source: Federal Reserve Bank of New York, 2004.

When you put money into a bank account, you are allowing the bank to lend the funds to someone else. So, through the bank, you are contributing to the supply of credit in the economy.

When you buy a U.S. Savings Bond, you are lending funds to the U.S. government. Again, you are contributing to the supply of credit.

On the other hand, when you borrow—to buy a car, for example, or by keeping a balance on a credit card account—you are contributing to the demand for credit.

Individual savers and borrowers aren't the only ones contributing to the supply of, and the demand for, credit. Business firms and governments in this country, and foreign organizations, too, affect the demand for, and supply of, credit.

Together, the actions of all of these participants in the credit market determine how high or low interest rates will be.

> ✔ **Quick Tip**
>
> For a chart showing how inflation and interest rates are related, see page 9 of "Points of Interest," available at www.chicagofed.org/publications/index.cfm#P.
>
> Source: Federal Reserve Bank of New York, 2004.

- All other things held constant, an increase in the demand for credit raises the price of credit, or interest rates, and a decrease in the demand for credit lowers interest rates.

- All other things held constant, an increase in the supply of credit lowers interest rates, and a decrease in the supply of credit raises interest rates.

How does inflation affect the level of interest rates?

Inflation is one reason interest exists; lenders must be compensated for the decline in the purchasing power of what they lend. So, rates generally are high when inflation is expected to be rapid.

Inflation expectations are based heavily on recent inflation. So, rates generally are high when inflation is rapid.

Why Do Interest Rates Differ?

Regardless of whether rates are generally high or low, some rates are higher than others.

The interest rate that you pay on a car loan typically is higher than the interest rate that you receive on an account in a savings bank, for example, and the interest rate on a credit-card balance is higher than the rate on a new-car loan.

Several major factors explain these rate differences: risk, duration, tax considerations, and other characteristics of a loan.

Risk. One risk that a lender faces is that of not being repaid. The greater the chance that you won't be repaid, the higher the interest rate you will have to charge as compensation for taking the risk. On the other hand, if a loan involves little risk, you would be willing to accept a lower interest rate. That's why the federal government can borrow at lower rates than can private parties. People are sure the government will pay its debts.

Some lenders reduce the risk of losing what they have lent by requiring the borrower to pledge *collateral,* property that the lender can take possession of if the borrower doesn't repay the loan. The risk is smaller in such "secured" loans than in unsecured loans, so the interest rates are lower, too. Auto loans, for example, carry lower rates than credit-card loans, because the lender can take possession of the car if the borrower fails to pay.

When you apply for a loan, you often have to fill out a form on which you provide information that the lender can use to determine how likely you are to be able to repay the loan. Similarly, there are business firms that rate the creditworthiness of individuals, other firms, and even governments; lenders use this information to determine what rates to charge on loans.

Duration. The longer the duration of a loan, the more likely the lender is to desire access to the funds. So lenders typically have to be compensated with higher interest rates for parting with their funds for longer periods.

The longer the duration of a loan, the greater the uncertainty over whether the borrower will be able to repay the loan. So, lenders have to be compensated for the greater risk with higher interest rates on longer-term loans.

Inflation is a major factor determining the level of interest rates. The longer the duration of the loan, the greater the risk that inflation can accelerate, reducing the purchasing power of the loan repayment. So, rates generally are higher on long-term loans than on short-term loans, because people who lend for longer periods have to be compensated for the risk that inflation might accelerate during the longer periods.

Tax Considerations. If you receive interest income, you are more concerned with how much of the income you can keep than with how much the borrower pays. You are concerned with after-tax income—that is, the interest you receive minus any taxes you have to pay on that interest.

Interest on some types of loans has some tax advantages. Interest on loans to state and local governments is exempt from the federal income tax, and interest on loans to the federal government (such as the interest you receive on U.S. Savings Bonds) is exempt from state and local income taxes. These tax advantages help governments borrow at lower interest rates than individuals or businesses.

Other Characteristics. When you put money into a bank account, you are allowing the bank to use the money. There are different types of bank accounts, though, and they pay different rates of interest. An account that allows you to write checks, for example, provides you with a benefit, so it pays a lower rate than a savings account, which does not offer this benefit.

If you agree to leave your funds in a savings account for a specified time— two years or five years, for example—you are providing the bank with some benefits. The bank knows for certain that it will keep your deposit, and it knows it can use the funds longer than if you had deposited them in, say, a checking account. In return, the bank will pay you a higher rate than on an account from which you can withdraw your funds at any time.

Suppose you lend to someone and suddenly you need the money back. It would be advantageous to you to be able to convert the loan into money quickly and without losing much of what you have lent. Loans that can be converted into money quickly and without a loss (either because you can

---

✔ Quick Tip

For a more detailed discussion of how interest rates are determined, see "Points of Interest," published by the Federal Reserve Bank of Chicago, available at www.chicagofed.org/publications/index.cfm#p.

Source: Federal Reserve Bank of New York, 2004.

demand that the borrower repay the loan at any time or because you can sell the loan to someone else) carry lower rates than other loans.

There are some differences in interest rates that not attributable to any of the reasons we have discussed. Just as some stores charge higher prices than other stores for the same items, some lenders charge higher rates than other lenders. In other words, while competition eliminates some price differences between similar goods and some interest-rate differences on similar loans, it doesn't eliminate all of them. So, if you are going to borrow, it might be a good idea to "shop around" to learn what interest rates different lenders charge.

Banks charge higher interest rates on the loans they make than they pay on deposits. They do that in order to make a profit.

So, why can't people cut out the bank as an intermediary and do the lending themselves, at the higher rates? There are several reasons:

- As an individual, you may not be able to find anyone who wants to borrow the amount you want to lend. Banks, though, can combine many people's funds to lend borrowers the amounts they want to borrow.

- As an individual, you may not be able to find anyone who wants to borrow for precisely the amount of time you want to lend. Banks, though, always have new deposits coming in, so they can lend for as long a period as people want to borrow for.

- Banks are much better than individuals at determining which potential borrowers are likely to repay loans, and which aren't.

Interest Rates And The Economy

Lower interest rates make it easier for people to borrow in order to buy cars and homes. Purchases of homes, in turn, increase the demand for other items, such as furniture and appliances, thus providing an additional boost to the economy.

Lower interest rates mean that consumers spend less on interest costs, leaving them with more of their income to spend on goods and services.

Lower interest rates make it easier for farmers, manufacturers, and other businesses to borrow to invest in equipment, inventories, and buildings. Also, the returns that investments will produce in future years are worth more today when rates are low than when rates are high. That gives business more of an incentive to invest when rates are low. Increased business investment, in turn, makes the economy grow faster, as productivity, or output per worker, increases faster.

Interest rates do not seem to affect the amount that people save. That's because higher interest rates have two conflicting effects on how much people save. First, the higher return that savings can earn gives people an incentive to save more. Second, however, the higher return makes savers feel richer, so they may spend more, rather than save more.

♣ It's A Fact!!
How does the health of the economy affect interest rates?

The health of the economy affects interest rates by influencing the supply of, and the demand for, credit. For example:

- People's incomes fall in a recession, so the amount they save also decreases.

- The demand for credit by business generally declines in a recession, as business spends less on new buildings, equipment, and inventories. Also, the Federal Reserve acts to reduce interest rates during recessions, in order to stimulate economic activity.

- The federal government's demand for credit generally rises in a recession, as the reduction in business and consumer incomes reduces tax revenues, and programs such as unemployment insurance require increased spending.

The net effect of all of these changes is that interest rates often go down in a recession.

In an expansion of the economy, the rising demand for credit pushes interest rates up. If the rates that consumers and businesses have to pay to borrow rise too rapidly, however, spending may decline, leading to an economic slowdown.

Source: Federal Reserve Bank of New York, 2004.

Simple Interest

Simple interest is interest paid only on the "principal" or the amount originally borrowed, and not on the interest owed on the loan.

For example, the simple interest due at the end of three years on a loan of $100 at a 10% annual interest rate is $30 (10% of $100, or $10, for each of the three years). No interest is calculated in the second year on the $10 interest that was due after the first year, and no interest is calculated in the third year on the interest that was due after two years.

Compound Interest?

Compound interest is interest calculated, not only on the principal, or the amount originally borrowed, but also on the interest that has accrued, or built up, at the time of the calculation.

Here's how the amount owed on a three-year loan at an interest rate of 10% would differ, depending on whether simple interest or compound interest was charged:

Compound interest is what depositors receive on bank accounts, and it makes their accounts grow faster than simple interest would.

Table 12.1. Comparison Of Simple And Compound Interest

	Simple Interest	Compound Interest
Amount of Loan	$100	$100
Amount Owed After One Year	$110	$110
Amount Owed After Two Years	$120	$121 ($110 + 10% of $110)
Amount Owed After Three Years	$130	$133.10 ($121 + 10% of $121)

Source: Federal Reserve Bank of New York, 2004.

The Magic Of Compounding

It doesn't take a fairy tale to achieve financial security. But if you start saving early and keep at it, you can benefit from the "magic" of compound interest that helps your money grow.

✔ Quick Tip

For more on compound interest, click on http://www.chicagofed.org/publications/abcinterest/index.cfm and go to "Compound interest."

Source: Federal Reserve Bank of New York, 2004.

Simply stated, compound interest means that you earn interest on the *original* amount you've saved, and then you continue to earn interest on the interest. This phenomenon goes on and on—packing your savings with power and moving you steadily toward your savings goals. Over time, the results can be dramatic.

To achieve lifetime financial security, you want your money to grow many times larger than its original value. With the magic of compounding at work, you can predict when you will double your money. It's called the Rule of 72—you simply divide 72 by the interest rate you'll earn on your investment. For instance, at a constant 6% interest rate, your money will double in approximately 12 years (72 ÷ 6).

The best news is that you can earn interest on even small amounts of savings—so you can start the magic of compounding today.

Start Early, Save More

The longer your money is invested, the better compounding works for you. It's not just that you give your money the chance to grow over many years, it's also the fact that the earlier you start, the less you have to save to reach your personal goal. The longer you wait or the more often you stop, the harder it is to make up for lost interest earnings.

☞ Remember!!

Compound interest means that you earn interest on the *original* amount you've saved, and then you continue to earn interest on the interest.

Source: ASEC, 2000.

Table 12.2. Start Early, Save More

Final Total	Amount Invested	Interest Earned
$159,557	$22,000	$137,557
Saved $2,000 per year from age 20 through age 30. Kept money in account until age 65.		
$337,746	$90,000	$247,746
Saved $2,000 per year from age 20 to age 65.		
$189,353	$70,000	$119,353
Saved $2,000 per year from age 30 to age 65.		
$99,254	$50,000	$49,254
Saved $2,000 per year from age 40 to age 65.		
$44,549	$30,000	$14,549
Saved $2,000 per year from age 50 to age 65.		

(*Assumes a 5% annual rate of return compounded monthly.*)

Source: ASEC, 2000.

If you're in the market for a house and you start saving a year or two before you want to move in, there's little time to make your money grow. But if you start saving when you get your first job and you aim to buy a house in ten years, the magic of compounding can put your money to work.

Say that you want to save $10,000 for a house down payment. Even in only two years, compounding makes a difference. If you try to save this amount of money in two years, you would have to save $401 a month, assuming you save in a vehicle earning a 4% rate of return compounded monthly. After two years, you've invested almost $9,624 and earned almost $376 in interest.

But, if you start earlier, and try to save the same $10,000 in ten years in the same vehicle earning 4%, your monthly savings requirement is only $68. That's a lot better than $83 a month without compounding ($10,000 ÷ 120). And, after ten years, you've invested about $8,160 and earned almost $1,840 in interest.

Manage Your Risks And Maximize Your Returns

When you start saving early and consistently, you can take a slow and steady route to your goals. Let's say that you have a goal to save $100,000. If you have 20 years to reach this goal, you could choose fairly conservative investments that earn, for example, a 4% rate of return. At this earnings rate, you need to invest $3,272 per year, and the magic of compounding helps you reach your goal.

But what if you shorten your savings period to just ten years? Then you have to save more and/or consider taking more risk. It would be almost impossible to earn a rate of return high enough to reach your $100,000 goal with the same amount of annual savings in just ten years. So, what if you invested your annual savings in a vehicle earning at 8% rate of return? You would need to save $6,559 each year to reach $100,000.

Go For The Savings Bonanza

When you start saving early *and* focus on tax-advantaged savings, you're way ahead of the game. With employer-sponsored 401(k) and similar plans and individual retirement accounts (IRAs), your money is not currently taxed as it grows—giving you even more money to save and invest. With more money and more time to save, there is even more magic in the "magic" of compounding.

☞ Remember!!

The higher the rate of return an investment vehicle has the potential to earn, the higher the risk that you could lose some or all of your money.

Source: ASEC, 2000.

Take Advantage Of Compound Interest

Compound interest helps you build wealth faster. Interest is paid on previously earned interest as well as on the original deposit or investment. For example, $5,000 deposited in a bank at 6 percent interest for a year earns $415 if the interest is compounded monthly. In just 5 years, the $5,000 will grow to $7,449.

Figure 12.1 shows how interest compounds on savings. Assume that a person saves $125 a month for 30 years and the interest on the savings is compounded monthly. The figure shows how compound interest at various rates would increase savings compared with simply putting the money in a shoebox. This is compound interest that you earn. And as you can see, compounding has a greater effect after the investment and interest have increased over a longer period.

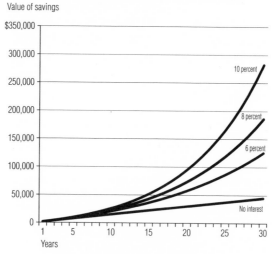

Figure 12.1. This chart demonstrates how compounding interest affects the value of an investment over time.

Part Four

Basic Investing For Teens

Chapter 13

Yes, Teens Actually Can Make Investments

When Time Is On Your Side

Investing when time is on your side is the absolutely best time to achieve your life's dreams and goals. It can mean the difference between an easy or difficult path your life will take. And while it may be the time in your life when you have the least amount of money, the time factor more than makes up for that. The miracle of compounding interest—a fundamental theme that runs through financial planning—can take a seemingly inconsequential investment and turn it into a major nest egg.

Another factor in your favor during the younger part of your life is that you can afford to take more risks—you can invest in riskier, and therefore higher yielding, investments, simply because you have the time to recoup your losses elsewhere if your investment goes bust. Again, this potentially greater return makes the most out of investing even small sums.

About This Chapter: This chapter includes text from "When Time Is On Your Side" reproduced with permission from CCH Financial Planning Toolkit™, January 2005, www.finance.cch.com; "Saving the Right Way," by Chris Stallman, © 1999 TeenAnalyst.com, LLC. All rights reserved. Reprinted with permission; "When Should I Start Investing?" by Chris Stallman, © 2001 TeenAnalyst.com, LCC. All rights reserved. Reprinted with permission; "Custodial Accounts," by Chris Stallman, © 1999 TeenAnalyst.com, LCC. All rights reserved. Reprinted with permission.

There you have it, the best of both worlds. Safer investments with lower risks and therefore lower returns have the time to build up into a substantial account. If you have a higher risk tolerance, you can invest in the riskier vehicles that older investors don't have time to take a shot at.

Sounds great, doesn't it? There's only one problem—the large majority of people at this point in their lives don't bother investing at all. They're too busy spending everything they make because they're "too young" to worry about investing. After all they're just starting to live—making and spending their own money—and they can barely make ends meet, whether they're earning $20,000 or over $100,000 annually.

☞ Remember!!

Remember, try your hardest to invest something, no matter how small it may seem, into the vehicle of your choice when time is on your side. Before you know it, you'll find yourself in the middle stage of your life.

Source: From CCH Financial Planning Toolkit™, January 2005.

Saving The Right Way

It's a known fact that if you can't save money, then it will be very difficult for you to invest any. So the first step in investing is to learn how to save money. Saving is a skill that a person carries throughout his or her lifetime and a person who does it correctly can become very rich. But how does one save correctly?

Saving The Wrong Way

In order to learn how to save the right way, we need to examine how to save the "wrong way."

Saving the wrong way is a lot like this: Your birthday was just last week and after collecting all of your birthday money from your generous relatives, you realize that you have earned a small fortune. Let's say $150. As you hold that money in your hand, your mind starts to race with plans of how you will spend it. You decide that you want that new CD. And maybe you've been eyeing that pair of jeans at Old Navy. As you think of how many things you can buy with this wealth of yours, you decide to make a trip to the local mall.

After a couple hours of shopping around, you find that you have only $10 left and think that you should just save it because there is nothing else that you want to spend it on.

What you just did was an example of saving the wrong way, which was not saving at all or not thinking about it until you had spent nearly all of your money.

Start To Save The Right Way

Now that you see how the wrong way to save works, understanding the right way is really rather easy.

People who save the right way realizes that saving money is very important, so they decide to save a portion of their money before they go out and spend all their money.

It's always important to have a plan to save and stick to it. If you want to save for that new stereo or for you college education, you need to tell yourself that you must save some money before you go out and spend the rest.

Instead of spending all of that $150 right away, a good saver would say "I really think that I should save first by setting aside $50." Then go to the mall and spend the rest on things that you really want.

It's really hard to set money aside and not touch it for a long time but it is really important to do this. Many goods such as cars are very expensive and most people cannot afford to buy one with just one paycheck so they have to save for it.

> ✔ **Quick Tip**
> **Save First,**
> **Then Invest**
>
> If you want to become a young investor, you have to have money to invest. So before you start to actually invest, you need to start yourself on a saving plan and decide how much you can save first. When you have enough money from your savings, you can use that money to buy stock in a company.
>
> Source: From "Saving the Right Way," by Chris Stallman, © 1999 Teen Analyst.com, LLC. All rights reserved. Reprinted with permission.

Over time, your savings habits will develop and will help you acquire your fortune.

When Should I Start Investing?

Question: *"Hey, I'm 17 and about to start college in the fall. I'm paying my way through college with scholarships so should I invest the money I had saved? Or should I just wait until after college to start investing?"*—Mark (Kalamazoo, Michigan)

Response: If the money you've set aside for college won't be used at all, then we recommend planning to start investing. But if you think you might need some of it for unforeseen expenses, then you might want to keep at least half of it in a traditional bank account or short-term CD.

But, really, now is the time to start thinking about investing, not after college. And here's why.

A long time ago, Albert Einstein called compounding "the eighth wonder of the world" because of its amazing abilities. Essentially, compounding is the idea that you can make money on the money you've already earned. The best way to explain this is through an example.

If you invest $1000 for 50 years at a 10% return that does NOT compound, you will receive $100 per year for 50 years. At the end of the 50 years, you would have $6,000 (the $1,000 investment + $5,000 in interest). Now, if you invested that $1000 for 50 years at a 10% return that *does* compound, you would have $117,390!

As you can see, compounding has a lot of value to investors. It makes their money grow a lot faster than it would if it didn't compound.

♣ It's A Fact!!

John decides to start investing when he gets out of college at age 22. He sets aside $1000 and earns a 10% return for 43 years (he retires at 65). At that time, he'll have $60,240. Jill decides to start investing too, but she does so at age 17, before she enters college. She sets aside $1000 she has earned and puts it into an investment with a 10% return for 48 years (she retires at 65). At that time, she'll have $97,017. That's a difference of nearly $37,000, even though Jill invested the same amount of money.

Source: © 2001 TeenAnalyst.com, LCC. All rights reserved. Reprinted with permission.

Compounding is also highly dependent on when you start investing and the smallest differences in when you start can make a big difference in your pocketbook when you retire.

Starting earlier can make a big difference in your pocketbook for when you retire. So our strongest advice to you is to begin investing early and set up a regular plan to invest a set amount (like, say, $50) per month.

👉 Remember!!

The way compounding works is that your money compounds slowly at first but it picks up speed the longer it's invested.

Source: © 2001 TeenAnalyst.com, LCC. All rights reserved. Reprinted with permission.

Custodial Accounts

When it comes to investing online or through a stockbroker, you can't just do it on your own...you actually have to have your parents' permission.

When you want to start investing in stocks, you have to set up what is known as a custodial account. In this account, you are named as the owner of the stocks but a person is appointed (usually a parent or guardian) to help you control the investments.

Keep in mind that this does not mean that the stocks aren't yours. You own them and you control them, but you have someone who will help you do this, and that is your custodian.

Once you reach the age of maturity for your state (usually 18 to 21) the custodian is removed from your account and you are given complete ownership of your account. But this doesn't mean that you can't take the money out at any time. You can tell your custodian that you want the money and they would have to withdraw it from your account for you. Also, the custodian can't take out any money from your account for himself.

I know it might seem like a drag to have a parent controlling your account because you want to do everything on your own but, believe me, this has some major benefits.

Benefits

It benefits you, the young investor, by offering you the opportunity to invest at such a young age. It also helps you in case you come across a situation involving your investments that you don't know how to handle. Your custodian would then help you out.

It benefits your parents or custodian because they are always aware of what you are investing in, which will help them sleep better at night knowing that little Johnny isn't risking all of his college money on a hot stock tip.

Disadvantages

For your parents or custodian, once they put money in your custodial account, they can't take it back. So if you decide to spend the money on that brand new sports car rather than your college education, they can't control that. So a lot of trust has to be given to you before they will risk that money.

Now that you know what kind of account to set up, you can talk to your parents about setting up a custodial account for you to get started in investing.

Chapter 14

Some Basics About Investing

Tools For Investing

Investing is not a get-rich-quick scheme. Smart investors take a long-term view, putting money into investments regularly and keeping it invested for five, 10, 15, 20, or more years.

Stocks—Owning Part Of A Company

Stocks. Shares of stock may be acquired on an organized exchange such as the Nasdaq or New York Stock Exchange, through a stockbroker, over the counter, or by direct purchase in some cases. When you buy stock, you become a part owner of the company and are known as a stockholder, or shareholder. Stockholders can make money in two ways—receiving dividend payments and selling stock that has appreciated. A dividend is an income

About This Chapter: "Tools For Investing," is excerpted from "Building Wealth: A Beginner's Guide to Securing Your Financial Future," 2002, a financial education publication of the Federal Reserve Bank of Dallas, http://www.dallasfed.org. "Investing 101: Portfolios and Diversification" is reprinted with permission from www.investopedia.com. © 2004 Investopedia, Inc. "Diversification Versus Concentration," by Chris Stallman, is © 2004 TeenAnalyst.com, LLC. All rights reserved. Reprinted with permission. "Understanding The Securities Markets" and "Reaching Financial Goals" are excerpted from *The Facts on Saving and Investing*, April 1999, published by the U.S. Securities and Exchange Commission. "How Do I Get There From Here?" excerpted and reprinted with permission from the American Savings Education Council, http://www.asec.org. © 2000. All rights reserved.

distribution by a corporation to its shareholders, usually made quarterly. Stock appreciation is an increase in the value of stock in the company, generally based on its ability to make money and pay a dividend. However, if the company doesn't perform as expected, the stock's value may go down.

There is no guarantee you will make money as a stockholder. In purchasing shares of stock, you take a risk on the company making a profit and paying a dividend or seeing the value of its stock go up. Before investing in a company, learn about its past financial performance, management, products and how the stock has been valued in the past. Learn what the experts say about the company and the relationship of its financial performance and stock price. Successful investors are well informed.

Stock Options. Some companies offer employees stock options, which they can use to buy stock in the company at a fixed price. For example, your employer, Wally's Widgets, offers a stock-option plan, and its stock is valued at $30 a share. The stock-option price is set at $40 a share. As part of your compensation for meeting company goals and contributing to increased profits, you receive options to purchase 100 shares. Over time the value of the Wally's Widgets shares appreciates to $50 a share. You may now want to exercise your stock options and purchase the shares valued at $50 for $40.

Bonds—Lending Your Money

Bonds. When you buy bonds, you are lending money to a federal or state agency, municipality or other issuer, such as a corporation. A bond is like an IOU. The issuer promises to pay a stated rate of interest during the life of the bond and repay the entire face value when the bond comes due, or reaches maturity. The interest a bond pays is based primarily on the credit quality of the issuer and current interest rates. Firms like Moody's Investor Service and Standard & Poor's rate bonds. With corporate bonds, the company's bond rating is based on its financial picture. The rating for municipal bonds is based on the creditworthiness of the governmental or other public entity that issues it. Issuers with the greatest likelihood of paying back the money have the highest ratings, and their bonds will pay an investor a lower interest rate. Remember, the lower the risk, the lower the expected return.

A bond may be sold at face value (called par) or at a premium or discount. For example, when prevailing interest rates are lower than the bond's stated rate, the selling price of the bond rises above its face value. It is sold at a premium. Conversely, when prevailing interest rates are higher than the bond's stated rate, the selling price of the bond is discounted below face value. When bonds are purchased, they may be held to maturity or traded.

Treasury Bonds, Bills And Notes. The bonds the U.S. Treasury issues are sold to pay for an array of government activities and are backed by the full faith and credit of the federal government. Treasury bonds are securities with terms of more than 10 years. Interest is paid semiannually. The U.S. government also issues securities known as Treasury bills and notes. Treasury bills are short-term securities with maturities of three months, six months or one year. They are sold at a discount from their face value, and the difference between the cost and what you are paid at maturity is the interest you earn. Treasury notes are interest-bearing securities with maturities ranging from two to 10 years. Interest payments are made every six months. Inflation-indexed securities offer investors a chance to buy a security that keeps pace with inflation. Interest is paid on the inflation-adjusted principal.

Bonds, bills and notes are sold in increments of $1,000.

Savings Bonds. U.S. savings bonds are government-issued and government-backed. There are different types of savings bonds, each with slightly different features and advantages. Series I bonds are indexed for inflation. The earnings rate on this type of bond combines a fixed rate of return with the annualized rate of inflation. Savings bonds can be purchased in denominations ranging from $50 to $10,000.

Some government-issued bonds offer special tax advantages. There is no state or local income tax on the interest earned from Treasury and savings bonds. And in most cases, interest earned from municipal bonds is exempt from federal and state income tax. Typically, higher income investors buy these bonds for their tax benefits.

Mutual Funds—Investing In Many Companies

Mutual funds are established to invest many people's money in many firms. When you buy mutual fund shares, you become a shareholder of a fund that has invested in many other companies. By diversifying, a mutual fund spreads risk across numerous companies rather than relying on just one to perform well. Mutual funds have varying degrees of risk. They also have costs associated with owning them, such as management fees, which will vary depending on the type of investments the fund makes.

Before investing in a mutual fund, learn about its past performance, the companies it invests in, how it is managed and the fees investors are charged. Learn what the experts say about the fund and its competitors.

👉 **Remember!!**

Remember, when investing in stocks, bonds and mutual funds:

• Find good information to help you make informed decisions.

• Make sure you know and understand all the costs associated with buying, selling and managing your investments.

• Beware of investments that seem too good to be true; they probably are.

Source: Federal Reserve Bank of Dallas, 2002.

Investing 101: Portfolios And Diversification

It's good to clarify how securities are different from each other, but it's more important to understand how their different characteristics can work together to accomplish an objective.

The Portfolio

A portfolio is a combination of different investment assets mixed and matched for the purpose of achieving an investor's goal(s). Items that are considered a part of your portfolio can include any asset you own—from real items such as art and real estate, to equities, fixed-income instruments, and cash and equivalents. For the purpose of this section, we will focus on the most liquid asset types: equities, fixed-income securities, and cash and equivalents.

An easy way to think of a portfolio is to imagine a pie chart, whose portions each represent a type of vehicle to which you have allocated a certain portion of your whole investment. The asset mix you choose according to your aims and strategy will determine the risk and expected return of your portfolio.

Basic Types Of Portfolios

In general, *aggressive* investment strategies—those that shoot for the highest possible return—are most appropriate for investors who, for the sake of this potential high return, have a high risk tolerance (can stomach wide fluctuations in value) and a longer time horizon. Aggressive portfolios generally have a higher investment in equities.

✎ What's It Mean?

Cash/Money Market: Any short-term, fixed-income investment, for example, money in a savings account or a certificate of deposit (CD).

Fixed-Income Instruments (or Fixed-Income Security): An investment that provides a return in the form of fixed periodic payments and eventual return of principle at maturity.

Futures: A financial contract that requires the sale of financial instruments or physical commodities for future delivery, usually on a commodity exchange. Futures contracts try to "bet" what the value of an index or commodity will be at some date in the future.

Inflation: The rate at which the general level of prices for goods and services is rising, and subsequently, purchasing power is falling.

Options: A privilege sold by one party to another that offers the buyer the right, but not the obligation, to buy (call) or sell (put) a security at an agreed-upon price during a certain period of time or on a specific date.

Portfolio: The group of assets—such as stocks, bonds, and mutuals—held by an investor.

Source: Excerpted from "Dictionary," and reprinted with permission from www.investopedia.com. © 2004 Investopedia, Inc.

The *conservative* investment strategies, which put safety at a high priority, are most appropriate for investors who have a lower risk tolerance and shorter time horizon. Conservative portfolios will generally consist mainly of cash and cash equivalents, or high-quality fixed-income instruments.

To demonstrate the types of allocations that are suitable for these strategies, we'll look at samples of both a conservative and a moderately aggressive portfolio.

The main goal of a conservative portfolio strategy is to maintain the real value of the portfolio, that is, to protect the value of the portfolio against inflation. The portfolio you see here would yield a high amount of current income from the bonds, and would also yield long-term capital growth potential from the investment in high quality equities.

A moderately aggressive portfolio is meant for individuals with a longer time horizon and an average risk tolerance. Investors who find these types of portfolios attractive are seeking to balance the amount of risk and return contained within the fund.

The portfolio would consist of approximately 50–55% equities, 35–40% bonds, 5–10% cash and equivalents.

You can further break down the above asset classes into subclasses, which also have different risks and potential returns. For example, an investor might divide the equity portion between large companies, small companies, and international firms. The bond portion might be allocated between those that are short-term and long-term, government versus corporate debt, and so forth. More advanced investors might also have some of the alternative assets such as options and futures in the mix. As you can see, the number of possible asset allocations is practically unlimited.

Why Portfolios?

It all centers around diversification. Different securities perform differently at any point in time, so with a mix of asset types, your entire portfolio does not suffer the impact of a decline of any one security. When your stocks go down, you may still have the stability of the bonds in your portfolio.

There have been all sorts of academic studies and formulas that demonstrate why diversification is important, but it's really just the simple practice of "not putting all your eggs in one basket." If you spread your investments across various types of assets and markets, you'll reduce the risk of catastrophic financial losses.

Diversification Versus Concentration

You've probably heard the saying, "don't put all of your eggs in one basket." Whoever came up with that was probably someone with a diversified investment portfolio because it's a very pertinent topic in personal finance.

Diversification is the strategy of spreading your money out among a number of investments. The thought is that if you own many stocks and one does poorly, your portfolio won't be affected as much. But also, if one stock does very well, your portfolio won't reap all of the benefits. So you are supported by all of your stocks, rather than depending on just one or two.

Concentration is the exact opposite strategy. Someone who has a concentrated portfolio may own just a couple stocks. If those stocks do really well, his portfolio will do really well too. But if they do poorly, he can end up losing a lot more money than planned. By having a concentrated portfolio, an investor is exposed to more risk but can earn higher returns.

It's highly unlikely that new investors will be able to achieve diversification on their own. Going out and buying 50–100 stocks is pretty difficult to do. If you invested $1,000 in each of them, you'd need $50,000–100,000. Not to mention that commissions will cost you a fortune. So your best way to do this is to invest in a mutual fund or exchange-traded fund (ETF) that will buy many stocks for you.

So which one is better? Well, it's pretty hard to say. Most investment advisors will tell people to own many stocks because putting all of your money in one or two stocks is too risky. However, some investment professionals will argue that concentrated portfolios are better because it's easier to keep up-to-date and follow your companies when there are just a few of them. They feel that people with diversified portfolios are clueless about the latest happenings with most of their stocks. So, again, which one is better? Especially for teens, a combination of diversification and concentration is recommended. We recommend you put at least half of your money into a diversified mutual fund. You can then open another account where you own just a few stocks and follow them closely. But the general rule of thumb is that it's better to be more diversified than concentrated. However, that's entirely up to you.

Understanding The Securities Markets

Not all investors are as informed as they should be on how the securities markets work, and the risks and rewards of investing.

For example, a study by the Investor Protection Trust concluded that "less than a fifth (18%) of investors surveyed are truly literate about financial matters specifically related to investing. Most lack basic knowledge about the meaning of financial terms and about the way different investment works."[1] Key findings of the study include:

- As many as 62% of investors mistakenly believe that a "no-load" mutual fund involves no sales charges or other fees.

- Only 38% of investors know that when interest rates go up the prices of bonds usually go down.

Similarly, a report on the financial literacy of mutual fund investors found that:

- Less than half of all investors correctly understand that the purpose of diversification is to balance both risk and return in achieving their financial goals.

- Approximately 45% of investors mistakenly believe that diversification provides "a *guarantee* that [their] portfolio won't suffer if the stock market falls."

- Nearly half of investors do not understand the impact of expenses on mutual fund results.[2]

Many investors today have unrealistic expectations of the long-term performance of the securities markets, some anticipating returns as high as

16–22% per year. They need to understand portfolio diversification and risk. A balanced mix of stocks, bonds, and cash provides investors with a cushion should any single asset class in their portfolio decrease in value during any given period. Because greater return usually correlates with greater risk, investors should know what their risk tolerance is and how risk fits in with their long- and short-term financial goals.

A study by Public Agenda found that "even when asked to include anything and everything they've stored in any type of savings vehicle, nearly half of all Americans report nothing or less than $10,000 in retirement savings."[3] While perhaps understandable in today's complex and difficult financial environment, the widespread failure to adequately plan does not bode well for Americans looking forward to the future.

Reaching Financial Goals

Reaching financial goals requires a considerable amount of thought, planning and discipline. How might you (1) gather the appropriate information; (2) formulate a realistic savings and investment plan; and (3) implement the plan with a program of disciplined saving and wise investment?

Get The Facts: Learn The Basics. The first step in reaching a financial goal is getting the right information. Making well-considered savings and investment decisions depends on knowing your own financial situation and needs. The following list, prepared by ASEC [American Savings Education Council], serves as a useful example of some of the primary areas that Americans need to address in retirement planning:[4]

- Cash reserves for emergencies

- Social Security benefits

- Employer-sponsored pensions or profit sharing plans

- Tax-sheltered savings plans such as 401(k)s

- Individual Retirement Accounts

- Savings

Make A Plan. Once an individual has gathered the basic information and has reasonably sound knowledge of the saving and investment options available, he or she is ready to formulate a plan, or road map, to serve as a financial guide in the coming years.

The Investor Protection Trust has suggested a five-step approach to help investors get started on developing a financial plan:[5]

- *Set goals.* Figure out what your major goals are, how much it will cost to reach them and the number of years that you have to build up your savings.

- *Start saving.* Your savings should not depend on what happens to be left over at the end of the month. Based on your goals and how much you need to save to reach them, start setting aside something toward each goal every month ... and put it in separate accounts. The best way to make sure that you have money to save is to put yourself on a budget based on your income and expenses.

- *Match investments to goals.* Take the time to learn about the best types of savings and investment products for each of your goals. An important point: Choosing the right type of investment is more important than choosing the very "best" product of that type. Never buy an investment that you do not understand. Always make sure that any investment you buy makes sense as part of your overall financial plan.

- *Do an annual check-up.* Have your goals changed? How are your investments doing? Could you save even more? These are the questions that you should ask at least once every year.

- *Choose help wisely.* You may be able to put together and carry out a financial plan on your own. Public libraries, bookstores and the Internet are good sources of information about financial planning strategies, as well as the savings and investment products used to carry them out. If you decide that you need the help of a financial professional, determine in advance what services you want to get

👉 **Remember!!**

Save And Invest Wisely

Investigate before you invest. Here are some tips individuals should follow to protect their hard-earned money:

1. **Ask Questions.** Call your state's securities regulators, and ask:

   • Is the investment registered?

   • Are the broker and the firm licensed to do business in your state? You can get that number by calling the North American Securities Administrators Association at 202-737-0900.

2. **Know Your Broker.** Ask your state's securities regulators if they've received complaints against the broker and the broker's firm. You can also call the National Association of Securities Dealers' toll-free public disclosure hotline at 800-289-9999 or visit their website at www.nasdr.com.

3. **Know The Investment.** How long has the company been in business? What are its products or services? Has the company made money for investors before?

4. **Get The Facts In Writing.** Don't get swept away by a sales pitch. Always ask for—and read carefully—the company's prospectus or latest annual report.

Source: SEC, 1999.

and then interview two or three properly licensed professionals who specialize in your needed services, are experienced, and have clean disciplinary records. Make sure you know how your financial adviser is going to be compensated and the total cost of getting his or her advice and putting it into action.

How Do I Get There From Here?

Are you overwhelmed by the number and variety of saving and investment vehicles available? You're not alone. Many of us believe there is more to learn about saving and investing than our busy schedules will allow. As a result, some of us stick to familiar vehicles (like a bank account) that may be appropriate for our short-term financial goals but make reaching our long-term goals more difficult. Others become poor financial consumers—buying inappropriate financial products they know very little about.

Fortunately, there is no need to feel overwhelmed. We'll let you in on a little secret—some of the most successful investment strategies are also simple and easy to understand. In fact, you will probably be surprised at how little time and effort it takes to master the fundamentals of saving and investing.

You'll want to take advantage of resources that teach the basics of saving and investing. These resources can be found at your local public library, on TV, or online from your home computer. If you need further assistance, a stockbroker, insurance agent, or financial planner can serve as your resource. Mastering the basics will help you work more effectively with your financial professional to create and maintain your saving and investing plan.

Once you understand the basics of investing you may still want guidance from a professional. Stockbrokers, insurance agents, and financial planners can assist you in developing an investment plan. But finding a qualified professional with whom you are comfortable is not easy. You must be prepared to identify several good candidates and interview each before making your selection.

You may begin by asking family and friends for recommendations. You can call or visit a local financial services firm to request information. Attend a free investment seminar given by a stockbroker, insurance agent, or a financial planner. If one of the speakers looks like a good candidate, call him or her for an interview.

Once you complete your investigation, narrow your list of potential candidates to those you wish to interview. Always conduct a personal interview to make sure you are comfortable with your final selection (in other words: you feel you will work well together—remember, this will be a long-term relationship).

A Guide For Do-It-Yourselfers

It is helpful to know what resources are available to help you make important decisions. [Some specific resources are listed at the end of this book.]

Your local newsstand and even the public library can be great sources of information on investing. There is a wide array of newspapers, magazines, and books written specifically for the individual investor.

More advanced individual investors can take advantage of a number of useful television programs. These programs typically cover events on Wall Street on a daily or weekly basis and are formatted to address issues confronting the individual investor.

Serious do-it-yourselfers may be interested in the wide range of budgeting and financial planning software available. These products help you with simple functions such as balancing a checkbook, and more advanced tasks like tracking your investment portfolio.

Online services are an excellent resource for any level of investor. Services such as America OnLine, CompuServe, and Prodigy offer chat rooms on personal finance as well as detailed information on investment companies, daily stock and mutual fund information, and access to the Internet, which offers a wealth of information.

If you prefer the classroom environment, there are virtually hundreds of classes, workshops, and seminars designed for all levels of investors from the novice to the expert. Local universities and community colleges offer many of these resources. Additionally, similar programs are often sponsored by stockbrokers, insurance agents, and financial planners.

Many of these courses can be located by looking through the business or finance section of your local newspaper, in a community college course catalog or simply by contacting a local financial services provider.

References

1. *Investor Knowledge Survey: A Report on the Findings,* Princeton Survey Research Associates for the Investor Protection Trust (March 1996).

2. The Vanguard Group, *Vanguard/Money Mutual Fund Literacy Test,* section 1, conducted by Edith C. Krieger, Ph.D. (January 1998) ("Mutual Fund Literacy Test").

3. Steve Farkas and Jean Johnson, *Miles to Go: A Status Report of American's Plans for Retirement, A Report From Public Agenda,* (1997).

4. ASEC and DOL, *Top 10 Ways to Beat the Clock and Prepare for Retirement* (www.asec.org/topten.htm).

5. Investor Knowledge (Press Release Packet).

Chapter 15

How To Become A Savvy Investor

Investment Choices Overview

Before beginning to invest, you also should know what your options are—and there are many: individual stocks and bonds, mutual funds, and more. Although these terms may already be familiar to you, do you really understand the variety of investment options and which are best for you?

Investing In Stocks

There are two types of stock shares: common and preferred. When you own a public company's common stock, you are entitled to vote in the election of company officers and on other important matters, and often you receive dividends on your shares. Common stock is usually riskier than preferred stock. Because of this, it offers greater potential returns and losses.

About This Chapter: This chapter begins with text excerpted from "Investment Choices Overview," © 2005 National Association of Securities Dealers, Inc. (NASD). Reprinted with permission from NASD. "U.S. Government Securities" is excerpted from *Investment Basics: Financial Institution Deposits and U.S. Government Securities,* by Joyce Jones, Ph.D., reprinted with permission of the Kansas State University Agricultural Experiment Station and Cooperative Extension Service, Manhattan, Kansas, http://www.oznet.ksu.edu/. Copyright © 1995. All rights reserved. "How To Avoid Problems With Investing" is excerpted from *The SEC's Roadmap to Saving and Investing,* Office of Investor Education and Assistance, U.S. Securities and Exchange Commission, October 8, 2004.

As a shareholder of preferred stock, you would not usually have voting rights, but you would receive a fixed dividend, which would be paid to you before common stockholders are paid. But owners of preferred stock pay for that privilege—usually your dividends wouldn't increase when the company's profits increase. When a company does well, the price of its preferred stock tends to underperform its common shares. However, when a company fails, preferred stockholders are ahead of common stockholders in recouping their investment.

The stock price is the amount at which you can buy one share of a public company's stock at a given moment. Outside events can make the price of a stock rise or fall. For instance, if another company or a big investor wants to buy the company you're invested in, the company's share price could rise quickly on that news. On the other hand, if your investment is in a pharmaceutical company and its competitor wins government approval for a drug similar to one that your company manufactures, the company's stock price might tumble. Other forces that can affect stock prices include interest rates, national and international issues or events, foreign exchange rates, financial forecasts, and new technologies. Retail stocks, for example, are subject to declines during recessions.

> ### ✎ What's It Mean?
>
> Market: A setting in which buyers and sellers establish prices for identical or very similar products, and exchange goods or services.
>
> Common stock: A share in the ownership of a corporation.
>
> Source: From "Glossary of Economic Terms" in *Outline of the U.S. Economy*, a publication of the Bureau of International Information Programs, U.S. State Department, February 2001.

The terms *large-cap, mid-cap,* and *small-cap* refers to the issuing company's market capitalization, that is the overall value of all shares of the company's stock. Stocks are also categorized by the way they perform. *Growth stocks* are shares of companies that have exhibited relatively fast growth in earnings, which generally causes the stock price to go up. Keep in mind, though, that growth stocks are the most volatile and are just as likely to go down in price quickly. That's because growth companies are typically in new or fast-growing industries such as the high-tech sector. Growth stocks are considered riskier and often pay you lower or no dividends but appeal to investors who will accept more volatility and risk in hopes of a greater appreciation in share price over time.

Income stocks, on the other hand, are characterized as those that would pay you high and regular dividends. Stable and well-established industries, including utilities and financial institutions, typically produce income stocks. Blue-chip stocks is the name applied to large, well-known, well-established companies with good reputations.

Value stocks are those considered to be selling at lower prices or "undervalued" because the companies that issue these shares have had business setbacks or are out of favor with investors. Value stocks have been known to outperform growth stocks in slow markets—and vice versa. But there is still a risk with value stocks because not all companies recover from setbacks.

Stocks are often referred to by a combination of the characteristics discussed above, such as shares of a "small-cap value" stock or of a "mid-cap growth" stock.

Dividends are the distribution of a company's profit or earnings back to the company's shareholders, or stockholders—the people and firms that have purchased that company's stock. Dividends are another way you can share in a company's growth; they are usually distributed quarterly. Most companies offer dividend reinvestment plans, which means that instead of paying you by sending you a check or depositing the money into your account, the amount of the dividend is used to buy more shares of the company's stock in your name. This is a good way to increase your investment in the company over time.

Utilities are an example of an industry with traditionally high dividend rates. Growth stocks and small cap stocks, on the other hand, tend to offer little, if any, dividends to their shareholders, as any profit the company makes is poured back into the growing company.

When selecting stocks, it's good to keep in mind factors that could influence the company's performance—and, therefore, the investment. [See chapters 18 and 19 for more information about stocks.]

✎ What's It Mean?

Growth Stocks: Shares in a company whose earnings are expected to grow at an above average rate relative to the market. A growth stock usually does not pay a dividend, as the company would prefer to reinvest retained earnings in capital projects. Most technology companies are growth stocks.

Income Stocks: A stock with a history of regular dividend payments that constitute the largest portion of the stock's overall return.

Large-Cap: Companies having a market capitalization between $10 billion and $200 billion.

Market Capitalization: The total dollar value of all outstanding shares. It's calculated by multiplying the number of shares times the current market price. This term is often referred to as "market cap."

Mid-Cap: Short for "Middle Cap," mid cap refers to stocks with a market capitalization of between $2 billion to $10 billion.

Preferred Stock: A class of ownership in a corporation with a stated dividend that must be paid before dividends to common stock holders. Preferred shareholders have priority over common stockholders on earnings and assets in the event of liquidation.

Small-Cap: Refers to stocks with a relatively small market capitalization. The definition of small cap can vary among brokerages, but generally it is a company with a market capitalization of between $300 million to $2 billion. Keep in mind that classifications such as "large cap" or "small cap" are only approximations that change over time. Also, the exact definition can vary between brokerage houses.

Value Stocks: A stock that tends to trade at a lower price relative to its fundamentals (i.e. dividends, earnings, sales, etc.) and thus considered undervalued by a value investor. Common characteristics of such stocks include a high dividend yield, low price-to-book ratio and/or low price-to-earnings ratio.

Source: Excerpted from "Dictionary," and reprinted with permission from www.investopedia.com. © 2004 Investopedia, Inc.

Investing In Bonds

Bonds are actually loans that investors—individuals like you, as well as institutions—make to the federal government, state governments, municipalities, companies, and government agencies. Investors who buy bonds become bondholders, or lenders. Bondholders get an "I.O.U." from the issuer of the bond, but the bondholder doesn't have any ownership rights like stockholders do.

Generally, bonds are fixed-income securities because they pay you, as the bondholder, a predetermined interest rate (also called "coupon rate"), regularly, that is set when the bond is issued. However, some bonds are issued with variable rates that can be affected by external economic factors. The borrower or issuer promises to pay back the loan in full on the maturity date. All bonds have set maturity dates—the date when it must be paid back to investors at its face amount, called "par value."

Bonds are usually sold in $1,000 units. Like its interest rate, a fixed-income bond's term is set when it is issued. Short-term bonds are usually one year or less. Intermediate-term bonds run 2 to 10 years and long-term bonds are generally for at least 20 to 40 years. In most cases, the longer the term, the higher the interest rate paid. Just as bank certificates of deposit (CDs) pay higher interest rates for the right to keep your money for a longer term than an ordinary savings account, so do bonds. Be aware, however, that the risk level increases the longer the bond is held because of its vulnerability to interest rate fluctuations and inflation, over time.

Different Types Of Bonds: Private corporations issue corporate bonds to raise money for capital expenditures, operations, and acquisitions. Corporate bond interest is taxable and the prices are well publicized (usually in newspapers), so it's easy to know what the bonds are worth. As with stocks, investing in corporate bonds carries risk. The value of the bond may change depending on changes in the company's credit rating and, in the event of a corporate bankruptcy, holders of corporate bonds suffer significant losses.

Municipal bonds issued by states, cities, counties, and towns pay for public works projects like new schools and highways. Your investment in municipal bonds is generally exempt from federal income taxes, and in many states, from state income taxes, too. This may be advantageous if you are in a high tax bracket. A tax-free bond usually has a lower yield than a taxable bond.

Secured bonds are backed by collateral that the issuer may sell to repay you if the bond is defaulted on at maturity. Unsecured bonds, called debentures, are backed by the promise and good credit of the bond's issuer. A convertible bond may at some time be exchanged for other securities from the issuing company under specified conditions.

Understanding Your Bond Investment: Interest rates affect bond prices—though, inversely. Usually, bond prices move in the opposite direction of national interest rates; when interest rates rise, bond prices fall. For example: you buy a 10-year, $1,000 bond issued at 7% today. Five years later, you want to sell that bond, but now interest rates have risen to 9% and new bonds are

---

✎ What's It Mean?

<u>Bond Rating</u>: A specification of a bond issuer's probability of defaulting based on an analysis of the issuer's financial condition and profit potential. Bond ratings start at AAA (denoting the highest investment quality) and usually end at D (meaning payment is in default).

<u>Dividends</u>: Distribution of a portion of a company's earnings, decided by the board of directors, to a class of its shareholders. Dividends may be in the form of cash, stock, or property. Most secure and stable companies offer dividends to their stockholders. Their share prices might not move much, but the dividend attempts to make up for this. High-growth companies don't offer dividends because all their profits are reinvested to help sustain higher-than-average growth.

<u>Fixed-Income Securities</u>: An investment that provides a return in the form of fixed periodic payments and eventual return of principle at maturity. Generally, these types of assets offer a lower return on investment because they guarantee income.

<u>Par Value</u>: The face value of a bond.

Source: Excerpted from "Dictionary," and reprinted with permission from www.investopedia.com. © 2004 Investopedia, Inc.

paying 9%. Few people would want
to buy a $1,000 bond paying
only 7%. So, you would probably have to sell that $1,000
bond for less than $1,000 to
make up for the higher interest rate now being paid
on other bonds.

☞ Remember!!

In extreme cases, the issuer of the bond
can suspend interest payments or default
entirely. Issuers can also buy back, or "call,"
the bonds before maturity if interest rates fall.
You should study the call provisions thoroughly before buying a bond.

Source: NASD, 2005.

Bond ratings measure credit
risk. Several private agencies, such
as Moody's and Standard & Poor's,
rate bonds based on their assessment of un-
derlying risk that the issuer may not be able to pay back the bond's principle
and interest. The better the rating, the lower the interest the bond will usually pay. Generally the higher the yield, the greater the risk.

Finally, some bonds, like U.S. Treasuries and municipal bonds, require
large minimum investments, usually $10,000. [See chapter 20 for more in-
formation about the bond market.]

Investing In Mutual Funds

Over the past decade, mutual funds—which are invested in everything
from stocks and bonds to commodities and money market securities—have
attracted millions of investors seeking both income and capital appreciation.
According to a recent study, investments in mutual funds have tripled since
1990. Today, more than 88% of investors own shares in mutual funds. Nearly
half of all investors own all their stocks through mutual fund shares and do
not own any stocks in individual firms.

A mutual fund is simply a pool of money invested for you by an investment
firm in a variety of instruments like stocks, bonds, or government securities. Each
mutual fund is different in its make-up and philosophy. As an investor, you should
look for funds with objectives and risk levels that match yours. If you're interested
in a diversified mutual fund covering a single class of investments, there are many
broad-based funds that invest in a wide variety of stocks. If you prefer to stick
with single industries, you might consider sector funds such as real estate

investment trusts (REITs), technology, and telecommunication funds, among others. Mutual funds are also a good way to invest in foreign stocks. Some funds own hundreds of different securities, while others may own only a few dozen.

The two most common types of mutual funds are equity funds that invest primarily in common stocks and fixed-income funds or "bond funds" that typically invest in bonds or money market securities. Less common are "balanced funds" invested in both equity and debt.

Most mutual funds require a minimum initial investment, sometimes as low as $250. Mutual fund shares trade like stocks, rising and falling in price depending on investor interest and the performance of stocks in the fund. The Net Asset Value (NAV) of a mutual fund indicates its value or price per share. Like stocks, mutual funds are liquid, meaning they can be bought and sold easily.

Before investing in a mutual fund, find out if it's a load or no-load mutual fund. Load funds charge a sales commission; no-load funds don't. When you pay a sales commission going in, that's called a front-end load. A commission paid when you sell is known as a back-end load. The advantage to a load fund is that there is usually staff available to explain the fund to you and advise you as to the appropriate time to buy more shares, or sell. If you're a new investor, it might be worth paying the commission for the extra guidance. With some no-load funds, a staff person merely takes your order to buy or sell, or can only offer limited support—you are fully responsible for understanding the investment.

Many mutual fund rates don't account for shareholder tax liability. Your actual return after-taxes might wind up much lower than the pre-tax one cited in the magazine or newspaper article rating the mutual funds. Remember, funds with high pre-tax returns don't necessarily offer the best after-tax returns. Not all funds create the same taxes for the investor. Smart investors look for the best total return.

A mutual fund that frequently trades its holdings pays more taxes than a fund that holds its investments long term. Unless you are invested in an Individual Retirement Account (IRA) or other tax-exempt account, you have to pay taxes whenever your fund sells a stock and profits. The more profitable the trades, the more taxes paid. Some fund managers count on attractive short-term returns to attract new investors. If your mutual fund investment is for your retirement, then tax liability may not be important for you now.

Index funds are mutual funds that are more conservative in their approach; they try to match their performance to the performance of the stock or bond markets as a whole. By purchasing the same securities held in an index such as Standard and Poor's 500 or the Russell 2000, these funds match the return on the markets they index. [See chapters 22 and 23 for more information about mutual funds.]

Futures And Options

Futures and options are not for most individual long-term investors. Futures commit the investor to buy or sell a commodity like wheat or silver on a set day for a set price. If the market value of the commodity increases, you profit. If it falls, you could lose all of your investment and more. There is great opportunity and great risk. That's why new investors tend to leave the futures markets to professionals or more experienced investors.

☞ Remember!!

There are dozens of kinds of mutual funds, each designed to meet the needs and preferences of different kinds of investors. Some funds seek to realize current income, while others aim for long-term capital appreciation. Some invest conservatively, while others take bigger chances in hopes of realizing greater gains. Some deal only with stocks of specific industries or stocks of foreign companies, and others pursue varying market strategies.

Source: From *Outline of the U.S. Economy*, a publication of the Bureau of International Information Programs, U.S. State Department, February 2001.

Options are an owner's right to buy or sell a specific item, like a stock, for a set price during a certain period of time. You can buy the right to purchase a security, say, for $50 during the next three months. If the stock increases in value, the option is worth more. If it falls, the option can expire, worthless. Options are traded in stocks, currencies, stock indexes, Treasury bills, and bonds.

Employer-Sponsored Retirement Plans

A good place to start investing for retirement is with your employer-sponsored retirement plan. Among these plans are defined contribution plans, such as the 457, the 403(b), and perhaps the most familiar, the 401(k). If your employer offers a retirement plan, you should consider participating in it, as it is one of the easiest and most beneficial means of helping you save for your retirement. It is also one of the best ways to defer paying taxes on your investments.

Contributing to a 401(k) is simple; your employer deducts the amount you designate from your pay, before federal taxes—in other words, the amount you contribute to the plan lowers your taxable income. In many companies, the employer matches all or part of your contribution. Let's say you make $4,000 each month and contribute 6% to your 401(k) plan account, or $240.00 If your employer's plan offers a 50% match—that is, half of the 6% you designate—your employer would put $120 into your 401(k) account for you each month.

As the employee, you usually get to choose how much you want to contribute within the restrictions of your particular plan; however, your employer or its plan administrator will manage the account. Many 401(k) plans also allow you to direct how the funds in your account are invested within the choices allowed by the plan. It is important that you read all the information provided to you about the plan and consult the plan administrator, if necessary, to ask questions and discuss the details. To learn more about 401(k)s, please read Smart 401(k) Investing.

A 403(b) plan is similar to a 401(k), but is offered to employees of public and private school systems—kindergarten through college—and non-profit, tax-exempt organizations, such as churches, libraries, etc. Your plan administrator can explain how it works and how it differs from the 401(k).

The 457 plan, offered only to state and local government employees, allows you to set aside a portion of your pay for use later—generally in retirement. You are not taxed on that income now; you pay taxes later, when you withdraw the money from the plan. A 457 plan reduces your current income taxes, while helping you save for retirement, and allows your earnings to accumulate tax-deferred.

Individual Retirement Accounts

You're probably already familiar with individual retirement accounts (IRAs). These tax-deferred accounts have been around since 1984 to help working people save for retirement.

Most IRAs allow you to direct how funds in your account are invested. You may be able to invest the funds in a variety of ways, including individual stocks and bonds, annuities, and mutual funds, though there are some restrictions on how you invest your IRA funds. Also, as long as you don't contribute more than your annual limit, you may diversify your IRA funds among different types of investments. Additionally, you cannot use your life insurance policies to fund your IRA.

There are two types of IRAs—traditional and Roth.

Traditional IRA: The earnings on your IRA are taxed-deferred. Depending on how much money you earn, you may be eligible to deduct your IRA contribution from your gross income for tax purposes. But, there are penalties for withdrawing money from your traditional IRA before you reach the age of 59½, and withdrawals will be taxed as ordinary income.

Roth IRA: This type of IRA was named after former Senator William Roth of Delaware, who championed the Taxpayer Relief Act of 1997. Eligibility is determined by the amount of your annual income. You may not deduct contributions to your Roth IRA from your taxable income, but growth in your Roth IRA is tax-free.

If you have had your Roth IRA for more than five years, you may be able to withdraw earnings from your Roth IRA without paying penalties and/or taxes, if: you have reached the age of 59½, you become fully disabled, or you are using the money to buy your first home ($10,000 life-time limit). You may also withdraw from your Roth IRA to pay for college—you will have to pay taxes on that withdrawal, but you will not be subject to the penalty for premature withdrawal.

In some cases, you may convert your traditional IRA to a Roth IRA, but you will have to pay income taxes on the converted amount not previously taxed. As with any retirement investment, you should consult a financial professional to learn all the details.

U.S. Government Securities

The U.S. Treasury Department issues a variety of marketable securities (bills, notes, and bonds), as well as nonmarketable securities (such as Series EE and HH savings bonds) to raise funds. All are backed by the full taxing power of the federal government; thus, the interest payments and the return of principal are fully guaranteed. Further, while interest earned on these Treasury securities is subject to federal income taxes, it is not subject to state or local taxes.

Treasury Bills. The major distinction between a Treasury bill, note, and bond is the term (or length of time until maturity) of the security. For example, Treasury bills (commonly called T-bills) are short-term securities issued with maturities of thirteen, twenty-six, and fifty-two weeks.

Treasury bills are currently issued to individuals in book-entry form, that means you receive a statement of account from the U.S. Treasury or a financial institution rather than an engraved certificate as evidence of your purchase. With book-entry securities, payment of interest and face (par) value is handled quickly and easily. Further, this system offers protection against loss, theft, and counterfeiting.

Initially, T-bills are sold at auction in minimum amounts of $10,000 and in multiples of $1,000 above the minimum. Generally, auctions for thirteen-week and twenty-six-week bills are held every week (on Monday). Auctions for fifty-two-week bills are held every four weeks (on Thursday). They are preceded by the announcement of an "offering" during the previous week.

Newly issued T-bills can be purchased through Federal Reserve banks and financial institutions. Previously issued T-bills (ones that other investors purchased when they were newly issued and now want to sell before they reach maturity) can be purchased and sold privately or in the secondary market through stockbrokers and other securities dealers. A fee is generally charged. Buying shares in mutual funds also offers a way to invest in T-bills, both newly issued and previously issued ones.

Secondary market bid (offers to buy) and ask (offers to sell) discount rates, as well as yield to maturity information, are often printed in daily newspapers and investor publications like *The Wall Street Journal* and *Barron's*.

The annualized yield to maturity information is probably of most interest to beginning investors because it can be used when comparing rates of return on other investments.

If you hold a T-bill until maturity, the face amount is paid to you through your financial institution. If you purchased one directly from a Federal Reserve bank (or branch), you also have the option to note on the original tender form that you wish to reinvest the funds automatically (roll-over) at maturity.

Treasury Notes And Bonds. Treasury notes and bonds have longer maturities than Treasury bills. Notes have a fixed maturity of two to ten years from date of issue. Bonds have a fixed maturity of over ten years. Both may be issued for $1,000 and multiples thereof (with the exception of two- and three-year notes, where the minimum is $5,000). Like T-bills, currently Treasury notes and bonds are issued to individuals in book-entry form (although there are some older, registered notes and bonds still in the hands of investors).

The specific terms of newly issued notes or bonds (term, auction date, maturity date, minimum purchase, and closing time for the offering) are provided in the public offering announcement. Federal Reserve banks can provide you with this information, as well as the results of recent auctions. This information can also be found in *The Wall Street Journal*. The schedule for the sale of notes and bonds vary. You can also write or call the Federal Reserve bank for a booklet about buying Treasury securities and help in establishing a "Treasury Direct" account.

After the sale of Treasury notes or bonds is publicly announced, a prospective purchaser may apply in person or by mail at a Federal Reserve bank (or branch), according to the time limits set by the Treasury for that particular offering. Newly issued notes and bonds may also be purchased through financial institutions—generally for a fee. Some mutual funds also invest in Treasury notes and bonds.

Treasury notes and bonds carry a fixed-interest (coupon) rate, which is established at the initial issue auction by competitive bidders. This fixed-interest rate enables purchasers to determine their annual interest earnings quickly by applying this rate to the face value of the note or bond. For example, a $1,000 note with a coupon rate of 9% provides earnings of $90 a year (as semiannual payments, in this case $45).

You receive interest payments up to the day the security is sold or at maturity, whichever occurs first. Treasury notes and bonds do not continue to earn interest after they reach maturity. Federal income taxes are payable on interest as received. Capital gains or losses occur if the purchase price and face value at maturity (or market value, if sold before maturity) differ.

Generally, Treasury notes and bonds are not "callable" (i.e., cannot be "called" or redeemed by the Treasury before maturity). However, they are highly marketable. Like T-bills, previously issued notes and bonds can be purchased and sold in the secondary market through stockbrokers and other securities dealers, as well as through mutual funds shares. A fee is often charged for these transactions.

If you hold a book-entry note or bond until maturity, the face amount is paid to you through your financial institution. Older, registered Treasury notes and bonds may be redeemed at Federal Reserve banks or through the Bureau of the Public Debt. If you purchased Treasury notes and bonds directly from a Federal Reserve bank, you also have the option to reinvest the funds automatically (roll-over) at maturity.

Savings Bonds. U.S. savings bonds are direct obligations of the U.S. Treasury and are considered to be a safe and secure savings vehicle. Over the years, the federal government has issued a variety of different series. Most series have been either replaced or discontinued. For example, Series E and H savings bonds are no longer being sold, although those less than forty years old continue to earn interest. Currently, Series EE and HH savings bonds are being issued. There are no purchase or sale fees charged when handling savings bonds transactions.

Bonds are registered Treasury securities and may be held in one of three ways: (1) Single ownership. Only the owner can redeem the bond or determine who inherits it at his or her death (although a payable on death, or POD, clause can be used to identify who the bond goes to in the event of the owner's death); (2)Two persons as co-owners. Either co-owner can redeem the bond and the surviving co-owner becomes sole owner at the death of the other co-owner; or (3) One owner and one beneficiary. Only the registered owner can redeem the bond during his or her lifetime, but the beneficiary becomes the owner of the bond when the original owner dies.

Only under limited circumstances, such as a divorce, can savings bonds be transferred and reissued with a change in registration.

- **Series EE.** Series EE savings bonds earn interest until they are redeemed (cashed), but not more than thirty years (final maturity). They are purchased for one-half of their face value (i.e., a $100 bond costs $50; a $200 bond costs $100) from financial institutions who are "qualified" as savings bonds agents and through employer-sponsored payroll savings plans. The issue date is the first day of the month in which the funds are received by the financial institution. Bonds are available in $50, $75, $100, $200, $500, $1,000, $5,000, and $10,000 denominations (although not all denominations are available through payroll savings plans).Bonds must be held for a least six months after the issue date before they can be redeemed. They can be redeemed at financial institutions, at which time the interest which has been earned is subject to federal income taxes (although the bond owner has the option to pay taxes on interest as it accrues, rather than wait until it is redeemed or at final maturity). When Series EE bonds (or E bonds) reach final maturity, the owner has one year to decide whether to redeem the bonds (and pay any income tax due on the accrued interest) or exchange the bonds for Series HH bonds (and further defer the tax liability on the accrued interest from the older bonds for up to twenty years, the total life of a Series HH bond).

- **Series HH.** Series HH bonds provide current income and are purchased at face value in denominations of $500, $1,000, $5,000, and $10,000. They cannot be purchased with cash, however, but must be obtained in exchange for Series EE bonds that are at least six months old (or Series E bonds, U.S. Savings Notes, or reinvested, matured Series H bonds). If the value of the savings bonds to be exchanged is more than $500, but not enough for the next larger size HH bond, enough cash may be added to purchase a bond of the next higher $500 multiple. Interest is paid semiannually at a fixed rate for the first ten years the bond is held. The rate can change for an additional ten years. After final maturity (twenty years), they no longer earn interest. Interest payments are deposited in the owner's financial institution by direct deposit.

The application for exchanging other bonds for Series HH bonds is handled by qualified financial institutions who can also process requests for redeeming (cashing) them. The Series HH bonds themselves are issued by a Federal Reserve bank. [See chapter 21 for more information about Savings Bonds.]

How To Avoid Problems With Investing

Choosing someone to help you with your investments is one of the most important investment decisions you will ever make. While most investment professionals are honest and hardworking, you must watch out for those few unscrupulous individuals. They can make your life's savings disappear in an instant.

Securities regulators and law enforcement officials can and do catch these criminals. But putting them in jail doesn't always get your money back. Too often, the money is gone. The good news is you can avoid potential problems by protecting yourself.

Let's say you've already met with several investment professionals based on recommendations from friends and others you trust, and you've found someone who clearly understands your investment objectives. Before you hire this person, you still have more homework.

Make sure the investment professional and her firm are registered with the Securities and Exchange Commission (SEC) and licensed to do business in your state. And find out from your state's securities regulator whether the investment professional or the person's firm have ever been disciplined, or whether they have any complaints against them. You'll find contact information for securities regulators in the U.S. by visiting the website of the North American Securities Administrators Association (NASAA) or by calling 202-737-0900. [See chapter 26 for more advice about choosing an investment professional.]

☞ **Remember!!**

Watch Out For Fraud

Think twice if you see any of these tell-tale signs of trouble:

- Pressure to invest before you've had an opportunity to investigate

- Sales people offering "inside" or "confidential" information

- Claims of a "once-in-a-lifetime opportunity" or a "limited time offer"

- Promises of spectacular profits or "guaranteed" returns

- Assurances that the investment is "risk-free" or "as safe as a certificate of deposit"

- Reluctance—or outright refusal—to send you written information about the investment

Complain Promptly. If you have problems, get help right away. Contact the broker's supervisor or the firm's compliance officer. If that does not work, write to:

U.S. Securities and Exchange Commission

Office of Investor Education and Assistance

450 5th Street, N.W.

Washington, DC 20549

E-mail: help@sec.gov

For tips on how to invest wisely and to protect yourself against investment fraud, call us toll-free at 800-SEC-0330, or visit our website at www.sec.gov.

Source: From *The Facts on Saving and Investing,* U.S. Securities and Exchange Commission, April 1999.

You should also find out as much as you can about any investments that your investment professional recommends. First, make sure the investments are registered. Keep in mind, however, the mere fact that a company has registered and files reports with the SEC doesn't guarantee that the company will be a good investment.

Likewise, the fact that a company hasn't registered and doesn't file reports with the SEC doesn't mean the company is a fraud. Still, you may be asking for serious losses if, for instance, you invest in a small, thinly traded company that isn't widely known solely on the basis of what you may have read online. One simple phone call to your state regulator could prevent you from squandering your money on a scam.

Be wary of promises of quick profits, offers to share "inside information," and pressure to invest before you have an opportunity to investigate. These are all warning signs of fraud.

Ask your investment professional for written materials and prospectuses, and read them before you invest. If you have questions, now is the time to ask:

- How will the investment make money?
- How is this investment consistent with my investment goals?
- What must happen for the investment to increase in value?
- What are the risks?
- Where can I get more information?

🖎 What's It Mean?

Investment Adviser: A person or entity who receives compensation for giving individually tailored advice to a specific person on investing in stocks, bonds, or mutual funds. Some investment advisers also manage portfolios of securities, including mutual funds.

Source: From "Invest Wisely: An Introduction to Mutual Funds," U.S. Securities and Exchange Commission (SEC), 2004.

What If I Have A Problem?

Finally, it's always a good idea to write down everything your investment professional tells you. Accurate notes will come in handy if ever there's a problem.

Some investments make money. Others lose money. That's natural, and that's why you need a diversified portfolio to minimize your risk. But if you lose money because you've been cheated, that's not natural—that's a problem.

Sometimes all it takes is a simple phone call to your investment professional to resolve a problem. Maybe there was an honest mistake that can be corrected. If talking to the investment professional doesn't resolve the problem, talk to the firm's manager, and write a letter to confirm your conversation. If that doesn't lead to a resolution, you may have to initiate private legal action. You may need to take action quickly because legal time limits for doing so vary. Your local bar association can provide referrals for attorneys who specialize in securities law. At the same time, call or write to the SEC and let them know what the problem was. You may think you're the only one experiencing a problem, but typically, you're not alone. Sometimes it takes only one investor's complaint to trigger an investigation that exposes a bad broker or an illegal scheme.

Part Five

Stocks, Bonds, And Mutual Funds

Chapter 16

Introduction To Capital Markets

Capital markets in the United States provide the lifeblood of the economy. Companies turn to them to raise funds needed to finance the building of factories, office buildings, airplanes, trains, ships, telephone lines, and other assets; to conduct research and development; and to support a host of other essential corporate activities. Much of the money comes from such major institutions as pension funds, insurance companies, banks, foundations, and colleges and universities. Increasingly, it comes from individuals as well.

Very few investors would be willing to buy shares in a company unless they knew they could sell them later if they needed the funds for some other purpose. The stock market and other capital markets allow investors to buy and sell stocks continuously.

The stock market and other capital markets enable vast numbers of sellers and buyers to engage in millions of transactions each day. These markets owe their success in part to computers, but they also depend on tradition and trust—the trust of one broker for another, and the trust of both in the good faith of the customers they represent to deliver securities after a sale or to pay for purchases. Occasionally, this trust is abused. But during the last half century, the federal government has played an increasingly important role in

About This Chapter: Text in this chapter is excerpted from *Outline of the U.S. Economy*, chapter 5, "Stocks, Commodities, and Markets," a publication of the Bureau of International Information Programs, U.S. State Department, February 2001.

ensuring honest and equitable dealing. As a result, markets have thrived as continuing sources of investment funds that keep the economy growing and as devices for letting many Americans share in the nation's wealth.

To work effectively, markets require the free flow of information. Without it, investors cannot keep abreast of developments or gauge, to the best of their ability, the true value of stocks. Numerous sources of

> **✎ What's It Mean?**
>
> Capital Market: The market in which corporate equity and longer-term debt securities (those maturing in more than one year) are issued and traded.
>
> Investment: The purchase of a security, such as a stock or bond.
>
> Source: U.S. State Department, 2001.

information enable investors to follow the fortunes of the market daily, hourly, or even minute-by-minute. Companies are required by law to issue quarterly earnings reports, more elaborate annual reports, and proxy statements to tell stockholders how they are doing. In addition, investors can read the market pages of daily newspapers to find out the price at which particular stocks were traded during the previous trading session. They can review a variety of indexes that measure the overall pace of market activity; the most notable of these is the Dow Jones Industrial Average (DJIA), which tracks thirty prominent stocks. Investors also can turn to magazines and newsletters devoted to analyzing particular stocks and markets. Certain cable television programs provide a constant flow of news about movements in stock prices. And investors can use the Internet to get up-to-the-minute information about individual stocks and even to arrange stock transactions.

The Stock Exchanges

There are thousands of stocks, but shares of the largest, best-known, and most actively traded corporations generally are listed on the New York Stock Exchange (NYSE). The exchange dates its origin back to 1792, when a group of stockbrokers gathered under a buttonwood tree on Wall Street in New York City to make some rules to govern stock buying and selling. By the late 1990s, the NYSE listed some 3,600 different stocks. The exchange has 1,366 members, or "seats," which are bought by brokerage houses at hefty prices and are used for buying and selling stocks for the public. Information travels electronically between brokerage offices and the exchange, which requires 200 miles of fiber-optic cable and 8,000 phone connections to handle quotes and orders.

How Are Stocks Traded?

Suppose a schoolteacher in California wants to take an ocean cruise. To finance the trip, she decides to sell 100 shares of stock she owns in General Motors Corporation. So she calls her broker and directs him to sell the shares at the best price he can get. At the same time, an engineer in Florida decides to use some of his savings to buy 100 GM shares, so he calls his broker and places a "buy" order for 100 shares at the market price. Both brokers wire their orders to the NYSE, where their representatives negotiate the transaction. All this can occur in less than a minute. In the end, the schoolteacher gets her cash and the engineer gets his stock, and both pay their brokers a commission. The transaction, like all others handled on the exchange, is carried out in public, and the results are sent electronically to every brokerage office in the nation.

Stock exchange "specialists" play a crucial role in the process, helping to keep an orderly market by deftly matching buy and sell orders. If necessary, specialists buy or sell stock themselves when there is a paucity of either buyers or sellers.

The smaller American Stock Exchange, which lists numerous energy industry-related stocks, operates in much the same way and is located in the same Wall Street area as the New York exchange. Other large U.S. cities host smaller, regional stock exchanges.

The largest number of different stocks and bonds traded are traded on the National Association of Securities Dealers Automated Quotation system, or Nasdaq. This so-called over-the-counter exchange, which handles trading in about 5,240 stocks, is not located in any one place; rather, it is an electronic communications network of stock and bond dealers. The National Association of Securities Dealers, which oversees the over-the-counter market, has the power to expel companies or dealers that it determines are dishonest or insolvent. Because many of the stocks traded in this market are from smaller and less stable companies, the Nasdaq is considered a riskier market than either of the major stock exchanges. But it offers many opportunities for investors. By the 1990s, many of the fastest growing high-technology stocks were traded on the Nasdaq. [See chapters 18 and 19 for more information about the stock exchange and how stocks are traded.]

A Nation Of Investors

An unprecedented boom in the stock market, combined with the ease of investing in stocks, led to a sharp increase in public participation in securities markets during the 1990s. The annual trading volume on the New York Stock Exchange, or "Big Board," soared and the portion of all U.S. households owning stocks, directly or through intermediaries like pension funds, rose dramatically.

Public participation in the market has been greatly facilitated by mutual funds, which collect money from individuals and invest it on their behalf in varied portfolios of stocks. Mutual funds enable small investors, who may not feel qualified or have the time to choose among thousands of individual stocks, to have their money invested by professionals. And because mutual funds hold diversified groups of stocks, they shelter investors somewhat from the sharp swings that can occur in the value of individual shares. [See chapters 22 and 23 for more information about mutual funds.]

✎ What's It Mean?

American Stock Exchange: One of the key stock exchanges in the United States, it consists mainly of stocks and bonds of companies that are small to medium-sized, compared with the shares of large corporations traded on the New York Stock Exchange.

National Association Of Securities Dealers Automated Quotation System (Nasdaq): An automated information network that provides brokers and dealers with price quotations on the approximately 5,000 most active securities traded over the counter.

New York Stock Exchange: The world's largest exchange for trading stocks and bonds.

Stock Exchange: An organized market for the buying and selling of stocks and bonds.

Source: U.S. State Department, 2001.

How Stock Prices Are Determined

Stock prices are set by a combination of factors that no analyst can consistently understand or predict. In general, economists say, they reflect the long-term earnings potential of companies. Investors are attracted to stocks of companies they expect will earn substantial profits in the future; because many people wish to buy stocks of such companies, prices of these stocks tend to rise. On the other hand, investors are reluctant to purchase stocks of companies that face bleak earnings prospects; because fewer people wish to buy and more wish to sell these stocks, prices fall.

When deciding whether to purchase or sell stocks, investors consider the general business climate and outlook, the financial condition and prospects of the individual companies in which they are considering investing, and whether stock prices relative to earnings already are above or below traditional norms. Interest rate trends also influence stock prices significantly. Rising interest rates tend to depress stock prices—partly because they can foreshadow a general slowdown in economic activity and corporate profits, and partly because they lure investors out of the stock market and into new issues of interest-bearing investments. Falling rates, conversely, often lead to higher stock prices, both because they suggest easier borrowing and faster growth, and because they make new interest-paying investments less attractive to investors.

A number of other factors complicate matters, however. For one thing, investors generally buy stocks according to their expectations about the unpredictable future, not according to current earnings. Expectations can be influenced by a variety of factors, many of them not necessarily rational or justified. As a result, the short-term connection between prices and earnings can be tenuous.

Momentum also can distort stock prices. Rising prices typically woo more buyers into the market, and the increased demand, in turn, drives prices higher still. Speculators often add to this upward pressure by purchasing shares in the expectation they will be able to sell them later to other buyers at even higher prices. Analysts describe a continuous rise in stock prices as a "bull" market. When speculative fever can no longer be sustained, prices start to fall. If enough investors become worried about falling prices, they may rush to sell their shares, adding to downward momentum. This is called a "bear" market.

Market Strategies

During most of the 20th century, investors could earn more by investing in stocks than in other types of financial investments—provided they were willing to hold stocks for the long term.

In the short term, stock prices can be quite volatile, and impatient investors who sell during periods of market decline easily can suffer losses.

✎ What's It Mean?

Bear Market: A market in which, in a time of falling prices, shareholders may rush to sell their stock shares, adding to the downward momentum.

Bull Market: A market in which there is a continuous rise in stock prices.

Source: U.S. State Department, 2001.

Peter Lynch, a renowned former manager of one of America's largest stock mutual funds, noted in 1998, for instance, that U.S. stocks had lost value in 20 of the previous 72 years. According to Lynch, investors had to wait 15 years after the stock market crash of 1929 to see their holdings regain their lost value. But people who held their stock 20 years or more never lost money. In an analysis prepared for the U.S. Congress, the federal government's General Accounting Office said that in the worst 20-year period since 1926, stock prices increased 3%. In the best two decades, they rose 17%. By contrast, 20-year bond returns, a common investment alternative to stocks, ranged between 1% and 10%.

The Regulators

The Securities and Exchange Commission (SEC), which was created in 1934, is the principal regulator of securities markets in the United States. Before 1929, individual states regulated securities activities. But the stock market crash of 1929, which triggered the Great Depression, showed that arrangement to be inadequate. The Securities Act of 1933 and the Securities Exchange Act of 1934 consequently gave the federal government a preeminent role in protecting small investors from fraud and making it easier for them to understand companies' financial reports.

The commission enforces a web of rules to achieve that goal. Companies issuing stocks, bonds, and other securities must file detailed financial registration statements, which are made available to the public. The SEC determines whether these disclosures are full and fair so that investors can make well-informed and realistic evaluations of various securities. The SEC also oversees trading in stocks and administers rules designed to prevent price manipulation; to that end, brokers and dealers in the over-the-counter market and the stock exchanges must register with the SEC. In addition, the commission requires companies to tell the public when their own officers buy or sell shares of their stock; the commission believes that these "insiders" possess intimate information about their companies and that their trades can indicate to other investors their degree of confidence in their companies' future.

The agency also seeks to prevent insiders from trading in stock based on information that has not yet become public. In the late 1980s, the SEC began to focus not just on officers and directors but on insider trades by lower-level employees or even outsiders like lawyers who may have access to important information about a company before it becomes public.

The SEC has five commissioners who are appointed by the president. No more than three can be members of the same political party; the five-year term of one of the commissioners expires each year.

✎ What's It Mean?

Over-The-Counter: Figurative term for the means of trading securities that are not listed on an organized stock exchange such as the New York Stock Exchange. Over-the-counter trading is done by broker-dealers who communicate by telephone and computer networks.

Securities And Exchange Commission (SEC): An independent, non-partisan, quasi-judicial regulatory agency with responsibility for administering the federal securities laws. The purpose of these laws is to protect investors and to ensure that they have access to disclosure of all material information concerning publicly traded securities. The commission also regulates firms engaged in the purchase or sale of securities, people who provide investment advice, and investment companies.

Source: U.S. State Department, 2001.

The Long Bull Market

Over the past few decades, the stock exchanges have initiated safeguards and new rules. These reforms have helped restore confidence, coupled with a strong performance by the economy. Partly as a result, the volume of trading has risen enormously. While trading of 5 million shares was considered a hectic day on the New York Stock Exchange in the 1960s, more than a *thousand-million* shares were exchanged on some days thirty years later.

Much of the increased activity was generated by so-called day traders who will typically buy and sell the same stock several times in one day, hoping to make quick profits on short-term swings. These traders are among the growing legions of persons using the Internet to do their trading.

♣ It's A Fact!!
Origin Of
The Stock Market

Did you know that investing has been around for over 200 years? In 1792, twenty-four men entered a room and signed a paper that said they would sell parts of companies among themselves and others. The parts of the companies were sold in the form of stocks. This marked the beginning of the stock market.

Although times have changed greatly in the past 200 years, the ideas of investing have basically remained the same. People still buy and sell stocks, bonds, and mutual funds.

Source: Excerpted from "An Introduction to Investing," by Chris Stallman, © 1999 TeenAnalyst .com, LLC. All rights reserved. Reprinted with permission.

Chapter 17

Learning The Language Of Stock

Stocks

When you buy stock, you are becoming an owner of the company. If the company does well, the value of your stock should go up over time. If the company does not do well, the value of your investment will decrease. Many companies distribute a portion of their profits to shareholders as dividends. As owners, shareholders generally have the right to vote on electing the board of directors and on certain other matters of particular significance to the company.

Companies issue two types of stock, common and preferred. Common stock is the basic form of ownership in a company. People who hold common stock have a claim on the assets and earnings of a firm after the claims of preferred stockholders and bondholders. The safety of the principal of preferred stock is greater than that of common stock, however, preferred stockholders cannot vote for the directors of the company.

About This Chapter: "Stocks" is excerpted from "Your Investment Options," reprinted with permission from the Office of the New York State Attorney General. [n.d.]. "Stock As Equity" is excerpted from *Investment Basics: Stocks*, by Joyce Jones, Ph.D., reprinted with permission of the Kansas State University Agricultural Experiment Station and Cooperative Extension Service, Manhattan, Kansas, http://www.oznet.ksy.edu/. Copyright © 1995. All rights reserved. "Market Capitalization Defined" is reprinted with permission from www.investopedia.com. © 2003 Investopedia, Inc. "Why Do Some Stocks Pay Dividends?" by Chris Stallman, is © 2004 TeenAnalyst.com, LLC. All rights reserved. Reprinted with permission.

There are five basic categories of stock:

1. *Income stocks* pay unusually large dividends that can be used as a means of generating income without selling the stock. Most utility stocks are considered income stocks.

2. *Blue chip stocks* are issued by very solid and reliable companies with long histories of consistent growth and stability. Blue chip stocks usually pay small but regular dividends and maintain a fairly steady price. Examples of blue chip stocks include IBM, Exxon, Kodak, GE, and Sears.

3. *Growth stocks* are issued by young, entrepreneurial companies that are experiencing a faster rate of growth than their general industry. Their stocks normally pay little or no dividend because the company needs all of its earning to finance expansion. Since they are issued by new companies, with no track record, growth stocks are riskier but offer more potential for growth than other kinds of stock.

4. *Cyclical stocks* are issued by companies that are affected by general economic treads. The prices of these stocks tend to go down during recessionary periods and increase during economic booms. Cyclical stocks include automobiles, heavy machinery, and home building.

5. *Defensive stocks* are the opposite of cyclical stocks. They are issued by companies producing staples such as food, beverages, drugs and insurance and they usually maintain their value.

Stock Splits

When a company increase the amount of its shares it is said to "split." A 2 for 1 split means that the company has doubled the amount of outstanding shares. The sale price will decrease proportionally to the split so if a stockholder held 100 shares of stock for $40 per share, after the spit she would have 200 shares at $20 a share. The stockholder's equity remains the same. The stock split is intended to reward shareholders. By making the company's stock less expensive, it is hoped to attract more investment, thus leading to an increase in the price of its stock.

Remember!!

The ups and downs of the stock market make the national news almost every night, and most people know someone who has made—or lost—money in the stock market. Most stock investors are motivated by a belief in the continued prosperity of American business and a desire to participate directly in the expected growth by being partial owners of these companies. Most experts agree that over the long run, stocks have performed better than most other financial assets.

Source: Kansas State University, 1995.

Stock As Equity

Shares of stock represent partial ownership of a corporation and are often referred to as "equities." Returns on investments in stocks are from stock price appreciation and/or dividends.

Stocks can appreciate in value as profits are earned and future expectations for growth are positive. Stocks can also depreciate in value if the company suffers losses or, in the extreme, goes bankrupt. Dividends may also increase or decrease. The stock market itself also affects the value of stocks.

Stocks have no maturity or expiration date, nor are there guarantees to repay your investment or to pay dividends. Shareholders share in the fortunes, good and bad, of the company.

Stock values also fluctuate with the general economy, with changes in the industry of which the company is a part, and with perceived changes in the future of the company. However, if the company thrives and makes a profit, so does the investor.

Stockholders include individual investors and institutional investors (who have large portfolios to invest, such as managers of pension funds, investment companies, and life insurance companies). Most individual stockholders own only a small fraction of a company.

Stockholders may or may not receive a stock certificate as evidence of ownership. Ownership information may be kept on computer files, rather than via printed stock certificates. When printed, a stock certificate can be made out for one share or a number of shares. The owner's name appears on the stock certificate and it is recorded on the stock books of the issuing corporation.

If your certificates are lost or destroyed, you can obtain new ones through the registrar for the corporation. There may be a significant cost to replace them, so stock certificates should be safeguarded. Stock certificates may be held in safekeeping by your stockbroker.

Types Of Stock

As mentioned above, companies issue two basic types of stock, common and preferred. Both preferred and common stockholders have limited liability for the debts of the corporation, up to the amount of their investment.

Preferred Stock. Preferred stock, as the name implies, gives the owner superior rights on dividend distribution. Dividends must be paid to preferred stockholders before they are paid to common stockholders. Also, in cases of bankruptcy, preferred stockholders have a prior claim on a company's assets (if there is anything left) after all debts (including bondholders) have been paid.

Preferred stock usually has a fixed dividend rate, which is established when the stock is issued. Thus, preferred stockholders are protected somewhat in times of low company profit. On the other hand, in peak performance times, preferred stockholders may receive lower dividends than common stockholders. Also, preferred stockholders do not usually have voting rights in the company.

The major purchasers of preferred stock are corporations, especially insurance companies and pension plans, who receive favorable tax treatment on the preferred dividends they receive from other corporations.

Many companies have issued convertible preferred stock, which is preferred stock that can be converted into (exchanged for) a specified amount of common stock.

Common Stock. The vast majority of stock is common stock. Common stock gives its owners a variable rate of return, depending on how well a company does in a given year. After a corporation has deducted its expenses, paid its income taxes, and paid dividends to preferred stock shareholders, the remainder is earnings on the common stock.

Common stock has several benefits for the individual investor. For example, returns in the form of both dividends and price appreciation may be quite good. Common stockholders have voting rights in the company—the weight of their vote is generally based on the number of shares owned—and may attend the annual meeting of a corporation and vote on major issues, such as electing directors. Most stockholders vote by proxy, which means that the stockholder gives someone else, usually the management of the corporation, authority to vote the stockholder's shares.

The major caution associated with common stock is its risk. Although the returns on common stock can be high, the risk or uncertainty of receiving this expected return also can be high. Generally, the greater the risk, the higher the potential return.

Distribution Of Earnings

Corporations may retain some earnings and distribute the rest in dividends. For example, if a corporation earns $6 per share on its stock in one quarter, it may pay only $4 per share in dividends in that quarter. Yet, the undistributed earnings of $2 per share are technically the stockholder's property.

By retaining part of current earnings, a company may be able to increase its future earnings through reinvestment for expansion. The retained earnings may also make it possible for the company to pay dividends in later years when there may be little or no profit.

- Cash dividends. Dividends are usually paid in cash to stockholders. Most are paid quarterly, although some are paid monthly, semiannually, or annually. Further, while many companies pay steady dividends regularly, some companies pay dividends that vary in amount and timing.

- Stock dividends and stock splits. Instead of (or in addition to) a cash dividend, a company may pay its shareholders a stock dividend. The corporation may choose to split the stock, generally to lower the price of the shares (making the stock more affordable to the general investor).

Neither of these actions affect the assets and liabilities of the company. However, they do affect the number of outstanding shares in the company. Stock dividends and stock splits lower the value of existing shares of stock because afterward there are more shares in existence.

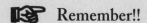 **Remember!!**

Categories Of Stock

Income Stocks. Income stocks stress income and generally pay higher, regular cash dividends. Growth of assets, and thus stock price appreciation, are less important to income stock shareholders than are dividends. These stocks appeal to the investor who needs current income. Income stocks are usually the least risky, so they fit into the portfolio of the more conservative investor.

Growth-And-Income Stocks. These are stocks that produce perhaps more modest dividends, but that also have a reasonable expectation of growth or appreciation. "Blue chip" stocks are growth-and-income stocks from companies that are well known and have strong records of growth, profit, and dividend payments. These are relatively safe investments and generally appeal to the investor with a lower tolerance for risk.

Growth Stocks. Growth stocks generally do not pay a high percentage of their earnings in dividends. Instead, the company reinvests some or all of its earnings back into the corporation (such as for expansion or research and development). This, in turn, can make your investment more valuable if the company is successful in achieving that growth. Growth stocks can have significant price fluctuations and are generally riskier than the two previously mentioned categories of stock.

Aggressive Growth Stocks. Like growth stocks, these stocks are of faster-growing companies that pay few or no dividends. They are considered high-risk stocks. Although the chances for loss of principal are high, so are the chances of rapid growth.

Source: Kansas State University, 1995.

For example, if you receive one stock dividend for each share of stock you own (or there is a two-for-one stock split), a share that was worth $100 now will be worth only $50. Thus, other things being equal, a stock dividend or stock split usually does not represent additional value to the investor.

Market Capitalization Defined

You often hear companies or different mutual funds being categorized as "small-cap," "mid-cap," or "large-cap." But what do these terms really mean? The "cap" is short for capitalization, which is a measure by which we can classify a company's size. Although the criteria for the different classifications are not strictly bound, it is important for investors to understand these terms, which are not only ubiquitous but also useful for gauging a company's size and riskiness.

Calculating Market Cap

Market capitalization is just a fancy name for a straightforward concept. Quite simply, it refers to the value of a company, that is, the market value of its outstanding shares. This figure is found by taking the stock price and multiplying it by the total number of shares outstanding. For example, if a corporation was trading at $20 per share and had 1 million shares outstanding, then the market capitalization would be $20 million ($20 x 1 million shares). It's that simple.

Why Is This Important?

A common misconception is that the higher the stock price, the larger the company. Stock price, however, may misrepresent a company's actual worth. If we look at two fairly large companies, IBM and Microsoft, we may see that their stock prices are $29 and $22.75 respectively. Although IBM's stock price is higher, it has approximately 1.73 billion shares outstanding while MSFT has 10.68 billion. As a result of this difference, we can see that MSFT ($243.5 billion) is actually quite larger than IBM ($127.8 billion). If we compared the two companies by solely looking at their stock prices, we would not be comparing their true values, which are affected by the amount of their outstanding shares.

The classification of companies into different caps also allows investors to gauge the growth versus risk potential. Historically, large caps have experienced slower growth with lower risk. Meanwhile small caps have experienced higher growth potential, but with higher risk.

Different Types of Capitalization

While there isn't one set framework for defining the different market caps, here are the widely published standards for each capitalization:

Mega Cap: This group includes companies that have a market cap of $200 billion and greater. They are the largest publicly traded companies and include names such as Microsoft, Exxon, Wal-Mart, and General Electric. Not many companies will fit in this category, and those that do are typically the leaders of their industry.

Big/Large Cap: These companies have a market cap between $10–$200 billion. Many well-known companies fall into this category, names such as Yahoo, IBM, and Citigroup. Typically, large-cap stocks are considered to be relatively stable and secure. Both mega and large cap stocks are often referred to as "blue chips," a security from a well-established and financially-sound company that has demonstrated its ability to pay dividends in both good and bad times. These stocks are usually less risky than other stocks. The stock price of a blue chip usually closely follows the S&P 500.

> ### ♣ It's A Fact!!
>
> The name "blue chip" came about because in the game of poker the blue chips were traditionally the most expensive ones.
>
> Source: Excerpted from "Dictionary," and reprinted with permission from www.investopedia.com. © 2004 Investopedia, Inc.

Mid Cap: Ranging from $2 billion to $10 billion, this group of companies is considered to be more volatile than the large and mega-cap companies. Growth stocks represent a significant portion of the mid caps. Some of the companies are not be industry leaders, but they may be well on their way to becoming one.

Small Cap: Typically new or relatively young companies, small caps have a market cap between $300 million to $2 billion. Although their track records won't be as lengthy as that of the mid to mega caps, small caps do present the possibility of greater capital appreciation—but at the cost of greater risk.

Micro Cap: Mainly consisting of penny stocks, this category denotes market capitalizations between $50 million to $300 million fall into this category. The upward potential of these companies is similar to the downside potential, so they do not offer the safest investment, and a great deal of research should be done before entering into such a position.

Nano Cap: Companies having market caps below $50 million are nano caps. These companies are the most risky, and the potential for gain is often relatively small. These stocks typically trade on the pink sheets or OTCBB.

Remember, these ranges are not set in stone, and they are known to fluctuate depending on how the market as a whole is performing.

Understanding the market cap is not just important if you're investing directly in stocks. It is also useful for mutual fund investors, as many funds will list the "average" or "median" market capitalization of its holdings. As the name suggests, this gives the middle ground of the fund's equity investments, letting investors know if the fund primarily invests in large, mid, or small cap stocks.

Why Do Some Stocks Pay Dividends?

Why do some companies pay dividends and others don't?

As you probably know, investors can earn a return on their investment through either dividends or capital gains. So it's important to know what affects dividends to get a sense of what kind of return you'll earn from a stock.

A company has an opportunity to pay its investors a dividend only after it has become profitable and can generate free cash flow. Free cash flow is the amount of cash a company generates from minus its capital expenditures. Basically, free cash flow is the amount of cash a company has left after it's made the necessary investments back into its business.

Free cash flow gives a company a lot of options. They have the option of using this excess cash to either invest it back into their business or pay it out as dividends. Sometimes companies will be trying to grow a new area of their business and they'll want to plow their cash back into the business

✎ What's It Mean?

Growth Stocks: Shares in a company whose earnings are expected to grow at an above average rate relative to the market. A growth stock usually does not pay a dividend, as the company would prefer to reinvest retained earnings in capital projects. Most technology companies are growth stocks.

OTC: Over the Counter—A security traded in some context other than on a formal exchange such as the NYSE, DJIA, TSX, AMEX, etc. A stock is traded over the counter usually because the company is small and unable to meet listing requirements of the exchanges. Also known as unlisted stock, these securities are traded by brokers/dealers who negotiate directly with one another over computer networks and by phone. The Nasdaq, however, is also considered to be an OTC market, with the tier 1 being represented by companies such as Microsoft, Dell and Intel.

Penny Stocks: A stock that sells for less than $1 a share but may also rise to as much as $10/share as a result of heavy promotion. All penny stocks are traded OTC or on the pink sheets. Penny stocks are highly speculative and risky. Many brokerages don't cover them simply because they are so difficult to track and predict.

Pink Sheets: A daily publication compiled by the National Quotation Bureau containing price quotations for over-the-counter stocks. Unlike companies on a stock exchange, companies quoted on the pink sheets system are not required to meet minimum requirements or file with the SEC. The pink sheets got their name because they were actually printed on pink paper. You can tell if a company trades on the pink sheets because the stock symbol will end in ".PK".

OTCBB: Over the Counter Bulletin Board—A regulated electronic trading service offered by the National Association of Security Dealers (NASD) that shows real-time quotes, last-sale prices, and volume information for over-the-counter (OTC) equity securities. An OTC security generally is not listed or traded on any other national securities exchange including the Nasdaq.

Source: Excerpted from "Dictionary," and reprinted with permission from www.investopedia.com. © 2004 Investopedia, Inc.

because they think they could get a strong return on their investments. Or sometimes companies won't have new areas to invest in and they feel that by paying a dividend, their shareholders can earn a better return on that cash than they can earn for them. This is why you typically see low-growth companies paying high dividends.

It's important to note that just because a company is highly profitable, it doesn't mean it has the capability to pay out a big dividend. Take Home Depot for example. During the 1990s, Home Depot had a strong net income but they weren't generating much free cash flow because they opted to use most of their operating cash to build new stores and expand into new markets.

Some companies flat-out hate paying dividends. One example is Microsoft. The company is sitting on about $30 billion in cash but hasn't found any suitable ways to put it to use. Common thinking is that they should pay a larger dividend, but management isn't too keen on that because of the tax consequences. When a company pays out a dividend, the investor has to pay taxes on it. So dividends often aren't the best way to put your cash to use, unless you have no other option.

Just remember: companies with strong free cash flow typically pay dividends when they feel it's the best use of the cash. If there's a better opportunity out there, they'll reinvest it.

Chapter 18

What Is A Stock Exchange?

Where Stock Trades Occur

Stocks are traded on the:

- New York Stock Exchange
- American Stock Exchange
- Nasdaq Stock Market
- Regional exchanges
- Over-the-counter market

Stock exchanges serve as central marketplaces. Stock (and other securities) orders to buy and sell are generally placed with local stockbrokers. Local brokers then contact other brokers of the firms who operate (have "seats") on the exchange floor. The floor broker then attempts to match buy and sell orders for individual stocks. The buyer and seller are notified that the purchase or sale has taken place. Prices fluctuate continually, based on supply and demand.

About This Chapter: This chapter begins with "Where Stock Trades Occur," excerpted from *Investment Basics: Stocks*, by Joyce Jones, Ph.D., reprinted with permission of the Kansas State University Agricultural Experiment Station and Cooperative Extension Service, Manhattan, Kansas, http://www.oznet.ksu.edu/. Copyright © 1995. All rights reserved. "The Tale Of Two Exchanges: NYSE And Nasdaq" is reprinted with permission from www.investopedia.com. © 2003 Investopedia, Inc. "Closing Price" is reprinted from a document dated August 30, 2004, published by the U.S. Securities and Exchange Commission.

New York Stock Exchange (NYSE). The New York Stock Exchange is the oldest and most well-known secondary market in the United States. Securities of large corporations are primarily listed there.

The New York Stock Exchange is a not-for-profit corporation whose members are primarily partners or directors of stock-brokerage firms. Most members of the NYSE act as brokers for customers or for their own accounts. Others are specialists who buy and sell shares of an assigned stock in such a way as to make sure the market in that stock remains "orderly."

American Stock Exchange (AMEX). The American Stock Exchange is also a major national exchange. The organization of AMEX is similar to that of the NYSE, except that fewer companies are listed there. Usually, the stocks that are traded on this exchange belong to smaller companies than those found on the NYSE.

✎ What's It Mean?

Equity: Equity is a term whose meaning depends very much on the context. In general, you can think of equity as ownership.

Market-Makers: A broker-dealer firm that accepts the risk of holding a particular number of shares of a particular security in order to facilitate trading in that security. Each market maker competes for customer order flow by displaying buy and sell quotations for a guaranteed number of shares. Once an order is received, the market maker immediately sells from its own inventory or seeks an offsetting order. This process takes place in mere seconds.

Specialist: A person on the trading floor of certain exchanges who holds an inventory of particular stocks. The specialist is responsible for managing limit trades, but does not make information on outstanding limit orders available to other traders. There is usually one specialist for each stock traded on the NYSE, except for lower volume stocks.

Source: Excerpted from "Dictionary," and reprinted with permission from www.investopedia.com. © 2004 Investopedia, Inc.

Nasdaq Stock Market. The Nasdaq Stock Market is the newest and fastest growing stock market. It uses computers and telecommunications networks for the trading of securities.

This stock market is distinguished from the exchanges described earlier by its use of multiple market makers—independent securities firms throughout the nation who compete with one another for investor orders in a "screen-based," floorless trading environment. Although the NYSE still has the largest dollar volume, Nasdaq now includes more issues and more companies than any other exchange or market.

When founded in 1971, the name Nasdaq stood for the National Association of Securities Dealers Automated Quotation system. This system was designed to enable more timely information and trading capability for the over-the-counter (OTC) securities.

Nasdaq (the name is no longer capitalized as an acronym) now has two tiers: the Nasdaq National Market, with larger companies whose securities are more actively traded (and with listing standards similar to the AMEX); and the Nasdaq Small Cap Market, with smaller, emerging growth companies.

Regional Exchanges. There are several regional exchanges located throughout the country. The listing requirements for these exchanges are not as stringent as those of the New York Stock Exchange. Usually, regional exchanges list smaller companies that have geographical interest.

Over-The-Counter (OTC) Market. Stocks of relatively small and new companies are listed on "Pink Sheets" published by the National Quotation Bureau for over-the-counter (OTC) trading. These stocks tend to be the most speculative and risky stocks in the secondary market.

The Tale Of Two Exchanges: NYSE And Nasdaq

Whenever someone talks about the stock market as a place where equities are exchanged between buyers and sellers, the first thing that comes to mind is either the NYSE or Nasdaq, and there's no debate over why. These two exchanges account for the trading of a major portion of equities in North America and the world. At the same time, however, the NYSE and Nasdaq are very different in the way they operate and in the types of equities that trade upon them. Knowing these differences will help you better understand the function of a stock exchange and the mechanics behind the buying and selling of stocks.

Location, Location, Location

The location of an exchange refers not so much to its street address but the "place" where its transactions take place. On the NYSE, all trades occur in a physical place, on the trading floor of the NYSE. So, when you see those guys waving their hands on TV or ringing a bell before opening the exchange, you are seeing the people through whom stocks are transacted on the NYSE.

The Nasdaq, on the other hand, is located not on a physical trading floor but on a telecommunications network. People are not on a floor of the exchange matching buy and sell orders on the behalf of investors. Instead, trading takes place directly between investors and their buyers or sellers, who are the market-makers through an elaborate system of companies electronically connected to one another.

Dealer Versus Auction Market

The fundamental difference between the NYSE and Nasdaq is in the way securities on the exchanges are transacted between buyers and sellers. The Nasdaq is a dealer's market, wherein market participants are not buying from and selling to one another but to and from a dealer, which, in the case of the Nasdaq, is a market maker. The NYSE is an auction market, wherein individuals are typically buying and selling between one another and there is an auction occurring; that is, the highest bidding price will be matched with the lowest asking price.

Traffic Control

Each stock market has its own traffic control police officer. That's right, just as a broken traffic light needs a person to control the flow of cars, each exchange requires people who are at the "intersection" where buyers and sellers "meet," or place their orders. The traffic controllers of both exchanges deal with specific traffic problems and, in turn, make it possible for their markets to work. On the Nasdaq, the traffic controller is known as the market-maker, who, we already mentioned, transacts with buyers and sellers to keep the flow of trading going. On the NYSE, the exchange traffic controller is known as the specialist, who is in charge of matching buyers and sellers together.

New York Stock Exchange Composite Transactions
(Quotations as of 5 p.m. Eastern Time, previous trading day)

(1)		(2)		(3)	(4)	(5)	(6)	(7)			
52 weeks					Yld		Vol				Net
Hi	Lo	Stock	(Sym)	Div	%	PE	100s	Hi	Lo	Close	Chg
58¾	45⅝	Kapstom (KPS)		1.2	2.8	18	169	58	57⅛	57⅜	+¼

Figure 18.1. Reading The Wall Street Journal.

1. *The highest and lowest prices over the last fifty-two weeks, not including the current quotation.*

2. *The name of the corporation and exchange ticker symbol used for that corporation (may be shortened or abbreviated).*

3. *Estimated annual per-share dividends in dollars and cents, based on last dividend.*

4. *Annual dividends as a percentage of the current per share price.*

5. *Price/earnings (P/E)—the relationship between the stock's current price and its earnings per share (for the last four quarters).*

6. *The number of shares traded the previous day, in hundreds of shares.*

7. *The highest, lowest, and closing prices of the stock for the previous day's trades. Net change compares the closing price quotation with the closing price for the previous trading day.*

Note: Various footnote symbols in The Wall Street Journal *provide additional information/exceptions.*

Source: Kansas State University, 1995.

The definitions of the role of the market maker and that of the specialist are technically different as a market maker "creates a market" for a security whereas the specialist merely facilitates it. However, the duty of both the market maker and specialist is to ensure smooth and orderly markets for clients. If too many orders get backed up, the traffic controllers of the exchanges will work to match the bidders with the askers to ensure the completion of as many orders as possible. If there is nobody willing to buy or sell, the market makers of the Nasdaq and the specialists of the NYSE will try to see if they can find buyers and sellers and even buy and sell from their own inventories.

Perception And Cost

One thing that we can't quantify but must acknowledge is the way in which the companies on each of these exchanges are generally perceived by investors. The Nasdaq is typically known as a high-tech market, attracting many of the firms dealing with the Internet or electronics. Accordingly, the stocks on this exchange are considered to be more volatile and growth oriented. On the other hand, the companies on NYSE are perceived to be more well-established. Its listings includes many of the blue chip firms and industrials that were around before our parents, and its stocks are considered to be more stable.

Whether a stock trades on the Nasdaq verses the NYSE is not necessarily a critical factor for investors when they are deciding on stocks to invest in. However, because both exchanges are perceived differently, the decision to list on a particular exchange is an important one for many companies. A company's decision to list on a particular exchange is affected also by the listing costs and requirements set by each individual exchange. The maximum listing fee you can pay on the NYSE is $250,000 while on the Nasdaq, the maximum is only $150,000. The maximum continual yearly listing fees are also a big factor: they are $500,000 and $60,000 respectively. So we can understand why the growth-type stocks (companies with less initial capital) would be found on the Nasdaq exchange.

Public Versus Private

The final major difference between these two exchanges is their type of ownership. Most of the time we think of the Nasdaq and NYSE as markets or exchanges, but these entities are both actual businesses providing a service to earn a profit for shareholders. The Nasdaq exchange is a publicly traded corporation whose shares, like those of any public company, can be bought and sold by investors on an exchange. (Incidentally, Nasdaq trades on itself.) As a public company, the Nasdaq must follow the standard filing requirements set out by the SEC. In contrast, the NYSE is not a public corporation. It is a private one owned by its private shareholders and is therefore not required to maintain the same filings as the Nasdaq. This ownership difference between the two exchanges, however, should not affect how they function as marketplaces for equity traders and investors.

Both the NYSE and the Nasdaq markets accommodate the major portion of all equities trading in North America, but these exchanges are by no means the same. Although their differences may not affect your stock picks, your understanding of how these exchanges work will give you some insight into how trades are executed and how a market works.

Closing Price

Many investors use closing prices reported in the newspapers to monitor their holdings. But not all closing prices are the same, and the differences may be important to you. Here's what you should know about closing prices.

"Closing price" generally refers to the last price at which a stock trades during a regular trading session. For many market centers, including the New York Stock Exchange, the American Stock Exchange, and the Nasdaq Stock Market, regular trading sessions run from 9:30 a.m. to 4:00 p.m. Eastern Time.

But a number of market centers offer after-hours trading. Some financial publications and market data vendors use the last trade in these after-hours markets as the closing price for the day. Others, however, publish the 4:00 p.m. price as the closing price and display prices for after-hours trading separately.

This discrepancy in the way the media and others report closing prices can cause confusion—especially when a single, low-volume after-hours trade occurs at a price that's substantially different from the 4:00 p.m. closing price.

For example, an investor might read on a company's website that its stock closed at one price but then see a much different price on the consolidated tape flashing across the bottom of her or his television screen. Or, the next day, the investor might hear that the stock opened "up" when, in fact, it opened "down" compared with the price at the 4:00 p.m. close.

How do current events affect the market?   ♣ It's A Fact!!

Bad News:

- **High interest rates:** High interest rates make it hard on companies to borrow money for expansion. Less growth may frighten away potential investors. Also, high interest rates may attract investors to other forms of investment, such as money market funds.

- **Increase in margin rates:** The Federal reserve (the "Fed") can increase the margin rate, thereby limiting the amount of money a broker may lend to his/her customers. For example, a 50% margin rate means that a person who wants to buy $10,000 of stock on margin must have $5,000 (50%) in cash, and may borrow the other $5,000 from the broker. If the FED raises the rate to 80%, the buyer must increase his/her contribution to $8,000. This would limit an investor's ability to purchase stocks.

- **Investigation by the SEC:** The Securities and Exchange Commission is the watchdog for the investment industry. If there are irregularities in its operation, the SEC will investigate. The investigation of a company by the SEC may warn investors of trouble and scare them off.

- **Government instability:** If a foreign country that supplies us with oil, for example, is going through a revolution, uncertainty would be created about the future of American companies which depend, either directly or indirectly, on oil.

- **Nationalization:** Occasionally, a foreign country will nationalize an industry in which American companies have a large stake. This may cause stock prices to drop dramatically. For example, Canada's nationalization of Gulf Oil Company's operation in that country sent shock waves through Gulf in the U.S.

To help clear up this confusion, the central distributor of transaction prices for exchange-traded securities—the Consolidated Tape Association (CTA)—implemented a system designed to make closing prices uniform. Under this system, the regular session closing price for stocks will be the 4:00 p.m. price. Sometimes orders come in before 4:00 p.m., but they can't be filled until

---

- **Accidents, health problems:** News about an accident or about a product which may cause health problems, may cause investors to fear that the company will not regain its customers or reputation.

Good News:

- **Take-over bids:** A take-over bid is an attempt by one company to buy another through stock acquisition, by buying enough stock to control it. The stock of the company being taken over becomes more valuable as the larger company makes offers. Investors want to own stock in the smaller company before the take-over, to share in the price rise.

- **Profits:** A report about the increased profits of a company usually indicates that the company is prospering and may increase its dividends. This my draw investors and increase the price of the stock.

- **Divestiture:** Large conglomerates often have one division of their corporation which does not make money. By announcing the sale of its losing interests, its potential for profit increases and its value will rise. For instance, a company might sell its unprofitable retail stores but retain its profitable communications division

- **New Product Line:** A company which produces a new product, such as a home computer, or a company that creates a new technique, such as splicing genes for the production of insulin, may draw investors who will bid up the price of the stock.

- **Government spending:** The U.S. government is the worlds leading consumer. If it decides to spend money on defense items, for example, the companies that produce those items are virtually assured of long-term profits, and the value of their stock will rise.

Source: Reprinted from *Kids Invest*, with permission from the State of Illinois Secretary of State, Securities Department. [n.d.]

after 4:00 p.m. Therefore, the CTA produces a 4:15 p.m. Market Summary for vendors and the media that includes regular session trades that are reported before 4:15 p.m. but should be included in regular session 4:00 p.m. prices. Any trades that take place during after-hours trading sessions will be "tagged" with the letter "T" on the consolidated tape and will not affect the regular session closing price (or the regular session high and low prices). The Nasdaq Stock Market, which operates a similar system for trades in its securities, uses similar conventions.

Because the closing price for the same stock may continue to be reported differently among various media and market data vendors, investors should try to understand what the reported price is based on. For example:

- Does the newspaper or vendor indicate that the closing price is based on the regular trading session price established on the security's primary market, such as the New York Stock Exchange, the American Stock Exchange, or the Nasdaq Stock Market?

- Does the closing price reflect the last trade reported over the consolidated tape as of the close of the regular trading session at 4:00 p.m. Eastern Time?

- Does the closing price reflect the last trade reported over the consolidated tape in after-hours trading?

Investors may be able to find this information if their newspaper or vendor system describes how the closing price is being reported.

Chapter 19

How To Buy A Stock

How Buying And Selling Stocks Works

Have you ever really wondered exactly how buying and selling stocks works? Ok, let's say that you have this feeling that McDonald's is going to go up soon. You, the young investor, remember that you have $350 that you have saved from Christmas presents, birthday presents, gifts, allowances, and whatever else you may have gotten the money from. You decide to invest in McDonald's so you would go to a person called a broker and tell them to buy stock in McDonald's. "Sure, I'll buy $325 worth of McDonald's and keep $25 for my commission," says the broker. Congratulations, you have just bought some stock.

About This Chapter: This chapter begins with "How Buying And Selling Stocks Works," excerpted from "Introduction to Investing," by Chris Stallman, © 1999 TeenAnalyst.com, LLC. All rights reserved. Reprinted with permission. "Buying And Selling Stock" and "Trade Execution: What Every Investor Should Know" are reprinted from documents dated January 26, 2000 and June 22, 2004, published by the U.S. Securities and Exchange Commission. "Stock Transactions" is excerpted from *Investment Basics: Stocks*, and "Dollar-Cost Averaging" is excerpted from *Investment Basics: Mutual Funds*, both by Joyce Jones, Ph.D., and reprinted with permission of the Kansas State University Agricultural Experiment Station and Cooperative Extension Service, Manhattan, Kansas, http://www.oznet.ksu.edu/. Copyright © 1995. All rights reserved. "What Are DRIPs?" is excerpted and reprinted with permission from http://www.directinvesting.com. Copyright © 2004 The Moneypaper, Inc. All rights reserved.

But what happens to the money I gave the broker? That's a good question. Well, after the broker takes your money, he puts in an order on his computer that is sent to the stock exchange. The order was given to a person called a floor broker. This person sees the order and runs to the area of the stock exchange where McDonald's stock is being bought and sold. He finds someone who is selling stock in McDonald's and buys the stock from that person. He then rushes back to one of the many computers and reports the trade. The report goes back to the broker and you are given ownership of the stock.

Buying And Selling Stock

When you call your broker to buy or sell a stock—or hit "enter" when placing an order through your online brokerage account—that's only the beginning of the transaction. Your broker's firm must then send your order to a market center to be executed. This process of filling your order is known as "trade execution."

Your broker generally has a choice of market centers to execute your trade:

Exchange. An exchange is a marketplace where traders can buy or sell stocks and bonds. For a stock that's listed on an exchange, such as the New York Stock Exchange (NYSE), your broker may direct the order to that exchange, to another exchange (such as a regional exchange), or to a firm called a "third market maker."

☞ **Remember!!**

No SEC regulations require a trade to be executed within a set period of time. But if firms advertise their speed of execution, they must not exaggerate or fail to tell investors about the possibility of significant delays.

Source: SEC, 2004.

Market Maker. A "market maker" is a firm that stands ready to buy or sell a stock at publicly quoted prices. Market makers in exchange-listed stocks are known as "third market makers." Market makers in stocks that trade in over-the-counter (OTC) markets, such as the Nasdaq, are known as "Nasdaq market makers" or simply "market makers."

Electronic Communications Network (ECN). An electronic communications network (ECN) is an electronic trading system that automatically matches buy and sell orders at specified prices.

Trade Execution: What Every Investor Should Know

When you place an order to buy or sell stock, you might not think about where or how your broker will execute the trade. But where and how your order is executed can impact the overall costs of the transaction, including the price you pay for the stock. Here's what you should know about trade execution.

Trade Execution Isn't Instantaneous

Many investors who trade through online brokerage accounts assume they have a direct connection to the securities markets. But they don't. When you push that enter key, your order is sent over the Internet to your broker—who in turn decides which market to send it to for execution. A similar process occurs when you call your broker to place a trade.

While trade execution is usually seamless and quick, it does take time. And prices can change quickly, especially in fast-moving markets. Because price quotes are only for a specific number of shares, investors may not always receive the price they saw on their screen or the price their broker quoted over the phone. By the time your order reaches the market, the price of the stock could be slightly—or very—different.

Your Broker Has Options for Executing Your Trade

Just as you have a choice of brokers, your broker generally has a choice of markets to execute your trade:

- For a stock that is listed on an exchange, such as the New York Stock Exchange (NYSE), your broker may direct the order to that exchange, to another exchange (such as a regional exchange), or to a firm called a "third market maker." A "third market maker" is a firm that stands ready to buy or sell a stock listed on an exchange at publicly quoted prices. As a way to attract orders from brokers, some regional exchanges or third market makers will pay your broker for routing your order to that exchange or market maker—perhaps a penny or more per share for your order. This is called "payment for order flow."

- For a stock that trades in an over-the-counter (OTC) market, such as the Nasdaq, your broker may send the order to a "Nasdaq market maker" in the stock. Many Nasdaq market makers also pay brokers for order flow.

- Your broker may route your order—especially a "limit order"—to an electronic communications network (ECN) that automatically matches buy and sell orders at specified prices. A "limit order" is an order to buy or sell a stock at a specific price.

Your broker may decide to send your order to another division of your broker's firm to be filled out of the firm's own inventory. This is called "internalization." In this way, your broker's firm may make money on the "spread"—which is the difference between the purchase price and the sale price.

Your Broker Has A Duty Of "Best Execution"

Many firms use automated systems to handle the orders they receive from their customers. In deciding how to execute orders, your broker has a duty to seek the best execution that is reasonably available for its customers' orders. That means your broker must evaluate the orders it receives from all customers in the aggregate and periodically assess which competing markets, market makers, or ECNs offer the most favorable terms of execution.

The opportunity for "price improvement"—which is the opportunity, but not the guarantee, for an order to be executed at a better price than what is currently quoted publicly—is an important factor a broker should consider in executing its customers' orders. Other factors include the speed and the likelihood of execution.

Here's an example of how price improvement can work: Let's say you enter a market order to sell 500 shares of a stock. The current quote is $20. Your broker may be able to send your order to a market or a market maker where your order would have the possibility of getting a price better than $20. If your order is executed at $20.05, you would receive $10,025.00 for the sale of your stock—$25.00 more than if your broker had only been able to get the current quote for you.

Of course, the additional time it takes some markets to execute orders may result in your getting a worse price than the current quote—especially in a fast-moving market. So, your broker is required to consider whether there is a trade-off between providing its customers' orders with the possibility—but not the guarantee—of better prices and the extra time it may take to do so.

You Have Options For Directing Trades

If for any reason you want to direct your trade to a particular exchange, market maker, or ECN, you may be able to call your broker and ask him or her to do this. But some brokers may charge for that service. Some brokers offer active traders the ability to direct orders in Nasdaq stocks to the market maker or ECN of their choice.

Ask your broker about the firm's policies on payment for order flow, internalization, or other routing practices—or look for that information in your new account agreement. You can also write to your broker to find out the nature and source of any payment for order flow it may have received for a particular order.

♣ **It's A Fact!!**

SEC rules require:

- All market centers that trade national market system securities must make monthly, electronic disclosures of basic information concerning their quality of executions on a stock-by-stock basis, including how market orders of various sizes are executed relative to the public quotes.

- These reports must also disclose information about effective spreads—the spreads actually paid by investors whose orders are routed to a particular market center.

- Market centers must disclose the extent to which they provide executions at prices better than the public quotes to investors using limit orders.

- Brokers who route orders on behalf of customers must disclose, on a quarterly basis, the identity of the market centers to which they route a significant percentage of their orders.

- Brokers must respond to the requests of customers interested in learning where their individual orders were routed for execution during the previous six months.

Source: SEC 2004.

If you're comparing firms, ask each how often it gets price improvement on customers' orders. And then consider that information in deciding with which firm you will do business.

Stock Transactions

The market for buying and selling stocks is primarily a secondary market. This means that most stocks are traded at resale among other investors. Initial public offerings (IPOs) are new stock issues of developing or expanding corporations and are usually speculative in nature (very risky) due to the limited history of the companies or their expanded operations.

Stocks are bought and sold through stockbrokers (and others authorized to buy and sell securities) who work with buyers and sellers as intermediaries and who receive commissions for their work. You may also be able to obtain stocks directly from a few companies through direct purchase or dividend reinvestment plans.

How Stock Trades Occur

Usually, you place an order to buy or sell stocks as a "market order," authorizing the stockbroker to complete your transaction at the best available price. To reduce the risk of prices going up (before you buy) or down (before you sell), you can place a "limit order," which specifies the maximum price you will pay (to buy) or the minimum price you will accept (to sell).

A "good until canceled order" stays in effect until the trade occurs or you cancel it, while a "day order" is only good for a day. These and other orders can provide the investor with some control over buy and sell transactions. Orders can be "round lots" (multiples of 100 shares) or "odd lots" (anything other than multiples of 100 shares). Odd lot orders usually involve higher sales costs.

A "cash account" allows a person to buy and sell stocks and other securities for cash or for payment within three business days. "Margin accounts" are brokerage credit accounts that allow investors to "leverage" their purchases by using credit (with 50% or more down). The investor signs a margin agreement or contract and pays interest on the loan amount. When the stock is sold, the loan is repaid. Because buying on margin can be very risky, it is not recommended for the beginning investor.

Dollar-Cost Averaging (DCA)

Dollar-cost averaging is a technique for purchasing mutual fund shares (or stocks) on a regular basis. It is one way to establish and follow a long-term investment plan.

By purchasing a specific dollar amount each time period (usually each month), you buy more shares when prices are down and fewer shares when prices are higher. This process actually leads to a greater return on your investment in the long-run (assuming share prices go up in the long-run).

Table 19.1 shows an example where an investor purchases $100 worth of shares each month. The average price was $10.67. If purchased at this price, the investor could have purchased 28.1 shares ($300 ÷ 10.67). However, the investor was able to purchase 28.5 shares at an average cost of $10.53 ($300 ÷ 28.5) because of dollar-cost averaging. Over the long run, these differences can add up.

Table 19.1. Dollar-Cost Averaging

	$ Invested	Share Price (NAV)	# Shares Purchased
		Share Price	
Month 1	$100.00	$10.00	10.0
Month 2	100.00	9.50	10.5
Month 3	100.00	12.50	8.0
	$300.00	$32.00 ÷ 3 = $10.67	28.5

Source: Kansas State University, 1995.

What Are DRIPs?

Direct investment plans, also known as dividend reinvestment plans (DRPs or DRIPs), are plans offered by companies to enable shareholders to invest cash and/or dividends directly through the company (or its agent) to buy additional shares of the company's stock.

Because you can invest through the DRIP, you don't have to contend with brokers or their commissions. Therefore, you can invest small amounts and accumulate shares slowly over a period of time—instead of making lump-sum investments.

✔ **Quick Tip**

Read more about DRIPs at The Motley Fool.com (http://www.fool.com/DRIPPort/WhatAreDRIPs.htm).

As a result of bypassing brokerage commissions, even a small investor can engage in two risk-reducing strategies—dollar-cost averaging and broad diversification of assets.

If you were to make small, regular investments in a diversified portfolio of companies through a broker, commissions might account for more of the investment than would the stock itself.

Chapter 20

The Bond Market

Add Balance With Bonds

Bonds belong in your investment plan for good reasons, but maybe not for the reasons you think:

- Economic forces that depress stock prices—the early stages of a recession, for instance—tend to boost bond prices.

- Bonds can generate impressive profits from capital gains. As we will point out, sometimes you can even calculate those gains years in advance on the day you buy the bonds.

- Bonds can provide a predictable stream of relatively high income you can use for living expenses or for funding other parts of your investment plan.

- Some kinds of bonds offer valuable tax advantages and unparalleled opportunities to take advantage of the time value of money, that is, to invest a modest amount with a reasonable prospect of collecting a large amount a few years later.

About This Chapter: This chapter begins with "Add Balance with Bonds," reprinted with permission from http://www.kiplinger.com. Copyright © 2005 Kiplinger Washington Editors, Inc. All rights reserved. Additional documents from Kiplinger Washington Editors are cited individually within the chapter.

Note that the word "safety" doesn't appear in this list. A lot of people think bonds are about the safest investment around, but as you'll see, such a notion can be costly.

How Bonds Work

Reprinted with permission from http://www.kiplinger.com. Copyright © 2005 Kiplinger Washington Editors, Inc. All rights reserved.

Bonds are IOUs issued by corporations, state and city governments and their agencies, and the federal government and its agencies.

When you buy a bond, you become a creditor of the corporation or government entity; it owes you the amount shown on the face of the bond, plus interest. (Bonds typically have a face value of $1,000 or $5,000, although some are larger.) You get a fixed amount of interest on a regular schedule—every six months, in most cases—until the bond matures after a specified number of years, at which time you are paid the bond's face value.

If the issuer goes broke, bondholders have first claim on the issuer's assets, ahead of stockholders.

In most cases, you won't receive the actual bond certificate. Bond ownership usually is in the form of a "book entry," meaning the issuer keeps a record of buyers' names but sends out no certificates. Treasury bonds, for instance, are issued in book entry form.

A long-term bond typically matures in 20 to 40 years, although some are issued for shorter periods. A bond that is due to mature in three to ten years is called an intermediate-term bond. Short-term bonds generally mature in three years or less.

After bonds are issued, they can be freely bought and sold by individuals and institutions in what's called the secondary market, which works something like a stock exchange.

All bonds share these basic traits, but they come in a variety of forms. Let's take a closer look.

Types Of Bonds

Secured Bonds. Secured bonds are backed by a lien on part of a corporation's plant, equipment or other assets. If the corporation defaults, those assets can be sold to pay off the bondholders.

Debentures. Debentures are unsecured bonds, backed only by the general ability of the corporation to pay its bills. If the company goes broke, debentures can't be paid off until secured bondholders are paid. Subordinated debentures are another step down the totem pole. Investors in these don't get paid until after holders of so-called senior debentures get their money.

Zero-Coupon Bonds. Zero-coupon bonds may be secured or unsecured. They are issued at a big discount from face value because they pay all the interest at maturity, with no payments along the way. (Although buying such a bond may sound nutty, in fact zero-coupon bonds offer a number of potential advantages to investors.)

Municipal Bonds. Municipal bonds are issued by state or city governments, or their agencies, and come in two principal varieties:

- *General obligation bonds* are backed by the full taxing authority of the government.

- *Revenue bonds* are backed only by the receipts from a specific source of revenue, such as a bridge or highway toll, and thus are not considered as secure as general obligation bonds.

The interest paid to holders of both revenue and general obligation municipal bonds is exempt from federal income taxes and, usually, income taxes of the issuing state.

U.S. Treasury Bonds. U.S. Treasury bonds, which when issued in maturities of a year or less are called Treasury bills and in maturities of under ten years may be called notes, are backed by the full faith and credit of the federal government.

♣ It's A Fact!!
Municipal Bonds

Municipal bonds (sometimes called "munis") are debt obligations of state and local governments (and state and local authorities such as school districts and airports). Typically, municipal bonds pay higher after-tax returns than U.S. government bonds of the same maturity, but less than corporate bonds.

Municipal bonds are only as safe as the issuer. There have been some defaults across the country.

Some municipal bonds are insured. However, these insured bonds tend to offer lower yields.

Municipal bonds can be more difficult to sell than U.S. government bonds. Small investors can find themselves at a disadvantage because they usually sell in large denominations (although you can buy municipal bonds through a mutual fund).

Source: Excerpted from "Part 4: Bonds," *Investment Basics: Mutual Funds*, by Joyce Jones, Ph.D., reprinted with permission of the Kansas State University Agricultural Experiment Station and Cooperative Extension Service, Manhattan, Kansas, http://www.oznet.ksu.edu/. Copyright © 1995. All rights reserved.

Agency Securities. Agency securities are issues from various U.S. government-sponsored organizations, such as Fannie Mae (formerly the Federal National Mortgage Association) and the Tennessee Valley Authority. Although they are not technically backed by the full faith and credit of the U.S. Treasury, they are widely considered to be moral obligations of the federal government, which presumably wouldn't let an agency issue fail.

Callable Bonds. Callable bonds are issues that can be redeemed, or "called," before they mature. A company might decide to call its bonds if, for instance, interest rates fell so far that it could issue new bonds at a lower rate and thus save money. This is obviously to the corporation's advantage, not yours. Not only would you lose your comparatively high yield, but you'd also have to figure out where to invest the unexpected payout in a climate of lower interest rates. And if the bond were called for more than you paid for it, you'd also owe tax on the difference.

Convertible Bonds. Convertible bonds are corporate bonds that can be swapped for the same company's common stock at a fixed ratio—a specified amount of bonds for a specified number of shares of stock. Convertible features make some companies' bonds more attractive by offering the possibility of an equity kicker: If the price of the stock rises enough after you buy the convertible bonds, you can profit by swapping your bonds for stock.

For example, suppose you buy five convertible bonds issued by AT&T at $1,000 each. The bonds pay 7% and each is convertible into 40 shares of AT&T stock. When you buy the bonds, AT&T is selling at $20 a share. Because break-even conversion price is $25, you've paid $5 a share for the conversion privilege. If AT&T stock climbs above $25, you can make a profit by converting your bonds to stock. If the price were to go to, say, $30, you could quickly turn your $5,000 bond investment into $6,000 worth of stock.

Because their fate is so closely tied to that of the stock price of the issuing firm, convertible bonds tend to be more closely in sync with the stock market than the bond market.

Unlocking The Potential Of Bonds

When a new bond is issued, the interest rate it pays is called the *coupon rate*, which is the fixed annual payment expressed as a percentage of the face value.

A 5% coupon bond pays $50 a year interest on each $1,000 of face value, a 6% coupon bond pays $60 and so forth. That's what the issuer will pay—no more, no less—for the life of the bond.

But it may or may not be the yield you can earn from that issue, and understanding why is the key to unlocking the real potential of bonds.

The Relationship Between Yield And Price

Take a new bond with a coupon interest rate of 6%, meaning it pays $60 a year for every $1,000 of face value. What happens if interest rates rise to 7% after the bond is issued? New bonds will have to pay a 7% coupon rate or no one will buy them. By the same token, you could sell your 6% bond only if you offered it at a price that produced a 7% yield for the buyer. So the price at which you could sell would be whatever $60 represents 7% of, which is $857.14. Thus, you'd lose $142.86 if you sell. Even if you don't sell, you suffer a paper loss because your bond is now worth $142.86 less than you paid for it. It is selling at a *discount.*

But what if interest rates were to decline? Say rates drop to 5% while you're holding your 6% bond. New bonds would be paying only 5% and you could sell your old bond for whatever $60 represents 5% of. Because $60 is 5% of $1,200, selling your 6% bond when interest rates are at 5% would produce a $200 capital gain. That $200 is called a *premium.*

Actual prices are also affected by the length of time left before the bond matures and by the likelihood that the issue will be called. But the underlying principle is the same, and it is the single most important thing to remember about the relationship between the market value of the bonds you hold and changes in current interest rates:

- As interest rates rise, bond prices fall; as interest rates fall, bond prices rise. The further away the bond's maturity or call date, the more volatile its price tends to be.

Varieties Of Yield

Because of this relationship, the actual yield to an investor depends in large part on where interest rates stand the day the bond is purchased, so the vocabulary of the bond market needs more than one definition for yield.

Coupon Yield. Coupon yield (the annual payment expressed as a percentage of the bond's face value) is only one way to look at a bond's payout. These are the others:

- *Current yield* is the annual interest payment calculated as a percentage of the bond's current market price. A 5% coupon bond selling for $900 has a current yield of 5.6%, which is figured by taking the $50 in annual interest, dividing it by the $900 market price and multiplying the result by 100.

- *Yield to maturity* includes the current yield and the capital gain or loss you can expect if you hold the bond to maturity. If you pay $900 for a 5% coupon bond with a face value of $1,000 maturing five years from the date of purchase, you will earn not only $50 a year in interest but also another $100 when the bond's issuer pays off the principal. By the same token, if you buy that bond for $1,100, representing a $100 premium, you will lose $100 at maturity.

The yield to maturity can dramatically affect investment results.

New York Exchange Bonds
Corporation Bonds Volume $23,700,000
(Quotations as of 4 p.m. Eastern Time, previous trading day)

(1)	(2)	(3)	(4)	(5)
Bonds	**Cur Yld**	**Vol**	**Close**	**Net Chg**
Balsat 8½00	8.6	32	99¼	+⅞

Figure 20.1. Reading The Wall Street Journal

1. *The company that issued the bond (may be shortened or abbreviated), the interest rate (8½%) and the year the bond matures (2000).*

2. *Annual interest payments divided by the current price of the bond.*

3. *Volume of the previous day's trading in thousands of dollars (in this case, $32,000 of bonds were traded).*

4. *Price of the bond at the close of the previous trading day, quoted in points ($10 a point; $1.25 per ⅛ point). Thus, 99¼ equals $992.50.*

5. *The closing price quotation compared with the closing price for the previous trading day (in this case, up ⅞ points or $8.75).*

Note: Various footnote symbols in The Wall Street Journal *provide additional information/exceptions.*

Source: Excerpted from "Part 4: Bonds," Investment Basics: Mutual Funds, *by Joyce Jones, Ph.D., reprinted with permission of the Kansas State University Agricultural Experiment Station and Cooperative Extension Service, Manhattan, Kansas, http://www.oznet.ksu.edu/. Copyright © 1995. All rights reserved.*

How To Reduce The Risks In Bonds

Interest-rate changes create one of the chief risks you face as an investor in bonds. The market value of the bonds you own will decline if interest rates rise.

This unalterable relationship suggests the first of several risk-reducing steps you can take as a bond investor:

- *Don't buy bonds when interest rates are low or rising.* Put your cash in a money-market fund or in certificates of deposit maturing in three to nine months. The ideal time to buy bonds is when interest rates have stabilized at a relatively high level or when they seem about to head down.

- *Stick to short- and intermediate-term issues.* Maturities of three to five years will reduce the potential volatility of your bond holdings. They fluctuate less in price than longer-term issues, and they don't require you to tie up your money for ten or more years in exchange for a relatively small additional yield.

♣ It's A Fact!!

Why Bonds Are Resold On The Market

Why would someone want to sell a $1,000 bond for less than its full value? Suppose you buy a bond for $1,000 that pays 10% interest and matures in ten years. Each year you would receive $100. After a few years, lets say interests rates in general rise to $15. Your $1000 investment could be paying $150 a year. You want to sell the bond to reinvest as much of the $1000 as you can, but who wants to pay $1000 for a bond only paying $100 a year when they could pay $1,000 for a bond paying $150 a year? To sell your bond you have to discount its price. On the other hand, if interest rates fall you would be able to sell it for more than $1,000.

Source: Excerpted from "Your Investment Options," reprinted with permission from the Office of the New York State Attorney General. [n.d.].

- *Acquire bonds with different maturity dates* to diversify your bond holdings. A mix of issues maturing in one, three and five years will protect you from getting hurt by interest rate movements you can't control. Mutual funds are an excellent way to achieve diversity in your bond investments.

Limit Default Risk

Interest-rate rises aren't the only potential enemy of bond investors. Another risk to consider is the chance that the organization that issued the bonds won't be able to pay them off. It's not realistic to expect that you could do the kind of balance-sheet analysis it takes to size up a company's ability to pay off its bonds in ten, 20 or even 30 years. Assessing the creditworthiness of companies and government agencies issuing bonds is a job for the pros, the best known of which are Standard & Poor's and Moody's. If the issuer earns one of the top four "investment grades" assigned by the companies— AAA, AA, A or BBB from Standard & Poor's, and Aaa, Aa, A or Baa from Moody's—the risk of default is considered slight. Table 20.1 gives a detailed breakdown of the companies' rating systems for issues considered to be worthy of the investment-grade designation. (Sometimes the ratings will be supplemented by a "+" or a "-" sign.)

Ratings below investment grade indicate that the bonds are considered either "speculative" (BB, Ba or B) or in real danger of default (various levels of C and, in the S&P ratings, a D, indicating that the issue is actually in default). You can consider any issue rated speculative or lower to be a "junk" bond, although brokers and mutual funds usually call them "high-yield" issues.

Individual junk bonds are very risky and it's best to avoid them unless you're willing to study the company's prospects closely. Alternatively, you could purchase shares in a junk bond mutual fund, which would ease the risk a bit through diversification. Even then, junk bonds should never occupy more than a sliver of your portfolio.

Check The Rating. Check the rating of any bond you're considering purchasing. A broker can give you the rating, or you can look it up in the Moody's or S&P bond guides found in many libraries. Online sources for ratings include S&P and Bondsonline.com. Moody's has a website, too, although you may find it difficult to search for ratings of individual companies.

For a mutual fund, the prospectus will describe the lowest rating acceptable to the fund's managers, and the annual reports should list the bonds in the fund's portfolio, along with their ratings.

In general, the lower the rating, the higher the yield a bond must offer to compensate for the risk.

Table 20.1. What The Ratings Mean

S&P	Moody's	What It Means
AAA	Aaa	The highest possible rating, indicating the agencies' highest degree of confidence in the issuer's ability to pay interest and repay the principal.
AA	Aa	A very high rating, only marginally weaker than the highest.
A	A	High capacity to repay debt but slightly more vulnerability to adverse economic developments.
BBB	Baa	The lowest investment-grade rating, indicating "adequate" capacity to pay principal and interest but more vulnerability to adverse economic developments.

Source: Kiplinger Washington Editors, © 2005.

Diversify. Diversify by buying bonds from several issuers. The fact that a municipal or corporate bond has a high rating is no guarantee that it is completely safe.

All of the major credit-rating agencies missed the signs of distress at Enron Corporation, failing to lower their safety ratings until just days before the giant company filed for bankruptcy protection in late 2001. The raters said they had been deceived by Enron and would have dropped their ratings much sooner if they had had the facts.

Diversify bond holdings across several different issuers, whether corporate or municipal. Bonds issued by the federal government are the only exceptions to this rule. They are as safe as you're going to get.

One way to diversify your bond investments is to buy shares in bond mutual funds.

Pay Attention To the News. Enron aside, the rating agencies do a good job of tracking the issues they've rated, raising or lowering ratings when they think a change is justified. Hundreds of "fallen angels" get downgraded each year, and hundreds get upgraded. The last thing you want is to have the rating of a bond issue lowered while you're holding it in your portfolio. Even a slight downgrade can affect a bond's value. To guard against downgrading, you have to pay attention to the company's prospects after you buy the bond.

♣ **It's A Fact!!**
Junk Bonds

"Junk Bond" is a term for speculative, high-risk, high interest rate corporate or municipal bonds. The default rate is much higher on junk bonds than on higher quality bonds.

Source: Excerpted from "Your Investment Options," reprinted with permission from the Office of the New York State Attorney General. [n.d.].

Consider Other Factors. Ratings aren't the final word on good bond buys. In fact, the market often recognizes problems with bond issues before the rating services can react.

Consider a bond's rating in the context of other information about bond issues you might buy:

- Compare the bond's price and yield with those of bonds with identical ratings to see which is the better buy.

- Make sure you're looking at the bonds' current credit rating. Buying on the basis of an outdated rating can be an expensive mistake.

- Make sure there's a market for the bond. This advice sounds obvious, but one thing that can cause junk bonds to lose so much of their value so fast is a situation in which there are suddenly many, many sellers and very few buyers, as when bad news hits.

Chapter 21

Savings Bonds

Savings bonds are issued by the U.S. Treasury Department. They are non-marketable securities. This means you may not sell savings bonds to or buy them from anyone except an issuing and paying agent authorized by the Treasury Department. Savings bonds are registered securities, meaning that they are owned exclusively by the person or persons named on them.

I Bonds and Series EE Savings Bonds are *accrual securities*. They earn, that is, *accrue* interest monthly at a variable rate and the interest is compounded semiannually. You receive your earnings when you redeem an I Bond or Series EE Savings Bond.

Series HH Savings Bonds are *current income securities*. You receive your earnings semiannually and you receive the face value of Series HH Savings Bonds when you redeem them. [Series HH Bonds are not available for purchase and are no longer available for reinvesting or exchanging.]

Overview Of Benefits Of Bond Ownership

- *Attractive interest rates.* The I Bond tracks inflation to prevent your earnings from being eroded by a rising cost of living. The Series EE Savings Bond earns market-based rates, keyed to five-year Treasury securities. Both series offer rates that are comparable to the rates of similar savings tools.

About This Chapter: Text for this chapter is excerpted from *The Savings Bond Owner's Manual*, published by the Bureau of the Public Debt, U.S. Treasury Department, August 2004.

- *Tax advantages.* Savings bond earnings are exempt from all state and local income taxes. You can defer federal income taxes on earnings until the savings bonds reach final maturity or you redeem them. If you use savings bonds to pay for qualified higher education expenses, your earnings may qualify for exclusion from federal income taxes, too.

- *Safety.* Savings bonds are backed by the full faith and credit of the United States. Your principal and earned interest are safe and cannot be lost because of changes in the market. Savings bonds are registered with the Treasury Department, so if yours are lost, stolen or destroyed, you may have them replaced at no cost to you.

- *Affordability.* You can buy savings bonds for as little as $25. Participants in Payroll Savings may buy them in even smaller installments. The Treasury Department never charges fees or service charges when you buy or redeem savings bonds. Because paper savings bonds come in eight denominations—$50, $75, $100, $200, $500, $1,000, $5,000 and $10,000—you can tailor your purchases to meet your goals and needs.

- *Accessibility.* The money you place in savings bonds is available whenever you want it after an initial holding period of 12 months for bonds issued February 2003 or later. However, if you redeem a savings bond earlier than five years from the issue date, you pay an early redemption penalty equal to the last three months of earned interest.

✎ What's It Mean?

<u>Accrual Bond</u>: A bond that earns interest until you cash it, but you don't get any of the money until you cash it (Series A, B, C, D, E, EE, F, I, or J).

<u>Current Income Bond</u>: A bond that pays you extra money (interest) every six months. For these bonds, the face amount always stays the same. For example, if the bond says $100 on it, then it's worth $100 when you decide you don't want it anymore. As long as you keep the bond, you'll get extra money (interest) in your bank account twice a year (Series H, HH, G, or K).

Source: From "Savings Bond Glossary For Kids," Bureau of the Public Debt, U.S. Treasury Department, August 2004.

- *Convenience.* You can buy savings bonds in several ways. The easiest is through an online account at TreasuryDirect or the traditional Payroll Savings Plan with an automatic allotment. You can also buy savings bonds at 40,000 financial institutions nationwide.

✎ What's It Mean?

<u>Bond</u>: A certificate reflecting a firm's promise to pay the holder a periodic interest payment until the date of maturity and a fixed sum of money on the designated maturing date.

Source: From "Glossary of Economic Terms" in *Outline of the U.S. Economy,* a publication of the Bureau of International Information Programs, U.S. State Department, February 2001.

How Does Interest Accrue On Savings Bonds?

Interest earned on I Bonds and Series EE Savings Bonds accrues monthly. This means that these savings bonds grow in value each month. The amount of this monthly growth is determined by the current interest rate and total value of a savings bond. Each month's earnings are applied to a savings bond's value on the first day of the next month. For example, interest earned in January is applied on February 1.

Interest accrued by I Bonds and Series EE Savings Bonds is compounded every six months—on a savings bond's semiannual anniversaries. When interest compounds, the savings bond's value on that date is used to calculate monthly interest accruals for the next six months. (Savings bond semiannual anniversaries are simply the months in which a savings bond is issued and six months from that. For example, a savings bond issued in January will have January and July as its semiannual anniversaries.)

Tax Exemption, Deferral And Reporting

Savings bond earnings are exempt from state and local income taxes.

You may defer payment of federal income taxes until an accrual-type savings bond (I Bond or Series EE Savings Bond) reaches final maturity—30 years from the issue date—or until you redeem it, whichever comes first.

The Internal Revenue Service requires that you report accrual-type savings bond earnings for federal income tax purposes no later than the year in which a savings bond reaches final maturity, even if you do not redeem it.

You may also elect to report your savings bonds earnings to the Internal Revenue Service and pay applicable federal income taxes annually. This is the only reporting method available for Series HH Savings Bonds.

Restrictions On Redemption. You may not redeem a savings bond until twelve months after its issue date for bonds issued February 2003 or later. For example, a savings bond with an issue date in February may be redeemed beginning the following February. Under extreme conditions, such as a widespread natural disaster, the Treasury Department may waive this holding period to assist people in a crisis.

After the initial holding period, you may redeem your savings bonds at any time. However, if you redeem I Bonds or Series EE Savings Bonds earlier than five years from the issue date, you pay an early redemption penalty equal to the last three months of earned interest.

Maturity Periods. I Bonds earn interest until they reach final maturity at thirty years from the issue date. At that time, they stop earning interest and you should redeem them. You must report your earnings for federal income tax purposes in the year in which your I Bonds reach final maturity.

The Education Tax Exclusion (Education Savings Bond Program). Your earnings from I Bonds and Series EE Savings Bonds may be excluded from federal income tax if you pay qualified higher education expenses in the year in which you redeem the savings bonds. Generally, tuition and fees at a postsecondary educational institution or program that receives federal tuition assistance qualify. Your household income in the year of redemption must meet guidelines for you to use the exclusion. Other restrictions apply.

Where To Buy Bonds

You can buy and hold savings bonds in a direct electronic account with the Treasury Department at TreasuryDirect (http://www.treasurydirect.gov). TreasuryDirect allows you to buy a single bond or schedule regular purchases for yourself or as gifts. In TreasuryDirect there are no paper bonds or paperwork.

Approximately 40,000 financial institutions are authorized as issuing and paying agents by the Treasury Department. You can buy paper savings bonds from any of these agents by filling out a purchase order and making a payment. The financial institution will process the order and you should receive your savings bond by mail within fifteen business days.

Owning Savings Bonds

Maintaining your paper savings bond holdings is very easy. Once you have bought a savings bond you do not have to do anything except let it grow and remember its final maturity date—30 years from issue.

If your paper savings bonds are lost, stolen or destroyed, you can easily have them replaced at no charge to you. The Treasury Department will replace them free of charge as long as it can establish that they have not been redeemed by someone authorized to do so. To ensure that your savings bonds can be easily replaced, you should keep a record of their serial numbers, issue dates, registration information and the Social Security number(s) that appear on them. Put the record in a safe place, separate from the savings bonds.

♣ It's A Fact!! Requirements For Buying U.S. Savings Bonds

If you belong in one of the following categories, you may buy savings bonds:

• Residents of the United States, its territories and possessions, or the Commonwealth of Puerto Rico, U.S. citizens residing abroad. (A non-citizen living outside the U.S. may be named as a co-owner or beneficiary as long as he or she does not live in an area restricted by the Treasury Department.)

• Civilian employees of the United States and members of its armed forces who have Social Security Numbers.

• Residents of Canada or Mexico who work in the United States, have Social Security Numbers and whose employers offer the Payroll Savings Plan.

Source: Bureau of the Public Debt, U.S. Treasury Department, August 2004.

Redeeming Savings Bonds

You can redeem paper savings bonds in any of the 40,000 financial institutions nationwide that are authorized as paying agents by the Treasury Department.

You can redeem any amount of I Bonds and Series EE Savings Bonds at an institution where you have had an account in good standing for at least six months or are personally known by the financial institution's staff.

Generally, other financial institutions may redeem no more than $1,000 in savings bonds for non-customers. In cases such as this, you may ask the institution to certify your signature and either forward your savings bonds to a Federal Reserve Bank or give you the address so that you may mail them yourself. The Federal Reserve Bank will mail you a check for the redemption value of the savings bonds.

You must send Series HH Savings Bonds to your servicing Federal Reserve Bank to redeem them. Your financial institution can help you by providing addresses or forwarding the savings bonds, certifying your signature and answering questions.

To redeem I Bonds and Series EE Savings Bonds, simply take your savings bonds into your financial institution with proper identification. A customer service representative will verify your identification, take your Social Security Number for tax reporting purposes and walk you through the process of redeeming your savings bonds.

To redeem Series HH Savings Bonds, take your savings bonds to your financial institution. A customer service representative will verify your identification, certify your signature on the savings bonds and take your

> ♣ **It's A Fact!!**
>
> HH Bonds are not available for purchase; these bonds were available only in exchange for matured EE/E Bonds with a total redemption value of at least $500, or by reinvesting the proceeds of a matured HH or H Bond.
>
> Source: From "Treasury HH Bonds FAQs," U.S. Treasury Department, 2005.

♣ It's A Fact!!

A bond may be registered in the name of individuals in three ways:

1. **One Owner Only.** Upon death, the bond becomes part of the owner's estate.

2. **Two Persons as Co-owner.** Either person may cash the bond without the knowledge or approval of the other. Upon the death of one owner, the other becomes the sole owner of the bond.

3. **One Owner and One Beneficiary.** The beneficiary, if he or she survives, automatically becomes the owner of the bond when the original owner dies.

Source: U.S. Treasury Department, 2005.

Social Security Number. The representative will either provide you with the address of your servicing Federal Reserve Bank or offer to send your savings bonds for you.

When You Should Redeem

The date at which savings bonds stop earning interest is called final maturity. I Bonds and Series EE Savings Bonds stop earning interest at thirty years from the issue date. Series HH Savings Bonds stop earning interest at twenty years from the issue date.

You should redeem I Bonds no later than the year in which they reach final maturity. Interest earnings are reportable for federal income taxes in that year.

How Redeeming Affects Your Taxes. Interest earned on savings bonds is exempt from state and local income taxes. Savings bonds are subject to federal income taxes and estate, inheritance, gift, or other excise taxes, both federal and state. You can report your income from I Bonds and Series EE Savings Bonds for federal income tax purposes in two ways: deferred reporting ("cash basis") and annual reporting ("accrual basis").

You can defer reporting and paying taxes on your earnings until the year in which you actually redeem your I Bonds and Series EE Savings Bonds. To choose this method, simply do nothing until the year in which you redeem your savings bonds or they reach final maturity. When you redeem your savings bonds, you will receive an IRS Form 1099-INT that shows the interest earned for the entire life of your savings bonds. Include your reportable interest earnings in your taxable income on your federal income tax return for the tax year in which you redeem your savings bonds.

Chapter 22

What Is A Mutual Fund?

What You Should Know About Mutual Funds

A mutual fund, also called an investment company, is an investment vehicle which pools the money of many investors. The fund's manager uses the money collected to purchase securities such as stocks and bonds. The securities purchased are referred to as the fund's portfolio.

When you give your money to a mutual fund, you receive shares of the fund in return. Each share represents an interest in the fund's portfolio. The value of your mutual fund shares will rise and fall depending upon the performance of the securities in the portfolio. Like a shareholder in a corporation, you will receive a proportional share of income and interest generated by the portfolio. You can receive these distributions either in cash or as additional shares of the fund. As a shareholder, you also have certain shareholder voting rights.

A mutual fund's portfolio is managed by a professional money manager. The manager's business is to choose securities that are best suited for the portfolio. Be aware, however, that even a professional money manager cannot insure against a loss of principal.

About This Chapter: This chapter begins with excerpts from "What You Should Know About Mutual Funds," reprinted with permission from the Secretary of the Commonwealth of Massachusetts, Securities Division, http://www.sec.state.ma.us/sct/sctidx.htm. Copyright 1996. "Invest Wisely" is excerpted from a brochure, "Invest Wisely: An Introduction to Mutual Funds," published by the U.S. Securities and Exchange Commission, November 2, 2004.

The mutual fund manager will invest in many different securities. This diversification of portfolio assets means that you as an investor have not pinned all your hopes on one company's success. Also, because the portfolio holds many securities, the negative impact that any one company may have on the fund is diminished. While diversification is a benefit of mutual fund investing, a mutual fund is still impacted, either favorably or unfavorably, by the ups and downs of the market in general.

☞ **Remember!!**

Mutual funds provide a relatively easy way to invest. Most funds have a minimum investment of $1000. In addition, a mutual fund stands ready to buy back, or redeem, your shares at any time. This liquidity allows you to get your money when needed. There is no guarantee, however, that your shares at the time of redemption will not have decreased in value.

Source: Massachusetts Secretary of the Commonwealth, 1996.

Types Of Mutual Funds

The types of mutual funds vary according to the fund's investment objective. A fund's investment objective will usually seek capital gains (gains from the sale of portfolio securities), income (interest and dividends earned on the portfolio securities) or a combination of both. While not a comprehensive list of all mutual funds, the basic types of funds are described below.

Money Market. A money market fund seeks safety of principal by investing in high quality, short-term securities. This type of fund is designed with the aim that an investor's principal should not decrease in value. There is no guarantee, how ever, that this will always be the case. A money market fund seeks to provide a regular distribution of income that is determined by short-term interest rates.

Growth. A growth fund invests primarily in the common stock of well-established companies. This type of fund may invest for long-term capital gains and is not intended for an investor who seeks income.

Aggressive Growth. Like a growth fund, an aggressive growth fund will invest primarily in common stock for long-term capital gains. An aggressive growth fund may invest in the common stock of small companies, out-of-favor companies or companies in new industries. It, therefore, has a higher degree of risk than a basic growth fund.

Income. An income fund invests in either corporate, government, or municipal debt securities. A debt security is an obligation that pays interest on a regular basis. Hence, this type of fund is designed for investors who desire periodic income payments. There are, however, substantial differences and varying degrees of risk among income funds depending on the credit quality of the debt issuer, the maturity of the debt instrument, and prevailing interest rates.

High Income. This category of income fund seeks to achieve a high degree of income by investing a material portion of its portfolio in below investment grade debt securities or junk bonds. These funds have a high degree of risk and should be purchased by investors who can incur the risk of loss of principal.

Balanced. A balanced fund, as the name implies, invests for both growth and income. The fund will invest in both equity and debt securities. A balanced fund seeks to provide long-term growth through its equity component as well as income to be generated by the portfolio's debt securities.

👉 Remember!!

- Mutual funds are not guaranteed or insured by the FDIC or any other government agency—even if you buy through a bank and the fund carries the bank's name. You can lose money investing in mutual funds.

- Past performance is not a reliable indicator of future performance. So don't be dazzled by last year's high returns. But past performance can help you assess a fund's volatility over time.

- All mutual funds have costs that lower your investment returns. Shop around, and use the SEC's Mutual Fund Cost Calculator at www.sec.gov/investor/tools.shtml to compare many of the costs of owning different funds before you buy.

Source: SEC, 2004.

Disclosure Documents

The Prospectus. The fund's prospectus is one of the most important documents to read when purchasing a mutual fund. It supplies the material information you will need to make an informed investment decision. Information is also available in the prospectus on certain administrative aspects of the fund, such as buying, redeeming and exchanging shares.

The Statement Of Additional Information (SAI). The SAI includes information that supplements what is disclosed in the prospectus. A fund's audited financial statement and a list of its portfolio holdings are included in the SAI, as well as in the annual report (see below). Because the SAI has been legally incorporated into the prospectus, it will be assumed that you have read it. Hence, you should always ask for a copy and read the SAI before investing in a mutual fund.

The Annual Report

The annual report is forwarded to a fund's shareholders at the end of each fiscal year. It includes the fund's audited financial statements and a list of the fund's portfolio securities. Unless otherwise included in the prospectus, a fund will include in its annual report a line graph comparing its performance to that of an appropriate broad-based securities market index, as well as a discussion of those events, strategies and techniques which affected its performance during the past fiscal year. An annual report includes material information that may not be available in other disclosure documents and, if available, should be read by a potential investor.

Mutual Fund Sales Charges

A mutual fund which sells its shares directly to investors without paying sales commissions to broker-dealers is referred to as a *no-load fund*. When you invest in a no-load fund your entire investment goes into buying shares of the fund. However, because you are not paying a commission to a broker-dealer, you will not receive financial advice.

When financial advice is needed, some investors choose a *load fund*. A load fund pays a broker-dealer a sales commission. The amount you invest in the fund is decreased by the payment of the sales commission. Some load funds, rather than charging the sales commission at the time of the sale,

✎ What's It Mean?

Aggressive Growth Fund: Also commonly referred to as a *capital appreciation fund* or *maximum capital gains fund*. A mutual fund that attempts to achieve the highest capital gains. Investments held in these funds are companies that demonstrate high growth potential with usually a lot of share price volatility. These funds are only for non risk-adverse investors willing to accept a high risk-return trade-off. Aggressive growth funds have a large positive correlation with the stock market. In times of economic upswings, they tend to perform very well and in times of economic downturns, they tend to do very poorly. An aggressive growth fund may invest in a company's IPO and then quickly turn around and re-sell the same stock to realize large profits. Some aggressive growth funds also invest in options to boost returns.

Balanced Fund: A mutual fund that invests its assets into the money market, bonds, preferred stock, and common stock with the intention to provide both growth and income. Also known as an *asset allocation fund*. A balanced fund is geared toward investors looking for a mixture of safety, income, and capital appreciation. The amount the mutual fund invests into each asset class usually must remain within a set minimum and maximum.

Growth Fund: A diversified portfolio of stocks that has capital appreciation as its primary goal, and thereby invests in companies that reinvest their earnings into expansion, acquisitions, and/or research and development. Most growth funds offer higher potential growth but usually at a higher risk.

Income Fund: A mutual fund that seeks to provide stable current income by investing in securities that pay interest or dividends. Income funds typically invest in utility stocks and blue chips.

Money Market Fund: A mutual fund that invests in short-term debt instruments. The fund's objective is to earn interest for shareholders while maintaining a net asset value of $1.00 per share. Generally sold with no load, money market funds may also offer low minimum investments to entice investors.

Source: Excerpted from "Dictionary," and reprinted with permission from www.investopedia.com. © 2004 Investopedia, Inc.

charge the fee when money is taken out of the fund. This fee is referred to as a *contingent deferred sales charge* or a *back-end load*. The back-end fee will usually decrease to zero the longer an investor remains in the fund.

Another sales-related expense, which is often overlooked by investors, is the *12b-1 fee*. This fee, which is disclosed in the fund's fee table, can be used by the fund for marketing, advertising or sales commissions. Because the 12b-1 fee is a charge against the fund on an annual basis, an investor could over the long term pay more in 12b-1 fees than would have been permissible as a maximum front end sales load.

Many load funds offer investors the option of paying the sales load up-front, back-end or a combination of a reduced sales commission and a 12b-1 fee. These sales-related options are called classes of fund shares. You should choose the class that best matches your needs and investment time frame. [See the next chapter for more about mutual fund fees.]

Invest Wisely

Some of the traditional, distinguishing characteristics of mutual funds include the following:

- Investors purchase mutual fund shares from the fund itself (or through a broker for the fund) instead of from other investors on a secondary market, such as the New York Stock Exchange or Nasdaq Stock Market.

- The price that investors pay for mutual fund shares is the fund's per share net asset value (NAV) plus any shareholder fees that the fund imposes at the time of purchase (such as sales loads).

- Mutual fund shares are "redeemable," meaning investors can sell their shares back to the fund (or to a broker acting for the fund).

- Mutual funds generally create and sell new shares to accommodate new investors. In other words, they sell their shares on a continuous basis, although some funds stop selling when, for example, they become too large.

- The investment portfolios of mutual funds typically are managed by separate entities known as "investment advisers" that are registered with the SEC.

Advantages And Disadvantages

Every investment has advantages and disadvantages. But it's important to remember that features that matter to one investor may not be important to you. Whether any particular feature is an advantage for you will depend on your unique circumstances. For some investors, mutual funds provide an attractive investment choice because they generally offer the following features:

- **Professional Management.** Professional money managers research, select, and monitor the performance of the securities the fund purchases.

- **Diversification.** Diversification is an investing strategy that can be neatly summed up as "Don't put all your eggs in one basket." Spreading your investments across a wide range of companies and industry sectors can help lower your risk if a company or sector fails. Some investors find it easier to achieve diversification through ownership of mutual funds rather than through ownership of individual stocks or bonds.

- **Affordability.** Some mutual funds accommodate investors who don't have a lot of money to invest by setting relatively low dollar amounts for initial purchases, subsequent monthly purchases, or both.

✎ What's It Mean?

<u>12b-1 Fee</u>: A provision that allows a mutual fund to collect from investors a small fee for promotions, sales, or any other activity connected with the distribution of the fund's shares. Originally it was believed that by marketing a mutual fund its assets would increase, which would ultimately lower management expenses because the cost would be spread out among more investors. However, this has yet to be proven. Most of the time the 12b-1 is just a way for fund companies to impose hidden costs on investors.

<u>Statement Of Additional Information (SAI)</u>: Conveys information about an open- or closed-end fund that is not necessarily needed by investors to make an informed investment decision, but that some investors find useful. Although funds are not required to provide investors with the SAI, they must give investors the SAI upon request and without charge. Also known as "Part B" of the fund's registration statement.

Source: SEC, 2004.

Mutual Fund Quotations

(1)	(2)	(3)	(4)	(5)	(6)			(7)
	Inv		Offer	NAV	—Total Return—			
	Obj	NAV	Price	Chg	YTD	13 wks	3 yrs	R
Quast	GRO	13.80	NL	+0.02	+1.5	− 0.01	+8.8	A

Figure 22.1. Reading The Wall Street Journal.

1. *Name of the mutual fund (may be shortened or abbreviated).*

2. *Investment objective, such as growth, growth and income, sector funds, and others.*

3. *Net asset value or dollar value per share as of the previous trading day.*

4. *Indicates this is a no-load fund (and thus, NAV is also offer price).*

5. *Change in the NAV between the closing quotation listed and that of the previous trading day.*

6. *Percentage return (+ or -), assuming all distributions are reinvested and excluding the sales charges. In this case, year-to-date, the last thirteen weeks, and the annual average over the last three years are given. YTD is calculated each business day; other time periods reported vary by day of the week, with expense ratios listed on Mondays.*

7. *Ranking of return performance, with "A" meaning the fund was in the top 20 percent over the last three years.*

Note: Various footnote symbols in The Wall Street Journal *provide additional information/exceptions.*

Source: Excerpted from "Part 5: Mutual Funds," Investment Basics: Mutual Funds, *by Joyce Jones, Ph.D., reprinted with permission of the Kansas State University Agricultural Experiment Station and Cooperative Extension Service, Manhattan, Kansas, http://www.oznet.ksu.edu/. Copyright © 1995. All rights reserved.*

- **Liquidity.** Mutual fund investors can readily redeem their shares at the current NAV—plus any fees and charges assessed on redemption—at any time.

But mutual funds also have features that some investors might view as disadvantages, such as:

- **Costs Despite Negative Returns.** Investors must pay sales charges, annual fees, and other expenses (which we'll discuss below) regardless of how the fund performs. And, depending on the timing of their investment, investors may also have to pay taxes on any capital gains distribution they receive—even if the fund went on to perform poorly after they bought shares.

- **Lack of Control.** Investors typically cannot ascertain the exact make-up of a fund's portfolio at any given time, nor can they directly influence which securities the fund manager buys and sells or the timing of those trades.

- **Price Uncertainty.** With an individual stock, you can obtain real-time (or close to real-time) pricing information with relative ease by checking financial websites or by calling your broker. You can also monitor how a stock's price changes from hour to hour—or even second to second. By contrast, with a mutual fund, the price at which you purchase or redeem shares will typically depend on the fund's NAV, which the fund might not calculate until many hours after you've placed your order. In general, mutual funds must calculate their NAV at least once every business day, typically after the major U.S. exchanges close.

Chapter 23

Buying And Selling Mutual Funds

How To Buy And Sell Shares

You can purchase shares in some mutual funds by contacting the fund directly. Other mutual fund shares are sold mainly through brokers, banks, financial planners, or insurance agents. All mutual funds will redeem (buy back) your shares on any business day and must send you the payment within seven days.

The easiest way to determine the value of your shares is to call the fund's toll-free number or visit its website. The financial pages of major newspapers sometimes print the NAVs for various mutual funds. When you buy shares, you pay the current NAV per share plus any fee the fund assesses at the time of purchase, such as a purchase sales load or other type of purchase fee. When you sell your shares, the fund will pay you the NAV minus any fee the fund assesses at the time of redemption, such as a deferred (or back-end) sales load or redemption fee. A fund's NAV goes up or down daily as its holdings change in value.

About This Chapter: "How To Buy And Sell Shares" is excerpted from a brochure entitled "Invest Wisely: An Introduction to Mutual Funds," published by the Securities and Exchange Commission (SEC), November 2, 2004. "Mutual Fund Fees And Expenses" is from a document published by the SEC on October 19, 2000.

Mutual Fund Fees And Expenses

As with any business, running a mutual fund involves costs. For example, there are costs incurred in connection with particular investor transactions, such as investor purchases, exchanges, and redemptions. There are also regular fund operating costs that are not necessarily associated with any particular investor transaction, such as investment advisory fees, marketing and distribution expenses, brokerage fees, and custodial, transfer agency, legal, and accountants fees.

Some funds cover the costs associated with an individual investor's transactions and account by imposing fees and charges directly on the investor at the time of the transactions (or periodically with respect to account fees). These fees and charges are identified in a fee table, located near the front of a fund's prospectus, under the heading "Shareholder Fees."

Funds typically pay their regular and recurring, fund-wide operating expenses out of fund assets, rather than by imposing separate fees and charges on investors. (Keep in mind, however, that because these expenses are paid out of fund assets, investors are paying them indirectly.) These expenses are identified in the fee table in the fund's prospectus under the heading "Annual Fund Operating Expenses."

Under the heading of "Shareholder Fees," you will find:

1. Sales Loads (including Sales Charge [Load] on Purchases and Deferred Sales Charge [Load])

2. Redemption Fee

3. Purchase Fee

4. Exchange Fee

5. Account Fee

☞ Remember!!

Remember that NAV stands for Net Asset Value. It is the value of the fund's assets minus its liabilities. Mutual funds must calculate the NAV at least once daily. The NAV per share is calculated by subtracting the fund's liabilities from its assets and then dividing the result by the total number of shares outstanding.

Source: SEC, 2004.

Under the heading of "Annual Fund Operating Expenses," you will find:

1. Management Fees

2. Distribution [and/or Service] (12b-1) Fees

3. Other Expenses

4. Total Annual Fund Operating Expense

> ### ♣ It's A Fact!!
>
> A frequently asked question is whether the Securities and Exchange Commission (SEC) imposes any specific limits on the size of the fees that a mutual fund may charge. In general, no, although the SEC limits redemption fees to 2% in most situations. The National Association of Securities Dealers, Inc. (NASD), however, does impose limits on some fees.
>
> Source: SEC, 2000.

Shareholder Fees

Sales Loads. Funds that use brokers to sell their shares must compensate the brokers. Funds may do this by imposing a fee on investors, known as a "sales load" (or "sales charge/load"), which is paid to the selling brokers. In this respect, a sales load is like a commission investors pay when they purchase any type of security from a broker. Although sales loads most frequently are used to compensate outside brokers that distribute fund shares, some funds that do not use outside brokers still charge sales loads.

The SEC does not limit the size of sales load a fund may charge, but the NASD does not permit mutual fund sales loads to exceed 8.5%. The percentage is lower if a fund imposes other types of charges. Most funds do not charge the maximum.

There are two general types of sales loads—a front-end sales load investors pay when they purchase fund shares and a back-end or deferred sales load investors pay when they redeem their shares.

Sales Charge (Load) On Purchases. The category "Sales Charge (Load) on Purchases" in the fee table includes sales loads that investors pay when they purchase fund shares (also known as front-end sales loads). The key point to keep in mind about a front-end sales load is it reduces the amount available to purchase fund shares. For example, if an investor writes a $10,000 check to a fund for the purchase of fund shares, and the fund has a 5% front-end sales load, the total amount of the sales load will be $500. The $500 sales load is first deducted from the $10,000 check (and typically paid to a selling broker), and assuming no other front-end fees, the remaining $9,500 is used to purchase fund shares for the investor.

Deferred Sales Charge (Load). The category "Deferred Sales Charge (Load)" in the fee table refers to a sales load that investors pay when they redeem fund shares (that is, sell their shares back to the fund). You may also see this referred to as a "deferred" or back-end sales load. When an investor purchases shares that are subject to a back-end sales load rather than a front-end sales load, no sales load is deducted at purchase, and all of the investors' money is immediately used to purchase fund shares (assuming that no other fees or charges apply at the time of purchase). For example, if an investor invests $10,000 in a fund with a 5% back-end sales load, and if there are no other "purchase fees," the entire $10,000 will be used to purchase fund shares, and the 5% sales load is not deducted until the investor redeems his or her shares, at which point the fee is deducted from the redemption proceeds.

Typically, a fund calculates the amount of a back-end sales load based on the lesser of the value of the shareholder's initial investment or the value of the shareholder's investment at redemption. For example, if the shareholder initially invests $10,000, and at redemption the investment has appreciated to $12,000, a back-end sales load calculated in this

> ✔ **Quick Tip**
> **A Word About Mutual Fund Fees And Expenses**
>
> As you might expect, fees and expenses vary from fund to fund. A fund with high costs must perform better than a low-cost fund to generate the same returns for you. Even small differences in fees can translate into large differences in returns over time. For example, if you invested $10,000 in a fund that produced a 10% annual return before expenses and had annual operating expenses of 1.5%, then after 20 years you would have roughly $49,725. But if the fund had expenses of only 0.5%, then you would end up with $60,858—an 18% difference.
>
> Source: SEC, 2000.

manner would be based on the value of the initial investment—$10,000—
not on the value of the investment at redemption. Investors should carefully
read a fund's prospectus to determine whether the fund calculates its back-
end sales load in this manner.

✎ What's It Mean?

Back-End Load: A fee an investor pays when selling a mutual fund within a
certain number of years, usually seven. Back-end mutual funds are OK if you
plan on investing for the long-term; otherwise, you'll pay high commission
to withdraw early. Remember that almost all mutual funds charge an annual
administration fee that is automatically withdrawn from your account, so
back-end funds aren't completely free.

Contingent Deferred Sales Charge (CDSC): In the context of mutual funds,
it is a back-end load charged only when a special circumstance occurs. A
good example of a CDSC is a charge applied when you decide to move your
money from one mutual fund into another company's fund. This sales charge
is "contingent" because it's only applied when the funds are prematurely moved
out of the original mutual fund.

Front-End Load: A mutual fund commission or sales fee that is charged at
the time shares are purchased. Loads are added to the net asset value of the
shares when the offering price is calculated. Remember, this fee is nothing
more than a sales commission. Its supporters (who are usually mutual fund
salespeople) argue that a load is the price you pay for a broker's expertise in
selecting the correct fund for you.

Load Fund: A mutual fund with shares sold at a price including a large sales
charge. This sales fee may range from 3% to as high as 8% of the full purchase. In exchange for paying your fees up front, mutual fund companies
don't usually make you pay high administration fees.

No-Load Fund: A mutual fund whose shares are sold without a commission
or sales charge as the shares are distributed directly by the investment company. Since there is no cost for you to enter a no-load fund, all of your money
is working for you. (*Most studies show that loads don't outperform no-loads.*)

Source: Excerpted from "Dictionary," and reprinted with permission from
www.investopedia.com. © 2004 Investopedia, Inc.

The most common type of back-end sales load is the "contingent deferred sales load," also referred to as a "CDSC," or "CDSL." The amount of this type of load will depend on how long the investor holds his or her shares and typically decreases to zero if the investor hold his or her shares long enough. For example, a contingent deferred sales load might be 5% if an investor holds his or her shares for one year, 4% if the investor holds his or her shares for two years, and so on until the load goes away completely. The rate at which this fee will decline will be disclosed in the fund's prospectus.

A fund or class with a contingent deferred sales load typically will also have an annual 12b-1 fee.

Redemption Fee. A redemption fee is another type of fee that some funds charge their shareholders when the shareholders redeem their shares. Although a redemption fee is deducted from redemption proceeds just like a deferred sales load, it is not considered to be a sales load. Unlike a sales load, which is generally used to pay brokers, a redemption fee is typically used to defray fund costs associated with a shareholder's redemption and is paid directly to the fund, not to a broker. The SEC generally limits redemption fees to 2%.

Purchase Fee. A purchase fee is another type of fee that some funds charge their shareholders when the shareholders purchase their shares. A purchase fee differs from, and is not considered to be, a front-end sales load because a purchase fee is paid to the fund (not to a broker) and is typically imposed to defray some of the fund's costs associated with the purchase.

Exchange Fee. An exchange fee is a fee that some funds impose on shareholders if they exchange (transfer) to another fund within the same fund group.

Account Fee. An account fee is a fee that some funds separately impose on investors in connection with the maintenance of their accounts. For example, some funds impose an account maintenance fee on accounts whose value is less than a certain dollar amount.

Annual Fund Operating Expenses

- *Management Fees*—fees that are paid out of fund assets to the fund's investment adviser for investment portfolio management, any other management fees payable to the fund's investment adviser or its affiliates, and administrative fees payable to the investment adviser that are not included in the "Other Expenses" category (discussed below).

- *Distribution [and/or Service] Fees ("12b-1" Fees)*—fees paid by the fund out of fund assets to cover the costs of marketing and selling fund shares and sometimes to cover the costs of providing shareholder services. "Distribution fees" include fees to compensate brokers and others who sell fund shares and to pay for advertising, the printing and mailing of prospectuses to new investors, and the printing and mailing of sales literature. "Shareholder Service Fees" are fees paid to persons to respond to investor inquiries and provide investors with information about their investments.

- *Other Expenses*—expenses not included under "Management Fees" or "Distribution or Service (12b-1) Fees," such as any shareholder service expenses that are not already included in the 12b-1 fees, custodial expenses, legal and accounting expenses, transfer agent expenses, and other administrative expenses.

- *Total Annual Fund Operating Expenses ("Expense Ratio")*—the line of the fee table that represents the total of all of a fund's annual fund operating expenses, expressed as a percentage of the fund's average net assets. Looking at the expense ratio can help you make comparisons among funds.

Be sure to review carefully the fee tables of any funds you're considering, including no-load funds. Even small differences in fees can translate into large differences in returns over time. For example, if you invested $10,000 in a fund that produced a 10% annual return before expenses and had annual operating expenses of 1.5%, then after 20 years you would have roughly $49,725. But if the fund had expenses of only 0.5%, then you would end up with $60,858—an 18% difference.

✎ What's It Mean?

Purchase Fee: A shareholder fee that some funds charge when investors purchase mutual fund shares. Not the same as (and may be in addition to) a front-end load.

Redemption Fee: A shareholder fee that some funds charge when investors redeem (or sell) mutual fund shares. Redemption fees (which must be paid to the fund) are not the same as (and may be in addition to) a back-end load (which is typically paid to a broker). The SEC generally limits redemption fees to 2%.

Shareholder Service Fees: Fees paid to persons to respond to investor inquiries and provide investors with information about their investments.

Source: SEC, 2004.

Part Six

Advanced Investing For Teens

Chapter 24

The Value Of Researching Before Investing

Information Matters

Information is the investor's best tool when it comes to investing wisely. But accurate information about the smallest of companies can be extremely difficult to find. Many of these very small companies do not register their securities or file financial reports with the SEC, which makes it almost impossible for investors to get the facts about the company's management, products, services, and finances.

Far too often, the lack of reliable, readily available, current information also opens the door to fraud. It's much easier for the unscrupulous to spread false information and to manipulate a stock's price when accurate information about the company is scarce. All it takes for a fraudster to make a killing is a handful of unwary investors who believed what they saw in spam E-mails, unsolicited faxes, chat room or bulletin board postings, newsletters, or questionable press releases.

About This Chapter: This chapter begins with "Information Matters" (August 3, 2004) and "Corporate Reports" (October 19, 2001), published by the U.S. Securities and Exchange Commission. "How To Analyze And Select Stock" is excerpted from *Investment Basics: Stocks*, by Joyce Jones, Ph.D., reprinted with permission of the Kansas State University Agricultural Experiment Station and Cooperative Extension Service, Manhattan, Kansas, http://www.oznet.ksu.edu/. Copyright © 1995. All rights reserved. The chapter concludes with information reprinted with permission from *How to Read a Prospectus: A Guide for Beginning Investors*, January 2005, a publication of the Missouri Secretary of State Securities Division. © 2005 State of Missouri.

The mere fact that a company files reports with the SEC does not make the company a "good" investment or immune to fraud. Conversely, the fact that a company does not file reports with the SEC does not mean the company lacks legitimacy. Many of the companies that don't file reports with the SEC are honest businesses with real products or services. The critical difference is the extra measure of risk you assume when you invest in a company about which little or no information is publicly available.

✔ **Quick Tip**
SEC Filings And Forms (EDGAR)

All companies, foreign and domestic, are required to file registration statements, periodic reports, and other forms electronically through EDGAR. Anyone can access and download this information for free. At http://www.sec.gov/edgar.shtml you'll find links to a complete list of filings available through EDGAR and instructions for searching the EDGAR database.

Source: U.S. Securities and Exchange Commission (SEC), 2004.

What information do I need?

Especially if you are investing on your own, be sure to research each investment opportunity thoroughly and ask questions—about both the company itself and the person or entity promoting it. These simple steps can help you make an informed investment decision:

1. **Research the company:** If you can't find the company on EDGAR [Electronic Data Gathering, Analysis and Retrieval], be sure to contact your state securities regulator to get the most recent reports the company has filed with its regulators. Make sure you understand the company's business and its products or services. Pay attention to the company's financial statements—particularly if they are not audited or not certified by an accountant. If the company does not file reports with the SEC, be sure to ask your broker for what's called the "Rule 15c2-11 file" on the company. That file will contain important information about the company.

2. **Know the owners:** Contact your state securities regulator to check out the people running the company. Be sure to find out whether they have a history of investor complaints or fraud charges. It pays to know whether the company's management has made money for investors in the past—or not.

3. **Check out your broker:** Make sure the broker and his or her firm are registered and licensed to do business in your state. And ask your state securities regulator whether the broker and the firm have ever been disciplined or have complaints against them.

When you ask questions, write down the answers you received and what you decided to do. If something goes wrong, your notes can help to establish who said what and when. Let your broker or investment adviser know you're taking notes. They'll know you're a serious investor and may tell you more—or give up trying to scam you.

How do I get information about companies?

If you're working with a broker or an investment adviser, he or she can provide you with information about the company and its disclosure documents. Be sure to read carefully the prospectus and the company's latest financial reports. Remember that unsolicited E-mails, message board postings, and company news releases should never be used as the sole basis for your investment decisions. You can also get information on your own from these sources:

- **From the company.** Ask the company if it is registered with the SEC. If the company is small and unknown to most people, you should also call your state securities regulator to get information about the company, its management, and the brokers or promoters who've encouraged you to invest in the company.

- **From the SEC.** A great many companies must file their reports with the SEC. Using the EDGAR database, you can find out whether a company files with us and get any reports in which you're interested. For companies that do not file on EDGAR, check with the SEC's Public Reference Room to see whether the company has filed an offering circular under Regulation A.

- **From your state securities regulator.** Contact your state securities regulator to find out whether they have information about a company and the people behind it. Look in the government section of your phone book or visit the website of the North American Securities Administrators Association to get the name and phone number. Even though the company does not have to register its securities with the SEC, it may have to register them with your state. Your regulator will tell you whether the company has been legally cleared to sell securities in your state. Too many investors could easily avoid heavy and painful financial losses if only they would call their state securities regulator before they buy stock.

- **From other government regulators.** Many companies, such as banks, do not have to file reports with the SEC. But banks must file updated financial information with their banking regulators. Visit the Federal Reserve System's National Information Center of Banking Information site at www.ffiec.gov/NIC, the Office of the Comptroller of the Currency at www.occ.treas.gov, or the Federal Deposit Insurance Corporation at www.fdic.gov.

- **From reference books and commercial databases.** Visit your local public library or the nearest law or business school library. You'll find many reference materials containing information about companies. You can also access commercial databases for more information about the company's history, management, products or services, revenues, and credit ratings. There are a number of commercial resources you may consult, including: Bloomberg, Dun & Bradstreet, Hoover's Profiles, Lexis-Nexis, and Standard & Poor's Corporate Profiles. Ask your librarian about additional resources.

- **From the secretary of state where the company is incorporated.** Contact the secretary of state where the company is incorporated to find out whether the company is a corporation in good standing. You may also be able to obtain copies of the company's incorporation papers and any annual reports it files with the state. Visit the National Association of Secretaries of State website at www.nass.org for contact information regarding a particular secretary of state.

What about bankruptcy?

Watch out for ticker symbols ending with a fifth letter "Q." The addition of a "Q" to a company's stock ticker symbol indicates that the company has filed for or is involved in bankruptcy proceedings. Investors often snatch up the low-priced shares of companies that have filed for Chapter 11 protection, speculating that the price will rise once the company emerges from bankruptcy. But that's not how bankruptcy typically works.

Be cautious when buying common stock of companies in Chapter 11 bankruptcy. Doing so is extremely risky and will likely lead to financial loss. Although a company may emerge from bankruptcy as a viable entity, in most instances, the company's plan of reorganization will cancel the existing equity shares. It is generally the creditors and the bondholders who become the new owners of the company's new shares—not the stockholders. This happens in bankruptcy cases because creditors are paid from the company's assets before common stockholders. And in situations where shareholders do participate in the plan, their shares are usually subject to substantial dilution.

Corporate Reports

Corporate reports are a treasure trove of information for investors: they tell you whether a company is making money or losing money and why. You'll find this information in the company's quarterly reports on Form 10-Q, annual reports (with audited financial statements) on Form 10-K, and periodic reports of significant events on Form 8-K.

It's usually easy to find information about large companies from the companies themselves, newspapers, brokerage firms, and the SEC. By

☞ Remember!!

Form 10-K is the report that most publicly traded companies file with the SEC on an annual basis. It provides a comprehensive overview of the company's business and financial condition and is available upon request. Some companies choose to send their Form 10-K to their shareholders instead of sending a separate annual report. You'll also find a company's Form 10-K in the SEC's EDGAR database.

Source: Adapted from "Form 10-K," U.S. Securities and Exchange Commission (SEC), 2002.

contrast, it can be extremely difficult to find information about small companies. Generally, smaller companies only have to file reports with the SEC if they have $10 million or more in assets and 500 or more shareholders, or list their securities on an exchange or Nasdaq.

How To Analyze And Select Stock

Fundamental Analysis. Fundamental analysis involves evaluating the stock's underlying value—its "fundamentals." Examining the overall economy and the securities market as a whole (such as economic growth, level of employment, level and direction of interest rate changes) is the first step. This becomes the baseline against which to measure the performance of a stock.

The second step in fundamental analysis involves examining the characteristics of the industry to which the prospective stock belongs. The final step, once an investor has determined that the time is right to invest in stocks and which industry has the most promising future, is to select the most promising stocks within that industry.

Information that can be helpful in this analysis includes such things as financial statements of the corporation. The balance sheet is like a snapshot of the company, showing assets and liabilities at a particular point in time. The income statement can provide insight into current management performance and estimate how profitable a company may be in the future.

✔ Quick Tip

You can get corporate reports from the following sources:

- The SEC. Find out whether a company files reports by using the SEC's database, EDGAR. For companies that do not file on EDGAR, you can contact the SEC at:

    Office of Public Reference
    450 5th Street, NW
    Room 1300
    Washington, DC 20549-0102
    phone: 202-942-8090
    fax: 202-628-9001
    e-mail: publicinfo@sec.gov

- The company.

- Other government regulators.

Source: SEC, 2001.

Technical Analysis. Technical analysis focuses on timing (when to buy and sell securities). It is based on the idea that common stock prices tend to move together. In addition, these prices are determined by the investors' demand for stocks and the supply of stocks available. Technical analysts are primarily interested in changes in stock prices. The assumption is that prices move in trends and that the trends last long enough to profit from them.

Market trends can be either "bullish" (meaning stock prices tend to go up overall) or "bearish" (meaning prices are falling overall). Bull markets reflect investor optimism and economic growth, while bear markets reflect investor pessimism and decline in economic growth.

Technical analysis also looks at other factors, such as the relationship of changes in stock prices and the volume of trading, the ratio of stocks advancing (or increasing) to stocks declining (or decreasing) in price, and the cycles that stock prices tend to take. Technical analysts use charts and computer models to track a stock's history and detect changes in trading trends.

Tax Treatment On Capital Gains And Losses

Capital gains (or capital losses) are the profits (or losses) resulting from your stock investments over and above any dividends you have received. Taxation of capital gains and losses has been treated differently over time. Therefore, it is important for the investor to be aware of what the current tax code is regarding capital gains and losses and to take it into account when making stock investment decisions.

At some points in time, individual investors with capital gains have received favored tax treatment. At other times, there is no favored tax treatment for short-term capital gains (on assets held for one year or less); they are treated as ordinary income, and long-term capital gains (on assets held for over a year) are taxed at a maximum tax rate. This provides a benefit for those taxpayers in higher tax brackets.

Capital losses can be used to offset capital gains, and excess capital losses can be deducted from ordinary income up to a maximum amount. Portions of that amount that are not used in the current tax year can be carried forward to future years.

> ☞ **Remember!!**
>
> While most people do not have the knowledge that is needed to perform sophisticated analysis on stocks before they invest, it is helpful to know what the experts study in giving investment advice. Making money in the stock market is not simple. Learn as much as you can about the market before you invest.
>
> • Check your local library or the business library of a nearby college or university for resources.
>
> • Read financial magazines, such as *Money, Business Week, Kiplinger's Personal Finance Magazine, Smart Money, Fortune,* and *Forbes.*
>
> • Check for current reference books, newsletters, and information services that provide more in-depth information, such as those by Standard & Poor, Moody, and Value Line.
>
> • Business sections of large daily newspapers, *The Wall Street Journal,* and *Barron's* can provide information on stock price movements and trading.
>
> Source: Kansas State University, 1995.

In addition, investors should realize that the criteria for defining capital gains have changed over time. Historically, the effect of the tax code has been a lower tax bite on capital gains than on earned income, interest, and dividends received. Investors may need to consult with an income tax adviser in regard to capital gains.

How To Read A Prospectus

Reading the prospectus is the best way to get detailed, precise information about a securities offering. There is no real shortcut.

In general a prospectus is a written document that provides all material information about an offering of securities, and is the primary sales tool of the company that issues the securities (called the issuer) and broker-dealers that market the offering for the issuer (called underwriters).

A prospectus is also a legal document that protects the issuer and underwriters because it serves as written proof that you were given all of the material facts as they are set out in the prospectus. For that reason, you should be certain that you understand the disclosures made to you, and that all verbal explanations are consistent with the disclosures contained in the prospectus.

In some instances, there may be other written material about a proposed investment that is not referred to as a prospectus, but contains the kind of information generally contained in a prospectus. For example, a mutual fund prospectus is a short summary of the statement of additional information (SAI), a document in which the detailed disclosures are made. If the security is not being offered for the first time, the annual report, "10-Q's," "10-K's" and "8-K's" will contain much the same information as a prospectus.

☞ Remember!!

• *Be skeptical.* If a claim or business plan does not look workable to you, perhaps it isn't.

• *Be assertive.* Make sure that you are given a copy of the prospectus before you decide to invest and insist on help in reviewing the prospectus if you feel you need it.

• *Be inquisitive.* Ask every question about the offering that occurs to you. If you need to, make a list of your questions. If you cannot get an answer to your questions, do not invest.

Source: Missouri Secretary of State Securities Division, 2005.

Parts Of A Prospectus

The front page gives general information such as the issuer's name, type and amount of securities offered and whether there are any existing shareholders who are selling their shares. It states whether there is or is not a public market. It names the underwriter(s), states the amount of underwriter's compensation, and notes whether the offering is "firm commitment" or "best efforts." The front page will also indicate whether the prospectus is effective with the Securities and Exchange Commission (the effective date will appear), or is still "preliminary" (marked in red).

Summary information is a summary of the matters to be disclosed more fully in the prospectus and audited financial statements. Take time to read the fine print in the footnotes.

Certain considerations is the risk factor section. Read it very carefully. If it is not included, be very skeptical about the investment. Each risk factor should have substantially more disclosure somewhere else in the prospectus. Look for each one.

A **litigation** section, which summarizes all ongoing material litigation, may or may not be included, depending on whether there is any. Although the risk factors will generally refer to this section, if there is one, it is a good idea to look for one even if it is not mentioned.

The **company** section gives the history, type of operation, location(s) of operations, and general business plan. This information is expanded in a subsequent section entitled "Business."

The **use of proceeds** section is very important. Don't invest unless this section can explain how your investment capital will be used.

A **capitalization table** gives the actual and *pro forma* (adjusted) financial position of the issuer for before and after it receives the funds from the offering. Read the footnotes to this table carefully.

The **dilution section** sets out the price at which shares in the company have been acquired and will be acquired in this offering. It contrasts the price per share paid by existing shareholders with the present offering price and contrasts the per share tangible book value (the value you will receive in your shares after the offering) with the offering price (that you will pay for those shares).

The **dividend policy** will reveal whether the stock is income or growth oriented. If income oriented, there should be a history of paying dividends. If growth oriented, there is generally no track record of dividend payments. Some companies may be restricted by their creditors from paying dividends. If you need income, don't invest in a security that doesn't pay dividends.

The **selected consolidated financial information** is an expansion of the financial information appearing in the summary information, but substantially less than that found in the financial statements and footnotes.

Management discussion and analysis of financial condition and results of operations is one of the most important sections in the prospectus, particularly if you have trouble following the financial statements. This section will tell you how management feels it has performed and gives some idea how the business is "trending" with the economy. Careful reading will reveal positive or negative trends on revenues, earnings and expenses. It pays to read this section closely to see where the issuer has been and where it might be going after the new capitalization.

Business is an expanded section of the information outlined under the "Company" heading and should provide more detailed disclosure as to the issuer's history, business plan and method(s) of operation. This section contains a subsection entitled "Competition." It is worthwhile to note who and what constitutes the competition against the issuer. This section will also have additional subsections such as Properties, Employees, Patents and Service Marks, and Legal Proceedings.

The **management** section lists the directors and executive officers, and gives their ages, positions and past experience. It also names the founders or promoters. In the subsection on compensation plans, note any special option plans, stock appreciation rights or other similar common stock equivalents to be paid to management or employers. These equivalents may provide necessary incentives to the employees, management and officers and directors, but an exceptionally larger number may eventually depress the price of your stock.

The **certain transactions** section discloses transactions between and among the issuer, principals and affiliates. Such transactions should be viewed skeptically since they can siphon operating capital and offering proceeds away from the business. Keep an eye open for questionable loans and promissory notes, use of business properties for personal benefit, less-than-competitive sales or acquisitions of plant and equipment or securities.

The **description of capital stock section** details the classes of stock and their voting rights. The section indicates which securities are authorized, issued and outstanding. This section provides insight as to the total supply of stock available for sale, which may increase and consequently depress the price of your stock (if earnings are poor or declining).

The **underwriting section** discloses the form of underwriting used and the amount of compensation the underwriter will receive. Firm underwriting is an underwriting in which the brokerage firm commits to buy the entire issue of stock being offered and therefore assumes all financial responsibility for any shares that go unsold.

This section also discloses whether the underwriter receives an option as compensation. Usually options are granted to underwriters as compensation when the issuer is small, new or weak. Note any finder's fees or other special consideration for selling the security. Keep in mind that

---

Signposts Of Value   ♣ It's A Fact!!

In a prospectus, look for signposts of value, a process frequently referred to as *fundamental analysis*. Search for the following strong fundamentals that indicate value:

- **The offering price.** The offering price should reasonably relate to the earnings per share, to similar companies already in the market and to the Standard & Poor's price earnings ratio for the market. If the price is higher, the stock may be overpriced.

- **Use of proceeds.** Look at the intended use of proceeds from the offering. If there is no particular specified use for the money being raised, the offering may be a "blind pool." Don't turn your money over to something without knowing how, in very specific terms, it will be used. Securities scams frequently involve entities with no particular plan of business.

- **Risk factors.** ("Certain Considerations") The title is a polite "tip off" to items you need to carefully consider as you read through the offering document. The items listed at the front of the prospectus are frequently the most risky features of the financing. Keep your eyes open for contingent liabilities that could affect the company after you've bought into it.

- **Age and track record of the company.** Note the company's age and its past success rate and how efficiently the company achieves its objectives (business costs versus revenues). Take special notice of whether earnings are steady

more compensation to the underwriter (and for organizational expenses) means less proceeds available to the issuer for business purposes. Generally, a sales commission in the range of 6–10% (plus any underwriters' options, and organization and offering costs in the neighborhood of 5%) is normal.

The **legal matters** and **experts sections** will indicate who performed the legal work on the offering and which accounting firms and other professionals participated. Parties listed in legal matters and experts have third-party liability in connection with the offering.

---

or erratic or whether they radically changed one way or the other recently. If there has been such a change, find out the reasons for it.

- **Capitalization of the issuer.** Check to see how much the issuer is worth. Start with the capitalization table and its footnotes in conjunction with the balance sheet and footnotes, which provide a good summary of any common stock equivalents that exist. The amount of common stock or common stock equivalent will directly affect the value of your common stock. The greater the pool of outstanding stock, the greater is the amount of earnings required to maintain or increase the price of the stock.

Check the amount of short-term, long-term and total debt, and review how much of each is carried on the books as a liability and when each type comes due. Check to see if the issuer's income is sufficient to pay its expenses. Particularly, note whether the issuer can pay its debts as they come due or whether it has borrowed too much. The issuer may have borrowed so much that even with the funds from this offering there will still be difficulty paying debts as they come due.

- **Management of company.** Examine how much experience in this type of business the management brings to the company and how much time each member of management will devote to the company. If the principals are not experienced or do not plan to devote their full time to the company, find a different investment.

Source: Missouri Secretary of State Securities Division, 2005.

Report of independent accountants is the auditors' opinion. Read it carefully for any qualification relating to management reporting practices that do not conform to generally accepted accounting principles. If the opinion mentions any specific footnotes to the financials, be sure to read them. Note the age of the financials, the date of which will appear under the accountant's signature.

Financial statements and **footnotes,** which includes the balance sheet, income statement, and statement of changes in financial position will provide strong insights into the business operations of the issuer, its solvency and any unique characteristics. The footnotes following the financials generally include operations, summary of significant accounting policies, inventories, property and equipment, leases, short-term borrowings and long-term debt, employee benefit plans, income taxes, related party transactions, litigation (if any), subsequent events (unaudited), authorization of common and preferred stock

Warning Signs

Insiders are getting out. The section after the management section indicates the amount of ownership of any of the principals and any other 5% or greater owners. By looking at this table and at principal and selling shareholders, you can tell whose ownership is changing because of the offering. If the company is not doing well and a number of the original investors are selling out, they may know something you don't. Try to figure out how much money the founders and early investors contributed to the company. To do this, check the same information you looked at to see what the company is worth, together with the dilution table. This will tell you how much the founders and early investors paid to the company versus how much you and the new investors are being asked to pay. If the original investors paid little, the company hasn't performed well or hasn't been around very long and you are paying significantly more than they did, you may not be getting much value for your dollar. These conditions are even more negative if the original investors are selling out.

Excess compensation. Check the compensation table, called "executive compensation," usually a subsection of the management section. Check for any information on stock options and benefit plans found in the "compensation pursuant to plans" subsection. If management is only part-time and receiving huge salaries and benefits or stock options, find a different company to invest in.

"Sweetheart deals." Check the "certain transactions" section to see what kinds of affiliated transactions are being engaged in by management and the issuer's principals. Are there any "sweetheart" contracts, land sales, personal use of company assets or questionable loans from the company to these parties? Are these transactions competitive and in the best interest of the company? Some of these transactions may not be in the best interest of the company and may constitute misappropriation of the company's assets.

Unexplained change in accounting methods. Certain accounting practices or changes will be disclosed in the footnotes to the financials. These practices or changes may make revenues and expenses appear different from what they really are. Although some such changes will make sense from a business standpoint, be sure that they weren't made simply to gloss over grim financial news.

Words To The Wise

Teach yourself to be a value shopper. Leave the urge to bet on the "longshot" at the track. If you do decide to gamble rather than invest, be prepared to lose your money. Always remember there are no guarantees and that there is always risk, no matter what anyone tells you.

☞ **Remember!!**

Offering features that should make you skeptical:

- No stated business purpose or plan.

- No specific use of proceeds.

- No specific restrictions on the use of the funds.

- A small aggregate offering amount, usually in the range of $75,000 to 250,000.

- Low offering share price, usually 1 to 10 cents.

- Inexperienced management.

- Limited time commitment by management.

- Little or no operating "track record."

- Unaudited financials, or financials that bear qualified opinions.

- Inadequate or difficult-to-obtain information or disclosure.

Source: Missouri Secretary of State Securities Division, 2005.

Chapter 25

What Are You Looking For In Your Research About Investments?

Stocks: Our Five Favorite Fundamentals

You don't need to be an industry insider to get the scoop on a company's stock. A degree in accounting or an MBA isn't necessary either. If you're trying to decide whether to buy a stock, hold one you already own or sell, you just need to pay attention to a few key details.

Below we list five of our favorite fundamentals that the pros use to evaluate stocks.

1. Price-Earnings Ratio (P/E Ratio)

One of the simplest methods of valuing a stock is to find its price-earnings ratio. This figure takes the price of the stock and divides it by its earnings-per-share (profits divided by number of shares)—essentially, it tells you how much an investor pays for each dollar-per-share a company earns.

About This Chapter: This chapter begins with "Stocks: Our Five Favorite Fundamentals," reprinted with permission from http://www.kiplinger.com. Copyright © 2005 Kiplinger Washington Editors, Inc. All rights reserved. "Questions You Should Ask About Your Investments" is reprinted from "Ask Questions," published by the U.S. Securities and Exchange Commission (SEC), June 18, 2002.

Investors should not only look at the previous year's earnings when calculating a P/E ratio, but also what analysts project the company will earn in future years. For example, if a company trades at $22 and earned 71 cents over the past 12 months, its trailing P/E is 31. If analysts expect it to earn 79 cents next year, its forward P/E is 28.

In general, the higher the P/E ratio, the faster and more consistently the market expects a company's earnings to rise. Larger P/Es can translate into more volatile investments because the lofty expectations have further to drop if the company falls short one quarter.

You can compare a stock's P/E with that of its past P/Es, the overall market or the average P/E of its industry. A P/E of 14, for example, may be high for an energy stock but low for a tech company.

> ☞ **Remember!!**
>
> The P/E ratio is calculated by dividing the current price of the stock by the earnings per share (generally those within the latest twelve months). This figure gives you some indication of what investors are paying for a company's earning power (i.e., are willing to pay for each dollar of earnings). Thus, a P/E ratio of 10 indicates that the stock is selling for ten times its earnings.
>
> Since companies within an industry tend to have similar P/E ratios, it's best to evaluate P/E ratios relative to other companies within the same industry. High P/E ratios are often found in rapidly growing, newer companies. Stocks with a low P/E ratio are usually in slow-growing, mature companies.
>
> Source: Excerpted from *Investment Basics: Stocks,* by Joyce Jones, Ph.D., reprinted with permission of the Kansas State University Agricultural Experiment Station and Cooperative Extension Service, Manhattan, Kansas, http://www.oznet.ksu.edu/. Copyright © 1995. All Rights Reserved.

2. Price-Earnings To Growth Ratio

Combining anticipated long-term earnings growth and P/E gives you a stock's PEG or price-earnings to growth ratio. It's figured by dividing a stock's P/E by analysts' projected percentage earnings-per-share growth over the coming three to five years.

For example, if analysts expect our company above to grow 14% annually over the next three to five years, the stock has a PEG ratio of 2.

Stocks with relatively low PEG ratios may be bargains—investors tend to favor stocks with PEGs below 1.

Another useful valuation measure is the *price-sales ratio.* You take the stock's price divided by the company's annual sales per share. *Price-to-book*—price divided by assets minus liabilities—is also a good tool and is often used to compare companies within an industry, such as insurance providers. As with the PEG ratio, lower is better for both price-sales and price-book ratios.

3. Margins

Gross margins hit at the core of a company's profitability—how much money it makes on what it sells, minus its basic costs. Avoid companies with seriously deteriorating gross margins.

To determine gross margins, analysts subtract the cost of goods sold from sales and then divide the result by sales. The figure is then multiplied by 100 and expressed as a percentage.

Operating margins tell you how well management controls expenses. Analysts figure this by dividing a company's earnings from operations by its sales, and then multiplying by 100 to get a percentage.

If management can keep down costs, its operating margins should hold fast or increase. Operating margins can also swell if a company raises prices without slowing sales.

4. Cash Flow

To get at the guts of a business, look at how much cash is coming in and how much is going out. Some professional investors say cash flow per share gives a clearer view than earnings per share of a company's essential profitability. It's especially handy when researching companies that don't have profits.

Cash flow's first cousin is *free cash flow.* Take cash flow from operations minus the money needed to maintain the business. Free cash flow is what's left over, or money the company can use to expand its business, invest in new ventures and pay dividends. If free cash flow runs negative, trouble looms.

5. Equity Efficiency

Don't overlook the *balance sheet numbers,* so-called because what a company owns, plus the stockholders' equity must exactly balance what the company owes. Stockholders' equity, by definition, is what remains after subtracting liabilities from assets. It's what shareholders have claim to.

The bigger the *return on equity*—net earnings divided by stockholders' equity—the better. A trend of rising ROE shows management has become increasingly efficient at investing the shareholders' stake in the company.

Debt levels can also provide vital clues to a company's future. While borrowed money can help companies grow faster, too much debt, particularly during an economic slowdown, can cripple a company's earnings or even send it into bankruptcy.

A good measure of debt is *debt to equity*—or how efficiently borrowed money is used to increase investors' stake. This figure takes a company's long-term debt and divides it by shareholders' equity. High debt levels can sometimes be inevitable in certain industries such as airlines and utilities. But a "clean balance sheet," which signals low debt, often gives a company a competitive edge.

✔ Quick Tip

The after-tax net income of the company, when divided by the number of common shares outstanding, is earnings per share (EPS). EPS is often used to judge how well a company is doing.

Source: Excerpted from *Investment Basics: Stocks,* by Joyce Jones, Ph.D., reprinted with permission of the Kansas State University Agricultural Experiment Station and Cooperative Extension Service, Manhattan, Kansas, http://www.oznet.ksu.edu/. Copyright © 1995. All Rights Reserved.

Questions You Should Ask About Your Investments

Avoid trouble and loss by asking basic questions from the start. Thoroughly evaluate the background of any brokerage firm or individual broker with whom you intend to do business—before you hand over your hard-earned cash.

It doesn't matter if you are a beginner or have been investing for many years, it's never too early or too late to start asking questions. It's almost impossible to ask a dumb question about how you are investing your money. Don't feel intimidated. Remember, it's your money at stake.

A good broker or investment adviser will welcome your questions, no matter how basic. Financial professionals know that an educated client is an asset, not a liability. They would rather answer your questions before you invest, than confront your anger and confusion later.

> ## ✎ What's It Mean?
> Price-Earnings Ratio (or P-E Ratio): The price of a stock as a multiple of its earnings per share. The P-E ratio is calculated by dividing the stock's last (closing) price by the earnings per share. For example, if the stock's closing price is $12 and earnings per share are $1, then the P-E ratio is calculated as follows:
>
> $$\text{P-E Ratio} = \text{closing price} \div \text{earning per share} = \$12 \div \$1 = 12.$$
>
> Source: Excerpted and reprinted from *KidsInvest*, reprinted with permission from the State of Illinois Secretary of State, Securities Department. n.d.

Questions About Products

- Is this investment product registered with the SEC and my state securities agency?

- Does this investment match my investment goals? Why is this investment suitable for me?

- How will this investment make money? (Dividends? Interest? Capital gains?) Specifically, what must happen for this investment to increase in value? (For example, increase in interest rates, real estate values, or market share?)

- What are the total fees to purchase, maintain, and sell this investment? After all the fees are paid, how much does this investment have to increase in value before I break even?

- How liquid is this investment? How easy would it be to sell if I needed my money right away?

- What are the specific risks associated with this investment? What is the maximum I could lose? (For example, what will be the effect of changing interest rates, economic recession, high competition, or stock market ups and downs?)

- How long has the company been in business? Is its management experienced? Has management been successful in the past? Have they ever made money for investors before?

- Is the company making money? How are they doing compared to their competitors?

> ✔ **Quick Tip**
> Investigate thoroughly before doing business with a broker or firm that has a history of complaints or problems with regulators. You should know that if your firm or broker goes out of business or declares bankruptcy, you might not be able to recover your money—even if an arbitrator or a court rules in your favor.
>
> Source: SEC, 2002.

- Where can I get more information about this investment? Can I get the latest reports filed by the company with the SEC: a prospectus or offering circular, or the latest annual report and financial statements?

For Mutual Funds

- How has this fund performed over the long run? Where can I get an independent evaluation of this fund?

- What specific risks are associated with this fund?

- What type of securities does the fund hold? How often does the portfolio change?

- Does this mutual fund invest in any type of securities that could cause the value to go up or down rapidly in a short period of time? (For example, derivatives?)

- How does the fund perform compared to other funds of the same type or to an index of the same type of investment?

- How much will the fund charge me when I buy shares? What other ongoing fees are charged?

Questions About The People Who Sell Investments

- Are you registered with our state securities regulator? Have you ever been disciplined by the SEC, a state regulator, or other organization (such as NASD [National Association of Securities Dealers] or one of the stock exchanges)?

- How long has your firm been in business? How many arbitration awards have been filed against your firm?

- What training and experience do you have? How long have you been in the business? What other firms have you been registered with? What is the status of those firms today?

- Have you personally been involved in any arbitration cases? What happened?

- What is your investment philosophy?

- Describe your typical client. Can you provide me with some names and telephone numbers of your long term clients?

- How do you get paid? By commission? Amount of assets you manage? Another method?

- Do I have any choices on how to pay you? Should I pay you by the transaction? Or a flat fee regardless of how many transactions I have?

- Do you make more if I buy this stock (or bond, or mutual fund) rather than another? If you weren't making extra money, would your recommendation be the same?

- Are you participating in a sales contest? Is this purchase really in my best interest, or are you trying to win a prize?

- You've told me what it costs me to buy this stock (or bond, or mutual fund); how much will I receive if I sell it today?

- Where do you send my order to be executed? Can we get a better price if we send it to another market?

- (If your broker changes firms, ask:) Did they pay you to change firms? Do you get anything for bringing me along?

Questions About the Progress Of Your Investments

- How frequently do I get statements? Do I understand what the statement tells me?

- Is the return on my investment meeting my expectations and goals? Is this investment performing as I was led to believe?

- How much money will I get back if I sell my investment today?

- How much am I paying in commission or fees?

- Have my goals changed? If so, are my investments still suitable?

- What criteria will I use to decide when to sell?

How To Handle Problems:

Act promptly! By law, you only have a limited time to take legal action. Follow these steps to solve your problem:

> **✔ Quick Tip**
>
> You can verify your broker's disciplinary history by checking the Central Registration Depository (CRD). Either your state securities regulator or NASD can provide you with CRD information. Your state securities regulator may give you more information from the CRD than NASD, especially when it comes to investor complaints, so you may want to check with them first. You can find out how to get in touch with your state securities regulator through the North American Securities Administrators Association, Inc.'s website. To contact NASD, visit its website, or call them toll-free at 800-289-9999.
>
> Source: SEC, 2002.

✔ **Quick Tip**

When you ask questions, write down the answers you receive and what you decided to do. If something goes wrong, your notes can help to establish what was said. Let your broker or investment adviser know you're taking notes. They'll know you're a serious investor and may tell you more.

Source: SEC, 2002.

1. Talk to your broker and explain the problem. Where is the fault? Were communications clear? Refer to your notes. What did the broker tell you? What do your notes say?

2. If your broker can't resolve your problem, then talk to the broker's branch manager.

3. If the problem is still not resolved, write to the compliance department at the firm's main office. Explain your problem clearly, and how you want it resolved. Ask the compliance office to respond to you within 30 days.

4. If you're still not satisfied, send a complaint to the SEC by using their online complaint form or by writing to them at the following address:

> Securities and Exchange Commission
> Office of Investor Education and Assistance
> 450 Fifth Street N.W.
> Washington, DC 20549-0213

If these steps don't work, you may need to take legal action on your own. The SEC can send you information on mediation, arbitration, and suggest how to locate a lawyer if you need one.

Chapter 26

Analysts, Brokers, And Other Financial Advisors: Understanding Their Roles And Limitations

How To Pick A Financial Professional

Are you the type of person who will read as much as possible about potential investments and ask questions about them? If so, maybe you don't need investment advice.

But if you're busy with your job or other responsibilities, or feel you don't know enough about investing on your own, then you may need professional investment advice.

Investment professionals offer a variety of services at a variety of prices. It pays to comparison shop.

You can get investment advice from most financial institutions that sell investments, including brokerages, banks, mutual funds, and insurance companies.

About This Chapter: "How To Pick A Financial Professional" is excerpted from *The SEC's Roadmap to Saving and Investing*, Office of Investor Education and Assistance, U.S. Securities and Exchange Commission, October 8, 2004. "If You Have A Problem" is excerpted from "Invest Wisely: Advice From Your Securities Industry Regulators," SEC, dated November 30, 2001 ("If You Have A Problem"). " How Do I 'Investigate' Before I Invest?" and "About Boiler Rooms: Where Investment Scams Are Always On Call" are © 2003 Arizona Corporation Commission. All rights reserved. Reprinted with permission.

You can also hire a broker, an investment adviser, an accountant, a financial planner, or other professional to help you make investment decisions.

Investment Advisers And Financial Planners

Some financial planners and investment advisers offer a complete financial plan, assessing every aspect of your financial life and developing a detailed strategy for meeting your financial goals. They may charge you a fee for the plan, a percentage of your assets that they manage, or receive commissions from the companies whose products you buy, or a combination of these. You should know exactly what services you are getting and how much they will cost.

People or firms that get paid to give advice about investing in securities generally must register with either the SEC or the state securities agency where they have their principal place of business. To find out about advisers and whether they are properly registered, you can read their registration forms, called the "Form ADV." The Form ADV has two parts. Part 1 has information about the adviser's business and whether they've had problems with regulators or clients. Part 2 outlines the adviser's services, fees, and strategies. Before you hire an investment adviser, always ask for and carefully read both parts of the ADV. You can view an adviser's most recent Form ADV online by visiting the Investment Adviser Public Disclosure (IAPD) website.

✔ **Quick Tip**
A *discount brokerage* charges lower fees and commissions for its services than what you'd pay at a full-service brokerage. But generally you have to research and choose investments by yourself.

A *full-service brokerage* costs more, but the higher fees and commissions pay for a broker's investment advice based on that firm's research. The best way to choose an investment professional is to start by asking your friends and colleagues whom they recommend. Try to get several recommendations, and then meet with potential advisers face-to-face. Make sure you get along. Make sure you understand each other. After all, it's your money.

Source: SEC, 2004.

Remember, there is no such thing as a free lunch. Professional financial advisers do not perform their services as an act of charity. If they are working for you, they are getting paid for their efforts. Some of their fees are easier to see immediately than are others. But, in all cases, you should always feel free to ask questions about how and how much your adviser is being paid. And if the fee is quoted to you as a percentage, make sure that you understand what that translates to in dollars.

Brokers

Brokers make recommendations about specific investments like stocks, bonds, or mutual funds. While taking into account your overall financial goals, brokers generally do not give you a detailed financial plan. Brokers are generally paid commissions when you buy or sell securities through them. If they sell you mutual funds make sure to ask questions about what fees are included in the mutual fund purchase. Brokerages vary widely in the quantity and quality of the services they provide for customers. Some have large research staffs, large national operations, and are prepared to service almost any kind of financial transaction you may need. Others are small and may specialize in promoting investments in unproven and very risky companies. And there's everything else in between.

You'll want to find out if a broker is properly licensed in your state and if they have had run-ins with regulators or received serious complaints from investors. You'll also want to know about the brokers' educational backgrounds and where they've worked before their current jobs. To get this information, you can ask either your state securities regulator or the NASD [National Association of Securities Dealers] to provide you with information from the CRD, which is a computerized database that contains information about most brokers, their representatives, and the firms they work for. Your state securities regulator may provide more information from the CRD than NASD, especially when it comes to investor complaints, so you may want to check with them first. You can find out how to get in touch with your state securities regulator through the North American Securities Administrators Association, Inc. website. You can go to the NASD website to get CRD information or call them toll-free at 800-289-9999.

Opening A Brokerage Account

When you open a brokerage account, whether in person or online, you will typically be asked to sign a new account agreement. You should carefully review all the information in this agreement because it determines your legal rights regarding your account.

Do not sign the new account agreement unless you thoroughly understand it and agree with the terms and conditions it imposes on you. Do not rely on statements about your account that are not in this agreement. Ask for a copy of any account documentation prepared for you by your broker.

The broker should ask you about your investment goals and personal financial situation, including your income, net worth, investment experience, and how much risk you are willing to take on. Be honest. The broker relies on this information to determine which investments will best meet your investment goals and tolerance for risk. If a broker tries to sell you an investment before asking you these questions, that's a very bad sign. It signals that the broker has a greater interest in earning a commission than recommending an investment to you that meets your needs. The new account agreement requires that you make three critical decisions:

1. Who will make the final decisions about what you buy and sell in your account?

You will have the final say on investment decisions unless you give "discretionary authority" to your broker. Discretionary authority allows your broker to invest your money without consulting you about the price, the type of security, the amount, and when to buy or sell. Do not give discretionary authority to your broker without seriously considering the risks involved in turning control over your money to another person.

2. How will you pay for your investments?

- Most investors maintain a "cash" account that requires payment in full for each security purchase. But if you open a "margin" account, you can buy securities by borrowing money from your broker for a portion of the purchase price.

- Be aware of the risks involved with buying stocks on margin. Beginning investors generally should not get started with a margin account. Make sure you understand how a margin account works, and what happens in the worst case scenario before you agree to buy on margin.

- Unlike other loans, like for a car or a home, that allow you to pay back a fixed amount every month, when you buy stocks on margin you can be faced with paying back the entire margin loan all at once if the price of the stock drops suddenly and dramatically. The firm has the authority to immediately sell any security in your account, without notice to you, to cover any shortfall resulting from a decline in the value of your securities. You may owe a substantial amount of money even after your securities are sold. The margin account agreement generally provides that the securities in your margin account may be lent out by the brokerage firm at any time without notice or compensation to you.

3. How mch risk should you assume?

- In a new account agreement, you must specify your overall investment objective in terms of risk. Categories of risk may have labels such as "income," "growth," or "aggressive growth." Be certain that you fully understand the distinctions among these terms, and be certain that the risk level you choose accurately reflects your age, experience and investment goals. Be sure that the investment products recommended to you reflect the category of risk you have selected.

- When opening a new account, the brokerage firm may ask you to sign a legally binding contract to use the arbitration process to settle any future dispute between you and the firm or your sales representative. Signing this agreement means that you give up the right to sue your sales representative and firm in court.

Your investment professional should understand your investment goals, and he or she should also understand your tolerance for risk. That is, how much money can you afford to lose if the value of one of your investments declines?

Ask Questions   ✔ **Quick Tip**

You can never ask a dumb question about your investments and the people who help you choose them, especially when it comes to how much you will be paying for any investment, both in upfront costs and ongoing management fees. Here are some of the most important questions you should ask when choosing an investment professional:

- What training and experience do you have? How long have you been in business?

- What is your investment philosophy? Do you take a lot of risks or are you more concerned about the safety of my money?

- Describe your typical client. Can you provide me with references, the names of people who have invested with you for a long time?

- How do you get paid? By commission? Based on a percentage of assets you manage? Another method? Do you get paid more for selling your own firm's products?

- How much will it cost me in total to do business with you?

Source: SEC, 2004.

An investment professional has a duty to make sure that he or she only recommends investments that are suitable for you. That is, that the investment makes sense for you based on your other securities holdings, your financial situation, your means, and any other information that your investment professional thinks is important.

How Should I Monitor My Investments?

Investing makes it possible for your money to work for you. In a sense, your money has become your employee, and that makes you the boss. You'll want to keep a close watch on how your employee, your money, is doing.

Some people like to look at the stock quotations every day to see how their investments have done. That's probably too often. You may get too caught up in the ups and downs of the "trading" value of your investment, and sell when its value goes down temporarily—even though the performance of the company is still stellar. Remember, you're in for the long haul.

Some people prefer to see how they're doing once a year. That's probably not often enough. What's best for you will most likely be somewhere in between, based on your goals and your investments.

But it's not enough to simply check an investment's performance. You should compare that performance against an index of similar investments over the same period of time to see if you are getting the proper returns for the amount of risk that you are assuming. You should also compare the fees and commissions that you're paying to what other investment professionals charge.

While you should monitor performance regularly, you should pay close attention every time you send your money somewhere else to work.

Every time you buy or sell an investment you will receive a confirmation slip from your broker. Make sure each trade was completed according to your instructions. Make sure the buying or selling price was what your broker quoted. And make sure the commissions or fees are what your broker said they would be.

☞ Remember!!

The best investment professional is one who fully understands your objectives and matches investment recommendations to your goals. You'll want someone you can understand, because your investment professional should teach you about investing and the investment products.

Source: SEC, 2004.

Watch out for unauthorized trades in your account. If you get a confirmation slip for a transaction that you didn't approve beforehand, call your broker. It may have been a mistake. If your broker refuses to correct it, put your complaint in writing and send it to the firm's compliance officer. Serious complaints should always be made in writing.

If You Have A Problem

If you have a problem with your sales representative or your account, promptly talk to the sales representative's manager or the firm's compliance officer. Confirm your complaint to the firm in writing. Keep written records of all conversations. Ask for written explanations.

If the problem is not resolved to your satisfaction, contact the appropriate regulators listed in this chapter. Investor complaint information assists these regulators in identifying violations of the securities laws and prosecuting violators. However, none of these organizations is authorized to provide legal representation to individual investors or to get your money back for you.

Obtain information on using arbitration to resolve your dispute by contacting the NASD, New York Stock Exchange, American Stock Exchange, Municipal Securities Rulemaking Board, Boston Stock Exchange, Chicago Board Options Exchange, Chicago Stock Exchange, Pacific Stock Exchange, or Philadelphia Stock Exchange. Each of these organizations operates a forum to resolve disputes between brokerage firms and their customers. It may be desirable to consult an attorney knowledgeable about securities laws. Your local bar association can assist you in locating a securities attorney.

☞ Remember!!

Your investment professional should not be recommending trades simply to generate commissions. That's called "churning," and it's illegal.

Source: SEC, 2004.

How Do I "Investigate" Before I Invest?

Before giving them your money, always investigate investment advisers (sometimes called investment or financial planners), securities salesmen (sometimes called brokers, stockbrokers, or agents), the firms for which they work (dealer or brokerage firms), and the investment they want you to buy.

Ask Questions About Your Adviser Or Salesman

Talk to your adviser or salesman and insist that he or she answers your questions to your satisfaction. Write down the answers you are given, the name of who gives you the answers, and the date. Ask:

- What commission or fee will you earn if I buy the investment?

- Who or what entity will be paying you?

- Will you be receiving any benefit other than your commission or fee if I buy the investment?

- Are you related to or involved with the investment in any way other than recommending that I buy it?

- Are you registered or licensed and, if so, with whom? If you are not registered or licensed with a regulatory agency, why not?

- Have you ever been sued, disciplined, or had any complaints filed relating to your work as a salesman or adviser?

> ✔ **Quick Tip**
> ## Get It In Writing
> Whatever an adviser or a securities salesman tells you about himself or herself, about the investment he or she is offering to you, or about the company or people in which you would be investing, get what you are told in writing. Anyone offering you an investment opportunity should give you an offering memorandum—a complete description of the investment and the people and risks involved with the investment. *Read the offering memorandum.* If you do not understand it, get help from an accountant, lawyer, or another independent third party who does understand how to read an offering memorandum.
>
> Source: Arizona Corporation Commission, 2003.

Ask Questions About The Investment

Ask your salesman, your adviser, and the officers or directors of the company in which you may make an investment all of the questions you have about the investment until you understand it and are comfortable. Write down the answers you are given, the name of the person who gives you the answers, and the date.

Ask: Is the investment registered with the Securities and Exchange Commission or your state securities division? If not, why not? If the investment is exempt from registration, what is the nature of the exemption? Is a notice regarding this exempt offering on file with the SEC or the securities division? If not, why not? (*Note*: The fact that a particular investment is properly registered, or exempt from registration, is not a guarantee as to how that investment will perform, or that it is an appropriate investment for you. If you need assistance understanding an investment and when it is suitable to invest in that type of investment, seek assistance from an accountant, attorney, or independent adviser.)

> ✔ **Quick Tip**
> **Protect Yourself**
>
> A high pressure sales pitch can mean trouble. Be suspicious of anyone who tells you, "Invest quickly or you will miss out on a once in a lifetime opportunity."
>
> Source: SEC, 2001.

Understand the fundamental nature of the investment. Understand the tax implications of the nature of the investment. Understand your rights as a creditor or an owner if the entity in which you are investing goes bankrupt.

Is it a debt offering? If you invest in a debt offering (notes, bonds, debentures), you will become a creditor. If the offered security is a debt obligation, who will repay your investment to you? Will you get interest? How much? Is your investment, the debt obligation, secured or guaranteed? If so, by what or whom?

Is it an equity (stock) offering? If you obtain an equity interest in an entity, you become an owner. Will you own shares of stock in a corporation? Will you own a partnership interest or a limited liability company membership interest? Will you have any control over how the entity is run? Will you receive dividends?

Is the investment "liquid"? Can you sell the investment if and when you want to? Is there a market—are other buyers interested in the investment? Will you be able to get your entire investment back? Do you have to hold the investment for a specific period of time? Will you have to pay penalties if you sell the investment earlier? (*Note*: Most securities offerings do not contain a "buy-back" feature and if you need to get your money back, you will likely have to attempt to sell the investment on the "secondary market" if one exists. If you have to sell your investment in a secondary market, you may have to sell for a substantial discount from the original amount of your investment.)

What type of business are you investing in? Is it an established business with an operating history? If so, what is that history? If not, does the proposed business make sense? Is it likely to be successful?

Who is responsible for operating the business in which you are investing? Do those persons have the necessary skill, experience, and training to operate the business?

What risks are you taking by making the investment? What factors may jeopardize the success of the business undertaking?

What factors may jeopardize your ability to recover your investment and make a return on that investment? (*Note*: Once you thoroughly understand the types of business risks and market risks involved with the investment, you need to assess your financial position and risk tolerance. Can you afford or are you willing to take those risks?)

Independently Research The Investment

Check the public records of the superior court to see if any of the people or entities involved have been or are involved in a lawsuit. Check the public records of the bankruptcy

> ☞ **Remember!!**
>
> For more information, consult one of the following offices:
>
> Securities and Exchange Commission
> 202-272-2800
> www.sec.gov
>
> National Association of Securities Dealers
> 202-728-8000
> 800-289-9999
> www.nasd.com
>
> North American Association of Securities Administrators
> 202-737-0900
> www.nasaa.org
>
> Alliance for Investor Education
> www.investoreducation.org
>
> Source: Arizona Corporation Commission, 2003.

court to see if any of the people or entities involved have filed bank-ruptcy. Call the Better Business Bureau to see if the entities involved are members and if any complaints have been filed. Call the office of your state attorney general to see if they have any information about the people or entities involved. Contact relevant departments of your state attorney general's office (such as real estate, insurance, securities) to see if people are appropriately licensed and if they have disciplinary histories. The se-curities division of your state attorney general's office may offer a direc-tory of telephone numbers of regulatory entities.

About Boiler Rooms: Where Investment Scams Are Always On Call

One of the most common types of securities fraud perpetrated against individual investors occurs far from plush corporate boardrooms and away from the big city trading centers. Rather, this type of investment scheme originates out of hundreds of largely invisible telemarketing offices located throughout the United States, Canada, and, more recently, as far away as Europe and Southeast Asia. These operations sell special "investment op-portunities" over the telephone, offering remarkably high, yet practically risk-free, rates of return. What these telemarketers invariably fail to mention is that these investment opportunities only provide these tremendous risk-free returns to a limited population: themselves.

The nerve center in most of these telemarketing schemes is the sales office, otherwise known as the "boiler room." The term "boiler room" origi-nated during an earlier era of telemarketing fraud, where managers of these operations would seek out cheap office space, such as in the basement of buildings, where the conditions were typically hot, uncomfortable, and crowded.

Today, the term boiler room is commonly understood to describe a com-mercial office setting involving a simple set-up of desks, computers, tele-phone lines, and salesmen employing a variety of high-pressure sales tactics to push their investment product to hundreds of potential investors across the country each day.

These offices can be established anywhere, but are often found in remote urban areas such as commercial parks, industrial parks, or other discrete locations. Beyond the low overhead and stealthy nature of these boiler rooms, the sparse set-up allows the operations to dissolve and resurface almost at will.

The types of boiler room investment scams are limited only by the promoter's imagination, and these operations are continually re-inventing and refining their bogus investment programs. Each operation ultimately relies on three basic elements to make the telemarketers and their telemarketing scams successful: the appearance of a legitimate investment program, investor leads, and unwary investors. Producers may design what appears to be an authentic investment opportunity in many ways. The "producers" who design these bogus investments for the boiler rooms often start by identifying a recently successful business operation or industry, and then mimic the blueprint of these business operations to construct their imaginary investment programs. As an example, telecommunication investment scams were epidemic in the early 1990s, and fraudulent "dot-com" investments were the telemarketing scam of choice during the late 1990s.

Once the fraudulent investment product is prepared and packaged, often as a "private placement" to investors, the salesmen begin targeting potential investors on their "lead lists." Lead lists are a listing of potential investors who are most likely to be interested in the fraudulent offering based on past investment patterns, internet-derived investor databases, or some other covert method of identifying potential investors. These lead leads can be sold to boiler room operators for as much as $3 to $5 per name. With the lead lists in hand, experienced salesmen then make "cold-calls," otherwise known as unsolicited calls, up to more than 200 potential investors per day.

The boiler room salesmen use any number of techniques to sell their fraudulent securities to unwary investors, their favorite quarry. A popular method is the "three-call" technique, where an initial caller will warm up the potential investor with descriptions of the company's past successes and the exciting offerings coming ahead. If the salesman detects a level of interest, brochure materials are sent to the prospect and a second "set-up" man calls to tell the prospect of the amazing opportunity currently available. The pressure is then turned up by the experienced "closer," who calls the prospect to say that the prospect must invest in the program now, using sales tactics and quick answers to any concerns the unwary prospect might have. Once the investment is made, usually through wire transfer or other immediate means of payment (after all, the salesman doesn't want the investor to have any time to reflect on a rash decision), the investor's name is often elevated to a highly valued "sucker list," which will often be resold to other boiler rooms for additional securities offerings to be hatched in the future.

Red Flags

Boiler room salesmen are glib and resourceful, and have a number of other techniques to help you part with your money. If the particular investment is "guaranteed," or if the salesman will buy back the investment "after a certain time period," a red flag should immediately go up.

Most, if not all, investments (perhaps other than certain low-yield government bonds and bank certificate of deposits), have at least some elements of risk. If a particular investment was not highly risky, the owners of the securities would not likely find it necessary to sell the investment through cold calls to unknown individuals. Similarly, when the salesman is suggesting that he will buy back the investment at a later date, he is again intimating that there is no risk associated with the investment; alarms should be sounding since the claim is not credible.

A similar alarm should sound when the investment is offering an exorbitant rate of return. As said many times, if something sounds to good to be true, it probably is. This mantra is the bane of all telemarketing scams; their success depends on the investor's belief that an investment may exist that has little or no risk but offers an extremely high rate of return. There is no such an animal, and even if did one exist, would a telemarketer have to call a stranger to sell it? The answer is a resounding "of course not!" Still another red flag is the salesman's dire warning that the "window of opportunity" is closing on the investment opportunity, and the prospective investor "must act now."

This routine ploy is usually nothing more than the salesman's attempt to prevent the investor from making sensible background checks, researching into the company further, checking with regulators, and/or reflecting on the rashness of the decision. This now-or-never pitch can often be translated as it applies to the investor's money: lose it to the salesman in the boiler room— now or never. The salesman will use any tactic in his repertoire, including formulated scripts and answers, levels of aggression, derision or flattery, anything it takes for the investor to swallow the bait and "act now."

An individual who becomes a target for one of these boiler rooms can take various steps to insulate himself from this type of securities fraud. The most obvious and effective strategy is to immediately decline the opportunity to invest with the boiler room caller, but this can, at times, be more difficult than it sounds. These telemarketers are experienced sellers who have heard practically every excuse, enabling them to develop what seems to be a rational answer to almost any question, concern, or reservation.

This being the case, if you begin to feel pressure to invest in a particular investment "opportunity," simply terminates the call. Hanging up the phone is the most effective way of having the telemarketer move onto another lead. Other policies should also be considered when dealing with a potentially fraudulent investment telemarketer. First, never be pressured into giving an immediate decision on investing. If that is the only alternative the salesman is offering you, then its time for you to go.

✔ Quick Tip

Be aware and have a healthy level of cynicism about any investment offer made over the phone. If an offering is very low risk and offers a high return, if you can't lose, or if the investment is sure to go public and double, triple, or quadruple, recognize that if that truly was the case, the "boiler room" on the other end of the line wouldn't have called you in the first place.

Source: Arizona Corporation Commission, 2003.

Next, make sure you receive everything in writing before making any investment decisions, particularly over the phone. You may be surprised to find that the verbal representations made by the salesmen are at odds with the documentation offered by the company. Alternatively, the written disclosures about this company may, in fact, be woefully inadequate and/or suspect.

With over-the-phone securities solicitations, another important policy is to always consult with the state and federal regulatory bodies charged with overseeing this activity. These agencies can often determine whether the securities being offered to you have been properly filed or registered, as well as determining whether the principals of the company have had any prior disciplinary problems within the industry. Often a fraudulent telemarketer may scold or threaten you for requesting to do such a check, a classic indication that something is amiss.

Chapter 27

Options For Investing Online

Investing Online: What Every Teen Needs To Know Before Logging On

The internet has become a round-the-clock source for financial products, services, and information. Electronic trading, or online investing, has become popular. If you use the Internet for personal financial management and investing, it is important to remember that it is just a tool. A working knowledge of basic personal finance, good decision-making skills, and an understanding of the potential risks are essential to investing, especially when investors enter cyberspace.

Tips For Teen Online Investors

1. **Trading is not as quick as the "click of the mouse."** Most likely, your home computer is not directly connected to the market and it may take more time than you expect for a trade to be completed and confirmed or an order to be canceled and confirmed.

About This Chapter: This chapter begins with "Investing Online: What Every Teen Needs to Know Before Logging On," reprinted with permission from the Secretary of the Commonwealth of Massachusetts, Securities Division, http://www.sec.state.ma.us/sct/sctidx.htm. Copyright 2004. "Online Trading: Both Short-Term And Long-Term Investments" is excerpted and reprinted with permission from "Tips for Online Investors," also by the Massachusetts Secretary of the Commonwealth, Securities Division. "Fast Markets" is excerpted from "Tips for Online Investors" (November 6, 2003) and "Tips For Avoiding Stock Scams On the Internet" (September 28, 2000); both these are produced by the U.S. Securities and Exchange Commission (SEC).

2. Be sure to check the stock quotes and account quotes that you receive. Are they **real-time** or **delayed?**

3. Is your online brokerage firm getting the **best price** for its investors? Check out the firm's website; most provide this information to the public.

4. **Put your online broker's claims to the test.** Order information from the firm to substantiate any advertised claims concerning the ease and speed of online trading.

5. Before you begin investing, be sure you have information on how to **enter and cancel orders** (market, limit, and stop loss). Also, gather information about the details and risks of margin accounts (borrowing to buy stocks).

✔ Quick Tip
Are You Ready to Invest Online?

If you're interested in online investing, but want to know if it is right for you, check out www.investingonline.org and do the following:

• Take the online investing quiz, "Are You Ready?"

• Try the account sign-up simulation so you will know what to expect.

• Learn about the things you need to know before investing online.

• Expose the myths about online investing.

• Get ratings from industry experts for online brokerage firms.

• Check out the online trading simulator.

• Get the facts on after-hours trading.

• Learn about the real costs of day trading.

• Link to the best resources on the Web.

• Access the online complaint center.

Source: Massachusetts Secretary of the Commonwealth, Securities Division, 2004.

---

6. Get information from the firm about how significant **website outages, delays, and other interruptions** may affect your ability to execute trades.

7. Review the firm's **privacy and security policies.** Some firms will sell your name to other companies for mailing lists and other promotional activities.

8. Receive clear information about **sales commissions, transaction fees, and conditions** that apply to any advertised discount and commissions.

9. Be sure you know, in advance, how to **contact a customer service representative** if problems occur. Request prompt attention and fair consideration, and be sure to keep good records so that you can substantiate any problem that occurs.

Myths And Realities Of Online Investing

Myth: I'm going to make a killing investing online.

Reality: Online investing isn't a surefire way to get rich. In fact, research shows that the vast majority of *day traders*—the handful of online stock traders who are the busiest—lose money. Though online investing isn't for everybody, it can be a powerful tool for investors who are disciplined about research, make carefully reasoned decisions, and maintain a balanced portfolio.

Myth: If I trade online, I can get in on all those high-flying IPOs.

Reality: IPOs (initial public offerings) consist of the shares of publicly traded companies that are being offered for the first time to investors. Because the price often rises rapidly in early trading, they are

> ✔ **Quick Tip**
> **Resources For**
> **Online Investors**
>
> The following resources may be helpful as you research investment products and services. Always consider the source of the information as you determine the accuracy and credibility of any information obtained online.
>
> • **Investing Online Resource Center** (www.investingonline.org)
>
> • **North American Securities Administrators Association, Inc.** (www.nasaa.org)
>
> • **U.S. Securities and Exchange Commission Online Investor Education** (www.sec.gov/investor/pubs/onlinetips.htm)
>
> • **National Association of Securities Dealers, Inc. Online Trading Information** (www.nasdr.com/online_trading.asp)
>
> Source: Massachusetts Secretary of the Commonwealth, Securities Division, 2004.

popular with many investors. Even though some online brokers are taking steps to get more IPO shares to individual investors, many investors will find it difficult or impossible to "get in on" a hot IPO in which they are interested. This is really a function of supply and demand—a relatively small number of IPO shares and a big demand on the part of interested investors.

Online Trading: Both Short-Term And Long-Term Investments

Some investors use the Internet to trade frequently with the hope of profiting from a rapidly changing market. Although the possibility of quick profits may be alluring to some investors, this strategy can be risky. Market volatility, inaccurate information about anticipated changes in stock prices, and delays in the execution of online trades may lead to financial losses.

Investors can also trade securities online as part of a long-term investment plan. Some investors research securities and then place trades without any professional guidance. Other investors use the Internet to manage a few of their investments on their own and then consult a broker or investment adviser for help in managing the rest of their portfolio in person.

✎ What's It Mean?

Day Trader: A stock trader who holds positions for a very short time (from minutes to hours) and makes numerous trades each day. Most trades are entered and closed out within the same day.

IPO: Initial Public Offering. The process of selling shares that were formerly privately held to new investors for the first time. IPOs are often smaller, younger companies seeking capital to expand their business.

Source: Excerpted from "Dictionary," and reprinted with permission from www.investopedia.com. © 2004 Investopedia, Inc.

Fast Markets

The price of some stocks, especially "hot" IPOs and high tech stocks, can soar and drop suddenly. In these fast markets when many investors want to trade at the same time and prices change quickly, delays can develop across the board. Executions and confirmations slow down, while reports of prices lag behind actual prices. In these markets, investors can suffer unexpected losses very quickly.

✔ **Quick Tip**
You can limit your losses in fast-moving markets if you know what you are buying and the risks of your investment; and know how trading changes during fast markets and take additional steps to guard against the typical problems investors face in these markets.

Source SEC, 2003.

Investors trading over the Internet or online, who are used to instant access to their accounts and near instantaneous executions of their trades, especially need to understand how they can protect themselves in fast-moving markets.

Online trading is quick and easy, but online investing takes time. With a click of mouse, you can buy and sell stocks from more than 100 online brokers offering executions as low as $5 per transaction. Although online trading saves investors time and money, it does not take the homework out of making investment decisions. You may be able to make a trade in a nanosecond, but making wise investment decisions takes time. Before you trade, know why you are buying or selling, and the risk of your investment.

Set your price limits on fast-moving stocks: market orders vs. limit orders. To avoid buying or selling a stock at a price higher or lower than you wanted, you need to place a limit order rather than a market order. A limit order is an order to buy or sell a security at a specific price. A buy limit order can only be executed at the limit price or lower, and a sell limit order can only be executed at the limit price or higher. When you place a market order, you can't control the price at which your order will be filled.

For example, if you want to buy the stock of a "hot" IPO that was initially offered at $9, but don't want to end up paying more than $20 for the stock, you can place a limit order to buy the stock at any price up to $20. By entering a limit order rather than a market order, you will not be caught buying the stock at $90 and then suffering immediate losses as the stock drops later in the day or the weeks ahead.

Remember that your limit order may never be executed because the market price may quickly surpass your limit before your order can be filled. But by using a limit order you also protect yourself from buying the stock at too high a price.

Online trading is not always instantaneous. Investors may find that technological "choke points" can slow or prevent their orders from reaching an online firm. For example, problems can occur where:

- an investor's modem, computer, or Internet Service Provider is slow or faulty;

- a broker-dealer has inadequate hardware or its Internet Service Provider is slow or delayed; or

- traffic on the Internet is heavy, slowing down overall usage.

A capacity problem or limitation at any of these choke points can cause a delay or failure in an investor's attempt to access an online firm's automated trading system.

Know your options for placing a trade if you are unable to access your account online. Most online trading firms offer alternatives for placing trades. These alternatives may include touch-tone telephone trades, faxing your order, or doing it the low-tech way—talking to a broker over the phone. Make sure you know whether using these different options may increase your costs. And remember, if you experience delays getting online, you may experience similar delays when you turn to one of these alternatives.

If you place an order, don't assume it didn't go through. Some investors have mistakenly assumed that their orders have not been executed and place another order. They end up either owning twice as much stock as they could afford or wanted, or with sell orders, selling stock they do not own. Talk with your firm about how you should handle a situation where you are unsure if your original order was executed.

If you cancel an order, make sure the cancellation worked before placing another trade. When you cancel an online trade, it is important to make sure that your original transaction was not executed. Although you may receive an electronic receipt for the cancellation, don't assume that that means the trade was canceled. Orders can only be canceled if they have not been executed. Ask your firm about how you should check to see if a cancellation order actually worked.

If you purchase a security in a cash account, you must pay for it before you can sell it. In a cash account, you must pay for the purchase of a stock before you sell it. If you buy and sell a stock before paying for it, you are freeriding, which violates the credit extension provisions of the Federal Reserve Board. If you freeride, your broker must "freeze" your account for 90 days. You can still trade during the freeze, but you must fully pay for any purchase on the date you trade while the freeze is in effect.

You can avoid the freeze if you fully pay for the stock within five days from the date of the purchase with funds that do not come from the sale of the stock. You can always ask your broker for an extension or waiver, but you may not get it.

If you trade on margin, your broker can sell your securities without giving you a margin call. Now is the time to reread your margin agreement and pay attention to the fine print. If your account has fallen below the firm's maintenance margin requirement, your broker has the legal right to sell your securities at any time without consulting you first.

Some investors have been rudely surprised that "margin calls" are a courtesy, not a requirement. Brokers are not required to make margin calls to their customers.

Even when your broker offers you time to put more cash or securities into your account to meet a margin call, the broker can act without waiting for you to meet the call. In a rapidly declining market your broker can sell your entire margin account at a substantial loss to you, because the securities in the account have declined in value.

No regulations require a trade to be executed within a certain time. There are no Securities and Exchange Commission regulations that require a trade to be executed within a set period of time. But if firms advertise their speed of execution, they must not exaggerate or fail to tell investors about the possibility of significant delays.

Tips For Avoiding Stock Scams On The Internet

One of the most common Internet frauds involves the classic "pump and dump" scheme. Here's how it works: A company's website may feature a glowing press release about its financial health or some new product or innovation. Newsletters that purport to offer unbiased recommendations may suddenly tout the company as the latest "hot" stock. Messages in chat rooms and bulletin board postings may urge you to buy the stock quickly or to sell before the price goes down. Or you may even hear the company mentioned by a radio or TV analyst.

Unwitting investors then purchase the stock in droves, creating high demand and pumping up the price. But when the fraudsters behind the scheme sell their shares at the peak and stop hyping the stock, the price plummets, and investors lose their money.

> **☞ Remember!!**
> You may be able to make a trade in a nanosecond, but making wise investment decisions takes time.
>
> Source: SEC, 2003.

Fraudsters frequently use this ploy with small, thinly traded companies because it's easier to manipulate a stock when there's little or no information available about the company. To steer clear of potential scams, always investigate before you invest:

Consider The Source. When you see an offer on the Internet, assume it is a scam, until you can prove through your own research that it is legitimate. And remember that the people touting the stock may well be insiders of the company or paid promoters who stand to profit handsomely if you trade.

Find Out Where The Stock Trades. Many of the smallest and most thinly traded stocks cannot meet the listing requirements of the Nasdaq Stock

Market or a national exchange, such as the New York Stock Exchange. Instead they trade in the "over-the-counter" market and are quoted on OTC systems, such as the OTC Bulletin Board or the Pink Sheets. Stocks that trade in the OTC market are generally among the most risky and most susceptible to manipulation.

Independently Verify Claims. It's easy for a company or its promoters to make grandiose claims about new product developments, lucrative contracts, or the company's financial health. But before you invest, make sure you've independently verified those claims.

Research The Opportunity. Always ask for—and carefully read—the prospectus or current financial statements. Check the SEC's EDGAR database to see whether the investment is registered. Some smaller companies don't have to register their securities offerings with the SEC, so always check with your state securities regulator, too.

Watch Out For High-Pressure Pitches. Beware of promoters who pressure you to buy before you have a chance to think about and fully investigate the so-called "opportunity." Don't fall for the line that you'll lose out on a "once-in-a-lifetime" chance to make big money if you don't act quickly.

Always Be Skeptical. Whenever someone you don't know offers you a hot stock tip, ask yourself: Why me? Why is this stranger giving me this tip? How might he or she benefit if I trade?

Chapter 28

Managing Your Portfolio

Beginner's Guide To Financial Statements

If you can read a nutrition label or a baseball box score, you can learn to read basic financial statements. If you can follow a recipe or apply for a loan, you can learn basic accounting. The basics aren't difficult and they aren't rocket science.

To manage your investment portfolio, you need to gain a basic understanding of how to read financial statements. Let's begin by looking at what financial statements do.

"Show Me The Money"

Financial statements "show you the money." They show you where a company's money came from, where it went, and where it is now.

There are four main financial statements. They are: (1) balance sheets; (2) income statements; (3) cash flow statements; and (4) statements of shareholders'

About This Chapter: This chapter begins with text from "Beginner's Guide to Financial Statements," U.S. Securities and Exchange Commission (SEC), July 13, 2004. "Reading the Financial Pages" is reprinted from *KidsInvest*, with permission from the State of Illinois Secretary of State, Securities Department. "Bond Quotations" and the accompanying tables are excerpted from "Investment Choices Overview," © 2005 National Association of Securities Dealers, Inc. (NASD). Reprinted with permission from NASD.

equity. Balance sheets show what a company owns and what it owes at a fixed point in time. Income statements show how much money a company made and spent over a period of time. Cash flow statements show the exchange of money between a company and the outside world also over a period of time. The fourth financial statement, called a "statement of shareholders' equity," shows changes in the interests of the company's shareholders over time.

Let's look at each of the first three financial statements in more detail.

Balance Sheets

A balance sheet provides detailed information about a company's assets, liabilities and shareholders' equity.

Assets are things that a company owns that have value. This typically means they can either be sold or used by the company to make products or provide services that can be sold. Assets include physical property, such as plants, trucks, equipment, and inventory. It also includes things that can't be touched but nevertheless exist and have value, such as trademarks and patents. And cash itself is an asset. So are investments a company makes.

Liabilities are amounts of money that a company owes to others. This can include all kinds of obligations, like money borrowed from a bank to launch a new product, rent for use of a building, money owed to suppliers for materials, payroll a company owes to its employees, environmental cleanup costs, or taxes owed to the government. Liabilities also include obligations to provide goods or services to customers in the future.

Shareholders' equity is sometimes called capital or net worth. It's the money that would be left if a company sold all of its assets and paid off all of its liabilities. This leftover money belongs to the shareholders, or the owners, of the company. A company's assets have to equal, or "balance," the sum of its liabilities and shareholders' equity.

Assets are generally listed based on how quickly they will be converted into cash. Current assets are things a company expects to convert to cash within one year. A good example is inventory. Most companies expect to sell their inventory for cash within one year. Noncurrent assets are things a company does not expect to convert to cash within one year or that would take longer than one year to sell. Noncurrent assets include fixed assets. Fixed assets are those assets used to operate the business but that are not available for sale, such as trucks, office furniture, and other property.

☞ Remember!!

A balance sheet shows a snapshot of a company's assets, liabilities and shareholders' equity at the end of the reporting period. It does not show the flows into and out of the accounts during the period.

Source: SEC, 2004.

Liabilities are generally listed based on their due dates. Liabilities are said to be either current or long-term. Current liabilities are obligations a company expects to pay off within the year. Long-term liabilities are obligations due more than one year away.

Shareholders' equity is the amount owners invested in the company's stock plus or minus the company's earnings or losses since inception. Sometimes companies distribute earnings, instead of retaining them. These distributions are called dividends.

Income Statements

An income statement is a report that shows how much revenue a company earned over a specific time period (usually for a year or some portion of a year). An income statement also shows the costs and expenses associated with earning that revenue. The literal "bottom line" of the statement usually shows the company's net earnings or losses. This tells you how much the company earned or lost over the period.

Income statements also report earnings per share (or "EPS"). This calculation tells you how much money shareholders would receive if the company decided to distribute all of the net earnings for the period. (Companies almost never distribute all of their earnings. Usually they reinvest them in the business.)

To understand how income statements are set up, think of them as a set of stairs. You start at the top with the total amount of sales made during the accounting period. Then you go down, one step at a time. At each step, you make a deduction for certain costs or other operating expenses associated with earning the revenue. At the bottom of the stairs, after deducting all of the expenses, you learn how much the company actually earned or lost during the accounting period. People often call this "the bottom line."

- At the top of the income statement is the total amount of money brought in from sales of products or services. This top line is often referred to as gross revenues or sales. It's called "gross" because expenses have not been deducted from it yet. So the number is "gross" or unrefined.

- The next line is money the company doesn't expect to collect on certain sales. This could be due, for example, to sales discounts or merchandise returns.

- When you subtract the returns and allowances from the gross revenues, you arrive at the company's net revenues. It's called "net" because, if you can imagine a net, these revenues are left in the net after the deductions for returns and allowances have come out.

- Moving down the stairs from the net revenue line, there are several lines that represent various kinds of operating expenses. Although these lines can be reported in various orders, the next line after net revenues typically shows the costs of the sales. This number tells you the amount of money the company spent to produce the goods or services it sold during the accounting period.

- The next line subtracts the costs of sales from the net revenues to arrive at a subtotal called "gross profit" or sometimes "gross margin." It's considered "gross" because there are certain expenses that haven't been deducted from it yet.

- The next section deals with operating expenses. These are expenses that go toward supporting a company's operations for a given period—

for example, salaries of administrative personnel, and costs of researching new products. Marketing expenses are another example. Operating expenses are different from "costs of sales," which were deducted above, because operating expenses cannot be linked directly to the production of the products or services being sold.

- Depreciation is also deducted from gross profit. Depreciation takes into account the wear and tear on some assets, such as machinery, tools and furniture, which are used over the long term. Companies spread the cost of these assets over the periods they are used. This process of spreading these costs is called depreciation or amortization. The "charge" for using these assets during the period is a fraction of the original cost of the assets.

- After all operating expenses are deducted from gross profit, you arrive at operating profit before interest and income tax expenses. This is often called "income from operations."

- Next companies must account for interest income and interest expense. Interest income is the money companies make from keeping their cash in interest-bearing savings accounts, money market funds and the like. On the other hand, interest expense is the money companies paid in interest for money they borrow. Some income statements show interest income and interest expense separately. Some income statements combine the two numbers. The interest income and expense are then added or subtracted from the operating profits to arrive at operating profit before income tax.

- Finally, income tax is deducted and you arrive at the bottom line: net profit or net losses. (Net profit is also called net income or net earnings.) This tells you how much the company actually earned or lost during the accounting period.

Did the company make a profit or did it lose money? How does this balance with the performance of other companies in which you have investments? Is your portfolio comprised of a balance of more profitable and less profitable companies?

Cash Flow Statements

Cash flow statements report a company's inflows and outflows of cash. This is important because a company needs to have enough cash on hand to pay its expenses and purchase assets. While an income statement can tell you whether a company made a profit, a cash flow statement can tell you whether the company generated cash.

A cash flow statement shows changes over time rather than absolute dollar amounts at a point in time. It uses and reorders the information from a company's balance sheet and income statement.

The bottom line of the cash flow statement shows the net increase or decrease in cash for the period. Generally, cash flow statements are divided into three main parts. Each part reviews the cash flow from one of three types of activities: (1) operating activities; (2) investing activities; and (3) financing activities.

Operating Activities. The first part of a cash flow statement analyzes a company's cash flow from net income or losses. For most companies, this section of the cash flow statement reconciles the net income (as shown on the income statement) to the actual cash the company received from or used in its operating activities. To do this, it deducts from net income any non-cash items (such as depreciation expenses) and any cash that was used or provided by other operating assets and liabilities.

Investing Activities. The second part of a cash flow statement shows the cash flow from all investing activities, which generally

♣ **It's A Fact!!**
Earnings Per Share (EPS)

Most income statements include a calculation of earnings per share or EPS. This calculation tells you how much money shareholders would receive for each share of stock they own if the company distributed all of its net income for the period.

To calculate EPS, you take the total net income and divide it by the number of outstanding shares of the company.

Source: SEC, 2004.

> ✎ **What's It Mean?**
>
> Asset: A possession of value, usually measured in terms of money.
>
> Dividend: Money earned on stock holdings; usually, it represents a share of profits paid in proportion to the share of ownership.
>
> Stock: Ownership shares in the assets of a corporation.
>
> Source: From "Glossary of Economic Terms" in *Outline of the U.S. Economy*, a publication of the Bureau of International Information Programs, U.S. State Department, February 2001.

include purchases or sales of long-term assets, such as property, plant and equipment, as well as investment securities. If a company buys a piece of machinery, the cash flow statement would reflect this activity as a cash outflow from investing activities because it used cash. If the company decided to sell off some investments from an investment portfolio, the proceeds from the sales would show up as a cash inflow from investing activities because it provided cash.

Financing Activities. The third part of a cash flow statement shows the cash flow from all financing activities. Typical sources of cash flow include cash raised by selling stocks and bonds or borrowing from banks. Likewise, paying back a bank loan would show up as a use of cash flow.

Read The Footnotes

It's so important to read the footnotes. The footnotes to financial statements are packed with information. Here are some of the highlights:

- *Significant accounting policies and practices*—Companies are required to disclose the accounting policies that are most important to the portrayal of the company's financial condition and results. These often require management's most difficult, subjective or complex judgments.

- *Income taxes*—The footnotes provide detailed information about the company's current and deferred income taxes. The information is broken down by level—federal, state, local and/or foreign, and the main items that affect the company's effective tax rate are described.

- *Pension plans and other retirement programs*—The footnotes discuss the company's pension plans and other retirement or post-employment benefit programs. The notes contain specific information about the assets and costs of these programs, and indicate whether and by how much the plans are over- or under-funded.

- *Stock options*—The notes also contain information about stock options granted to officers and employees, including the method of accounting for stock-based compensation and the effect of the method on reported results.

Read The MD&A

You can find a narrative explanation of a company's financial performance in a section of the quarterly or annual report entitled, "Management's Discussion and Analysis of Financial Condition and Results of Operations." MD&A is management's opportunity to provide investors with its view of the financial performance and condition of the company. It's management's opportunity to tell investors what the financial statements show and do not show, as well as important trends and risks that have shaped the past or are reasonably likely to shape the company's future.

The SEC's rules governing MD&A require disclosure about trends, events or uncertainties known to management that would have a material impact on reported financial information. The purpose of MD&A is to provide investors with information that the company's management believes to be necessary to an understanding of its financial condition, changes in financial condition and results of operations. It is intended to help investors to see the company through the eyes of management. It is also intended to provide context for the financial statements and information about the company's earnings and cash flows.

Financial Statement Ratios And Calculations

You've probably heard people banter around phrases like "P/E ratio," "current ratio" and "operating margin." But what do these terms mean and why don't they show up on financial statements? Listed below are just some of the many ratios that investors calculate from information on financial statements and then use to evaluate a company. As a general rule, desirable ratios vary by industry:

- *Debt-to-equity ratio* compares a company's total debt to shareholders' equity. Both of these numbers can be found on a company's balance sheet. To calculate debt-to-equity ratio, you divide a company's total liabilities by its shareholder equity. If a company has a debt-to-equity ratio of 2 to 1, it means that the company has two dollars of debt to every one dollar shareholders invest in the company. In other words, the company is taking on debt at twice the rate that its owners are investing in the company.

- *Inventory turnover ratio* compares a company's cost of sales on its income statement with its average inventory balance for the period. To calculate the average inventory balance for the period, look at the inventory numbers listed on the balance sheet. Take the balance listed for the period of the report and add it to the balance listed for the previous comparable period, and then divide by two. (Remember that balance sheets are snapshots in time. So the inventory balance for the previous period is the beginning balance for the current period, and the inventory balance for the current period is the ending balance.) To calculate the inventory turnover ratio, you divide a company's cost of sales (just below the net revenues on the income statement) by the average inventory for the period. If a company has an inventory turnover ratio of 2 to 1, it means that the company's inventory turned over twice in the reporting period.

- *Operating margin* compares a company's operating income to net revenues. Both of these numbers can be found on a company's income statement. To calculate operating margin, you divide a company's income from operations (before interest and income tax expenses) by its net revenues. Operating margin is usually expressed as a percentage. It shows, for each dollar of sales, what percentage was profit.

- *P/E ratio* compares a company's common stock price with its earnings per share. To calculate a company's P/E ratio, you divide a company's stock price by its earnings per share. If a company's stock is selling at $20 per share and the company is earning $2 per share, then the company's P/E Ratio is 10 to 1. The company's stock is selling at 10 times its earnings.

✎ What's It Mean?

Balance Sheet: A company's financial statement. It reports the company's assets, liabilities and net worth at a specific time.

Liability: A legal debt or obligation estimated via accrual accounting. (Recorded on the balance sheet, liabilities include loans, accounts payable, mortgages, deferred revenues, and accrued expenses. For example, the unpaid value of a mortgage or outstanding money owed to suppliers would be considered a liability. Current liabilities are debts payable within one year, while long-term liabilities are debts payable over a longer period.)

Portfolio Management: The art and science of making decisions about investment mix and policy, matching investments to objectives, asset allocation for individuals and institutions, and balancing risk vs. performance.

Source: Excerpted from "Dictionary," and reprinted with permission from www.investopedia.com. © 2004 Investopedia, Inc.

- *Working capital* is the money leftover if a company paid its current liabilities (that is, its debts due within one-year of the date of the balance sheet) from its current assets.

Bringing It All Together

Although this chapter discusses each financial statement separately, keep in mind that they are all related. The changes in assets and liabilities that you see on the balance sheet are also reflected in the revenues and expenses that you see on the income statement, which result in the company's gains or losses. Cash flows provide more information about cash assets listed on a balance sheet and are related, but not equivalent, to net income shown on the income statement. And so on. No one financial statement tells the complete story. But combined, they provide very powerful information for investors. And information is the investor's best tool when it comes to investing wisely.

Reading The Financial Pages

The financial pages are set up in columns as you see on Table 28.1.

Table 28.1. Reading The Financial Page

(A)	(B)	(C) Yld %	(D) P-E Ratio	(E) Sales 100s	(F) High	(G) Low	(H) Close	(I) Net Chg
Stock	Div	%	Ratio	100s	High	Low	Close	Chg
GnDyn	.32	3.2	20	225	10.25	10	10.13	-⅛

Source: Illinois Secretary of State, Securities Office.

Column A is the name of the corporation selling the stock ["Gndyn"]. Most of these names are abbreviated.

Column B is the dividends. On the example, the dividend was .32. That means last year it paid a dividend of 32 cents on each share of stock. (A dividend is what the company pays its stockholders from that year's profits. Usually the higher the dividend, the more profits the company is making.) If the column is empty, the company did not pay a dividend.

Column C, headed Yld. % (an abbreviation for yield) tells what you earned on your investment that day. This figure, shown as a percentage, represents the total amount of annual dividend divided by the current price of the stock.

Column D is the P-E (or price-earnings) ratio, a figure that helps the investor judge whether a stock is priced too high or too low. Corporations get this figure by dividing the corporation's earnings for the year by the number of shares of stock outstanding (that have been sold throughout the corporation's history and are still out in the hands of investors). That gives an "earnings per share" figure. To get the price-earnings ratio, the earnings per share is divided into the current price of the stock. If GnDyn stock is selling for $10.00 a share and the company is earning 50 cents per share, you divide 50 cents into $10.00 and get 20. The P-E ratio is 20 to 1, and the number 20 will be listed in the P-E ratio column.

Column E tells how many shares of the stock were sold that day. 100s means hundreds. In our example, 22,500 shares were sold (add 00 to the number in this column).

Columns F, G, H and I are the columns most people are interested in, the price information. Our example shows "high," 10.25; "low," 10; "close," 10.13; and "net change," - ⅛. On this particular day, GnDyn stock sold for as much as $10 ¼ a share, dropped to as little as $10 a share, and had risen to $10.13 a share when the stock market closed and trading stopped at 4:00 p.m. EST.

Column I "Net Chg." tells how much the price of the stock changed from the time the market opened until it closed. If the price was 10 ¼ when the market opened, changed some during the day then closed at 10 ¼, the column would show "..." meaning there was no change. In our example, we can see that the stock opened at 10 ¼ and closed at 10.13 a ⅛ decrease, so the ⅛ has a minus sign before it. If it had closed at 10 ¾, the net change would be + ½.

Bond Quotations

Bond price quotations use eighths, but with a difference. Bonds are sold in units of $1,000 but are quoted as 100s. To find the correct dollar value, move the decimal one place to the right.

For example, a bond quoted at 98 ¼ is equivalent to 98.25. Move the decimal one place the right to find the dollar price of the bond, which is $982.50. This bond is selling for less than $1,000 so it is selling at a discount, probably because of a low rate of interest.

A bond quoted at 102 ⅜ (102.375) equals $1,023.75. This bond is selling at a premium, probably because of a high interest rate or yield.

What is the dollar price of a bond quoted at 97 ⅞? _____

Table 28.2. Bond Quotations

1	2	3	4	5
Bonds	Cur. Yld.	Vol.	Close	Net Change
Chiquita 101/204	10.7	144	98 1/4	+ 3/8
K Mart 6.2s17	cv	50	91	+ 1/4
Disney zr05	...	414	45 3/4	+ 3/4

What It Says:

Column 1: Bond, Coupon Rate, Date of Maturity

A bond issued by Chiquita which matures in 2004 has a coupon rate of 101/ 2. This stated annual interest rate represents the 10.5% paid on the bond's $1,000 face value. The holder of this bond will receive $105 annually.

The "s" in the K Mart quotation separates the 6.2% rate from the 2017 maturity date. Note this bond is listed in fractions of 10s instead of 8s.

The Disney bonds are zero coupon bonds as indicated by the "zr." They do not pay annual interest.

Column 2: Current Yield

At this day's price, the holder of a Chiquita bond annually will receive 10.7 percent or $10.70 for every $100 invested. The current yield is calculated by dividing the annual interest by the closing price.

"cv" indicates the K Mart bond is convertible and can be exchanged for K Mart stock.

Column 3: Volume

On this day, 500,000 K Mart bonds were sold. The number 50 has been multiplied by 10,000.

Column 4, 5: Close, Net Change

The final price for Chiquita bonds was $982.50 which was $3.75 more than the final price on the day before.

Source: © 2005 National Association of Securities Dealers, Inc. (NASD).

Table 28.3. Mutual Fund Quotations

1	2	3	4
Fidelity Investments	NAV	Net Chg.	YTD % Ret.
MAGLN	83.35	-0.21	+5.8
OVRSE	32.15	+0.03	+4.2
Vanguard Group			
SELVALU	11.07	-0.03	+1.5
STAR	16.67	-0.03	+5.1

What It Says:

Column 1: Fund Family

Magellan and Overseas are names of mutual funds within the Fidelity Investment family. Fund Family Select Value and STAR are mutual funds within the Vanguard Group of funds.

Column 2: NAV

The NAV stands for the net asset value per share of the fund at the close of the previous NAV business day. A fund's NAV is calculated by adding up the value of all stocks or other securities owned by the fund, subtracting the liabilities, and then dividing by the number of fund shares available. However, sales commissions are not subtracted from the NAV.

Column 3: Net Change

The net change column shows the change in the NAV from the preceding day's quote. In Net Change this example, there was a 21-cent loss in net asset value of the Fidelity Magellan Mutual Fund as compared to the previous day. Both of the listed Vanguard funds lost three cents a share.

Column 4: YTD% Return

YTD % Return refers to the year-to-date percentage change in the value of the fund. That YTD% Return includes re-investment of all distributions, subtracting annual expenses charged to investors.

Readers of *Wall Street Journal* stock tables will sometimes find one-letter "codes" by certain funds. To interpret these codes, look for the "explanatory notes."

Source: © 2005 National Association of Securities Dealers, Inc. (NASD).

Chapter 29
Leveraged Trading

Small investors fare best if they can put their money into a diversified portfolio of stocks and hold them for the long term. But some investors are willing to take risks in hopes of realizing bigger gains in the short term. And they have devised a number of strategies for doing this.

Buying On Margin. Americans buy many things on credit, and stocks are no exception. Investors who qualify can buy "on margin," making a stock purchase by paying 50% down and getting a loan from their brokers for the remainder. If the price of stock bought on margin rises, these investors can sell the stock, repay their brokers the borrowed amount plus interest and commissions, and still make a profit. If the price goes down, however, brokers issue "margin calls," forcing the investors to pay additional money into their accounts so that their loans still equal no more than half of the value of the stock. If an owner cannot produce cash, the broker can sell some of the stock—at the investor's loss—to cover the debt.

Buying stock on margin is one kind of leveraged trading. It gives speculators—traders willing to gamble on high-risk situations—a chance to buy more shares. If their investment decisions are correct, speculators can make a greater profit, but if they are misjudge the market, they can suffer bigger losses.

About This Chapter: Text in this chapter has been excerpted and adapted from "Chapter 5: Stocks, Commodities, and Markets," *Outline of the U.S. Economy,* a publication of the Bureau of International Information Programs, U. S. State Department, February 2001.

The Federal Reserve Board ("the Fed"), the U.S. government's central bank, sets the minimum margin requirements specifying how much cash investors must put down when they buy stock. The Fed can vary margins. If it wishes to stimulate the market, it can set low margins. If it sees a need to curb speculative enthusiasm, it sets high margins. In some years, the Fed has required a full 100% payment, but for much of the time during the last decades of the 20th century, it left the margin rate at 50%.

Selling Short. Another group of speculators are known as "short sellers." They expect the price of a particular stock to fall, so they sell shares borrowed from their broker, hoping to profit by replacing the stocks later with shares purchased on the open market at a lower price. While this approach offers an opportunity for gains in a bear market, it is one of the riskiest ways to trade stocks. If a short seller guesses wrong, the price of stock he or she has sold short may rise sharply, hitting the investor with large losses.

Options. Another way to leverage a relatively small outlay of cash is to buy "call" options to purchase a particular stock later at close to its current price. If the market price rises, the trader can exercise the option, making a big profit by then selling the shares at the higher market price (alternatively, the trader can sell the option itself, which will have risen in value as the price of the underlying stock has gone up). An option to sell stock, called a "put" option, works in the opposite direction, committing the trader to sell a particular stock later at close to its current price. Much like short selling, put options enable traders to profit from a declining market. But investors also can lose a lot of money if stock prices do not move as they hope.

Commodities And Other Futures

Commodity "futures" are contracts to buy or sell certain goods at set prices at a predetermined time in the future. Futures traditionally have been linked to commodities such as wheat, livestock, copper, and gold, but in recent years growing amounts of futures also have been tied to foreign currencies or other financial assets as well. They are traded on about a dozen commodity exchanges in the United States, the most prominent of which include the Chicago Board of Trade, the Chicago Mercantile Exchange, and several exchanges in New York City. Chicago is the historic center of America's agriculture-based industries. Overall, futures activity rose to 417 million contracts in 1997, from 261 million in 1991.

Commodities traders fall into two broad categories: hedgers and speculators. Hedgers are business firms, farmers, or individuals that enter into commodity contracts to be assured access to a commodity, or the ability to sell it, at a guaranteed price. They use futures to protect themselves against unanticipated fluctuations in the commodity's price. Thousands of individuals, willing to absorb that risk, trade in commodity futures as speculators. They are lured to commodity trading by the prospect of making huge profits on small margins (futures contracts, like many stocks, are traded on margin, typically as low as 10 to 20% on the value of the contract).

Speculating in commodity futures is not for people who are averse to risk. Unforeseen forces like weather can affect supply and demand, and send commodity prices up or down very rapidly, creating great profits or losses. While professional traders who are well versed in the futures market are most likely to gain in futures trading, it is estimated that as many as 90% of small futures traders lose money in this volatile market.

Commodity futures are a form of "derivative"—complex instruments for financial speculation linked to underlying assets. Derivatives proliferated in the 1990s to cover a wide range of assets, including mortgages and interest rates. This growing trade caught the attention of regulators and members of Congress after some banks, securities firms, and wealthy

✎ What's It Mean?

Derivatives: Stock options are known as derivative investment instruments because their value derives from the security on which they are based. Stock options are contracts giving the purchaser the right to buy or sell a stock at a specific price within a certain period of time. Like all futures contracts, a stock option can be a very complicated and risky investment.

Futures: A futures contract is a commitment to buy or sell a specific amount of a commodity at a specific future date and price.

Source: Excerpted from "Your Investment Options," and reprinted with permission from the Office of the New York State Attorney General.

individuals suffered big losses on financially distressed, highly leveraged funds that bought derivatives, and in some cases avoided regulatory scrutiny by registering outside the United States.

Regulators

The Commodity Futures Trading Commission oversees the futures markets. It is particularly zealous in cracking down on many over-the-counter futures transactions, usually confining approved trading to the exchanges. But in general, it is considered a more gentle regulator than the SEC. In 1996, for example, it approved a record 92 new kinds of futures and farm commodity options contracts. From time to time, an especially aggressive SEC chairman asserts a vigorous role for that commission in regulating futures business.

Chapter 30

Other Investments

Investment information is focused primarily on stocks, bonds, and mutual funds. However, additional types of investments exist. This chapter provides an overview of them.

Insurance As An Investment

Although some insurance products have an investment component, such as variable life policies and some annuities, we don't suggest you consider insurance as one of your options for investment vehicles that make money. But if you really stop to ponder the role of insurance, you'll quickly realize that it's theoretically one of the most important purchases you make because it protects your other investments. When you buy health insurance or homeowner's insurance, you are making an investment toward realizing your goals.

For example, if you did not purchase health insurance and found that you had to undergo major surgery, you would be responsible for the hospital and doctor bills on your own. Most of us faced with this situation would have to

About This Chapter: "Insurance As An Investment" is reproduced with permission from CCH Financial Planning Toolkit, www.finance.cch.com, January, 2005. "Annuities" and "Variable Annuities" are excerpted and reprinted from documents published by the U.S. Securities and Exchange Commission dated June 5, 2000 and October 8, 2004 respectively. "Land," and "Tangible Assets" are excerpted from "Your Investment Options," reprinted with permission from the Office of the New York State Attorney General, n.d.

tap into our investments (our home's equity, sell some bonds and mutual funds) and, in a worst-case scenario, could end up unable to meet our financial obligations and lose our precious assets. Insurance is a type of investment that anticipates adverse events and mitigates or even eliminates the potential consequences, which can range from inconvenient to financial ruin.

Annuities

An annuity is a contract between you and an insurance company, under which you make a lump-sum payment or series of payments. In return, the insurer agrees to make periodic payments to you beginning immediately or at some future date.

There are two types of annuities—fixed and variable. In a fixed annuity, the insurance company guarantees that you will earn a minimum rate of interest during the time that your account is growing. The insurance company also guarantees that the periodic payments will be a guaranteed amount per dollar in your account. These periodic payments may last for a definite period, such as 20 years, or an indefinite period, such as your lifetime or the lifetime of you and your spouse.

In a variable annuity, by contrast, you can choose to invest your purchase payments from among a range of different investment options, typically mutual funds. The rate of return on your purchase payments, and the amount of the periodic payments you will eventually receive, will vary depending on the performance of the investment options you have selected.

Annuities also offer tax-deferred growth of earnings and a death benefit that will pay your beneficiary a guaranteed minimum amount, such as your total purchase payments.

Variable annuities are securities regulated by the SEC. Fixed annuities are not securities and are not regulated by the SEC.

Variable Annuities

[Variable annuities are not likely to be part of a young person's portfolio, but you might want to know that they are available.] Variable annuities have become a part of the retirement and investment plans of many Americans. Before you buy a variable annuity, you should know some of the basics—and be prepared to ask your insurance agent, broker, financial planner, or other financial professional lots of questions about whether a variable annuity is right for you.

A variable annuity offers a range of investment options. The value of your investment will vary depending on the performance of the investment options you choose. The investment options for a variable annuity are typically mutual funds that invest in stocks, bonds, money market instruments, or some combination of the three.

Although variable annuities are typically invested in mutual funds, variable annuities differ from mutual funds in several important ways:

1. Variable annuities let you receive periodic payments for the rest of your life (or the life of your spouse or any other person you designate). This feature offers protection against the possibility that, after you retire, you will outlive your assets.

2. Variable annuities have a death benefit. If you die before the insurer has started making payments to you, your beneficiary is guaranteed to receive a specified amount—typically at least the amount of your purchase payments. Your beneficiary will get a benefit from this feature if, at the time of your death, your account value is less than the guaranteed amount.

3. Variable annuities are tax-deferred. That means you pay no taxes on the income and investment gains from your annuity until you withdraw your money. You may also transfer your money from one investment option to another within a variable annuity without paying tax at the time of the transfer. When you take your money out of a variable annuity, however, you will be taxed on the earnings at ordinary income tax rates rather than lower capital gains rates. In general, the benefits of tax deferral will outweigh the costs of a variable annuity only if you hold it as a long-term investment to meet retirement and other long-range goals.

Other investment vehicles, such as IRAs and employer-sponsored 401(k) plans, also may provide you with tax-deferred growth and other tax advantages. For most investors, it will be advantageous to make the maximum allowable contributions to IRAs and 401(k) plans before investing in a variable annuity.

The tax rules that apply to variable annuities can be complicated—before investing, you may want to consult a tax adviser about the tax consequences to you of investing in a variable annuity.

Land

The most common investment people hold is real estate (in the form of home ownership). Over two-thirds of American's own their homes. Generally, home ownership is a good investment, as real estate prices generally rise. However, as the purchase of a home is usually the largest single investment a person makes, if real estate prices fall owners may have a hard time keeping up with their mortgages.

Tangible Assets

Assets that you can hold onto or touch are called tangible. They include gold coins and collectible items such as dolls, baseball cards, or stamps. Generally collectibles pay no interest and may or may not increase in value over the years. There is no regulated market for collectibles and should be used for enjoyment rather than investment.

☞ Remember!!

Variable annuities are designed to be long-term investments, to meet retirement and other long-range goals. Variable annuities are not suitable for meeting short-term goals because substantial taxes and insurance company charges may apply if you withdraw your money early. Variable annuities also involve investment risks, just as mutual funds do.

Source: SEC, 2004.

✎ What's It Mean?

Annuity: A series of fixed payments paid at regular intervals over the specified period of the annuity. The fixed payments are received after a period of investments that are made into the annuity.

Insurance: A contract (policy) under which a corporation (the insurer) provides financial protection against losses to an individual, business or organization (the insured) in exchange for periodic payments of a sum of money, known as a premium. For example, car insurance in exchange for a premium provides reimbursement for any damages in the event of an accident.

Real Estate: Land plus anything permanently fixed to it, including buildings, sheds, and other items attached to the structure. Unlike other investments, real estate is dramatically affected by the condition of the immediate area where the property is located. With the exception of a global recession, real estate is affected primarily by local factors.

Tangible Asset: An asset that has a physical form such as machinery, buildings and land.

Source: Excerpted from "Dictionary," and reprinted with permission from www.investopedia.com. © 2004 Investopedia, Inc.

Chapter 31

There's Always More To Learn About Investing

In this book, you have read about various savings vehicles as well as stocks, bonds, and mutual funds. There are other types of investment companies as well.

Other Types Of Investment Companies

Legally known as an "open-end company," a mutual fund is one of three basic types of investment companies. You should be aware that other pooled investment vehicles exist and may offer features that you desire. The two other basic types of investment companies are:

1. *Closed-end funds*, which, unlike mutual funds, sell a fixed number of shares at one time (in an initial public offering) that later trade on a secondary market; and

About This Chapter: "Other Types Of Investment Companies" is excerpted from a brochure entitled "Invest Wisely: An Introduction to Mutual Funds," published by the Securities and Exchange Commission (SEC), November 2, 2004. "Exchange-Traded Funds (ETFs)" is from a SEC fact sheet dated November 30, 2000. "Get Active—Join A Club," by Jason Van Bergen, is reprinted with permission from www.investopedia.com. © 2004 Investopedia.Inc. "Some Do's And Don'ts For Investors," is reprinted from *KidsInvest*, with permission from the State of Illinois Secretary of State, Securities Department [n.d.]; "More Do's And Don'ts" is excerpted from "10 Do's and Don'ts for Investors," reprinted with permission from the Secretary of the Commonwealth of Massachusetts, Securities Division, http://www.sec.state.ma.us/sct/sctidx.htm. Copyright 2000.

2. *Unit Investment Trusts* (UITs), which make a one-time public offering of only a specific, fixed number of redeemable securities called "units" and which will terminate and dissolve on a date specified at the creation of the UIT.

"Exchange-traded funds" (ETFs) are a type of investment company that aims to achieve the same return as a particular market index. They can be either open-end companies or UITs, but ETFs are not considered to be, and are not permitted to call themselves, mutual funds.

Exchange-Traded Funds (ETFs)

An exchange-traded fund, or ETF, is a type of investment company whose investment objective is to achieve the same return as a particular market index. An ETF is similar to an index fund in that it will primarily invest in the securities of companies that are included in a selected market index. An ETF will invest in either all of the securities or a representative sample of the securities included in the index. For example, one type of ETF, known as Spiders or SPDRs, invests in all of the stocks contained in the S&P 500 Composite Stock Price Index.

Although ETFs are legally classified as open-end companies or Unit Investment Trusts (UITs), they differ from traditional open-end companies and UITs in the following respects:

✎ What's It Mean?

ETF: A security that tracks an index and represents a basket of stocks like an index fund, but trades like a stock on an exchange, thus experiencing price changes throughout the day as it is bought and sold. The most widely known ETFs are SPDR (Spider), which tracks the S&P 500 index, and QQQ, which tracks the Nasdaq-100 Trust.

SPDRs (Spiders): Shares in a trust that owns stocks in the same proportion as that represented by the S&P 500 stock index. [The name comes from Standard & Poor's depository receipts—SPDRs.]

Source: Excerpted from "Dictionary," and reprinted with permission from www.investopedia.com. © 2004 Investopedia, Inc.

- ETFs do not sell individual shares directly to investors and only issue their shares in large blocks (blocks of 50,000 shares, for example) that are known as "Creation Units."

- Investors generally do not purchase Creation Units with cash. Instead, they buy Creation Units with a basket of securities that generally mirrors the ETF's portfolio. Those who purchase Creation Units are frequently institutions.

- After purchasing a Creation Unit, an investor often splits it up and sells the individual shares on a secondary market. This permits other investors to purchase individual shares (instead of Creation Units).

- Investors who want to sell their ETF shares have two options: (1) they can sell individual shares to other investors on the secondary market, or (2) they can sell the Creation Units back to the ETF. In addition, ETFs generally redeem Creation Units by giving investors the securities that comprise the portfolio instead of cash. So, for example, an ETF invested in the stocks contained in the Dow Jones Industrial Average (DJIA) would give a redeeming shareholder the actual securities that constitute the DJIA instead of cash. Because of the limited redeemability of ETF shares, ETFs are not considered to be—and may not call themselves—mutual funds.

- An ETF, like any other type of investment company, will have a prospectus. All investors that purchase Creation Units receive a prospectus. Some ETFs also deliver a prospectus to secondary market purchasers. ETFs that do not deliver a prospectus are required to give investors a document known as a Product Description, which summarizes key information about the ETF and explains how to obtain a prospectus. All ETFs will deliver a prospectus upon request. ETFs do not use profiles. ETFs that are legally structured as open-end companies (but not those that are structured as UITs) must also have statements of additional information (SAIs). Open-end ETFs (but not UIT ETFs) must provide shareholders with annual and semi-annual reports. Before purchasing ETF shares, you should carefully read all of an ETF's available information, including its prospectus.

The Nasdaq Stock Market also provides detailed information about ETFs, including how they work and the different types of ETFs. An ETF will have annual operating expenses and may also impose certain shareholders fees that are disclosed in the prospectus.

✔ Quick Tip
Investment Games Online

You can practice your investment skills for free and without risk by playing online trading, or investment, games. The services that maintain the sites make registration easy; most will provide you with $100,000 in virtual money to invest in real markets.

You can watch your profits rise and fall as you learn to develop the best-performing portfolio using a live trading simulation. You will learn to research and evaluate stocks, why specific stocks perform in certain ways, and why the market as a whole moves up and down.

There are hundreds of investment games online. Here is a sampling:

• The Stock Market Game (http://www.smg2000.org/). The granddaddy of educational investment games.

• FleetKids (http://www.fleetkids.com/) Choose from seven online games.

• Investopedia Simulator (http://simulator.investopedia.com/)

• Virtual Stock Exchange (http://game.marketwatch.com/Home/default.asp)

• nVe$stor (The League of American Investors) (http://investorsleague.com/index.html)

(See "Websites About Saving And Investing Money" for more investment games.)

—by KRD

Get Active—Join A Club

Most mutual fund investors would be hard pressed to name more than one or two of the top holdings within their favorite funds. This is because fund investors tend to compare mutual funds on the basis of their performance, without giving much thought to the specific stocks, bonds, and other financial instruments held within the fund. By their nature, mutual funds are a passive form of investment: we trust that the mutual fund manager has the expertise to choose the "right" investments that will provide the best returns in our portfolios.

As individual investors, we rarely have a large enough portfolio to make individual equity or bond selections on our own. As a result, the average retail portfolio is usually insufficiently diversified with individual stock picks, and we mutual fund holders are subjected to undue risk from one or two bad choices forming a large percentage of our total holdings. For these reasons, retail investors who are dissatisfied with the passive approach of mutual funds and want to take a more active role in choosing equities would do well to join an investment club.

The Benefits Of An Investment Club

You can think of an investment club as a small-scale mutual fund where decisions are made by a committee of non-professionals. In fact, an investment club can be established as a legal entity, either as a legal partnership or as a limited liability corporation, making its framework similar in principle to that of a mutual fund. Best of all, an investment club avoids the often burdensome management fees that all mutual funds levy on their unit-holders—fees that can have a significant impact on the overall return provided by mutual funds.

But the benefits of an investment club come with a major caveat: the returns (or losses) that the club realizes entirely depend on club members and their abilities to choose the right investments for their pooled funds. When we purchase mutual funds from the major fund companies, we are effectively purchasing the education, experience, skills, and discipline of the mutual fund managers entrusted with our money. When we join an investment club, we are attempting to replicate (and improve upon) some of those management attributes, but in a non-professional setting.

A typical investment club will meet on a regular basis (usually every month) to review its existing portfolio and to take suggestions from club members regarding new investment opportunities. The monthly meeting is an open floor, where each club member is able to voice his or her opinion about the suitability of new investments and other concerns regarding the performance of the pooled funds. Unlike any mutual fund, the investment club is a true democracy: here, the collective wisdom of the club members, combined with information they've gathered through intensive research, serves (in theory) to produce the best investment decisions.

Principles Of A Successful Investment Club

The National Association of Investors Corporation (NAIC) is the pre-eminent advocate of collaborative investing. It maintains extensive archives of information for starting and maintaining investment clubs. The NAIC advocates four simple principles that apply as much to making excellent individual investment decisions as they do to making democratic decisions in a club setting:

- Invest regularly.
- Reinvest dividends and capital gains.
- Discover and own leadership growth companies.
- Prudently diversify by company size and industry.

These principles are very much in keeping with a buy-and-hold strategy, characterized by low portfolio turnover rates. The average holding period for equities within NAIC-advocated portfolios is more than six years. The NAIC's principles and strategies have enabled it to claim that "on average, the long-term performance of NAIC members has generally outperformed market benchmarks." The NAIC boasts a large membership consisting of both individual investors and investment clubs, and it offers services for introducing individuals to clubs in their area.

You don't need to belong to the National Association of Investors Corporation to see the value in its overarching principles of discipline, diversification, reinvestment, and careful selection of top companies. Indeed, you don't even need to belong to an investment club to adopt these principles as part of your individual investment strategy.

♣ It's A Fact!!

What Is An Investment Club?

An investment club is a group of people who pool their money to make investments. Usually, investment clubs are organized as partnerships and, after the members study different investments, the group decides to buy or sell based on a majority vote of the members. Club meetings may be educational and each member may actively participate in investment decisions.

To learn more about investment clubs or investing, you may want to contact the National Association of Investors Corporation (NAIC) website. This membership organization provides education for individuals and members of investment clubs.

Source: Excerpted from "Investment Clubs and the SEC," U.S. Securities and Exchange Commission (SEC), 2004.

But there are clear benefits to the discipline and decision-making typical of investment clubs. By maintaining a strict regimen of regular meetings, investment clubs force individual investors to adopt an active investment style, in which portfolio review is ongoing and investment decisions—whether to buy, sell, or hold—are constantly made.

Furthermore, the decision-making power of the investment club resides in its democracy. Each member brings his or her own education, experience, and skills to the group, all of which are used to their fullest when evaluating and debating a decision. The power of the mutual fund comes from professional management that may be able to beat average market returns. The power of the investment club comes from the collective talents of numerous individual members.

Some Do's and Don'ts For Investors

• Never invest more than you can afford to lose.

• Never send cash or a cashier's check through the mail or give it to a messenger sent by the salesperson. Never give your credit card number over the phone.

• Deal only with firms and individuals you have researched and trust.

- Beware of any investment offered by a stranger over the phone. Never send money for the purchase of an investment as a result of a telephone sales pitch.

- Do your homework. Don't invest in something you don't understand. Make sure the product and the salesperson are properly registered.

- A high-pressure sales pitch means trouble. Be suspicious of anyone who encourages you to make an investment decision immediately.

- Beware of promises of spectacular profits. Investments with great profit potential also have a great amount of risk.

- Do not invest on the basis of tips and rumors. Obtain all the facts, know your rights and demand information in writing.

- Never write a check to the sales representative.

- Be suspicious of sending checks to addresses that are different from the brokerage firm address, especially P.O. box addresses.

- Insist on transaction confirmations and regular account statements. Review them promptly and verify that the information is correct. If you find an error, insist in writing that it be corrected immediately.

- Don't make any unwarranted assumptions. If it is not in the prospectus, you cannot assume it to be accurate.

- Save all records of transactions and correspondence with the broker/advisor and the firm. Never part with original documents.

- Take notes of your conversations with your broker/advisor(and include the date).

- If in doubt—do not invest.

More Do's And Don'ts For Investors

- Look with doubt on promises that you can double your money or even expect a high return on your investment within a short period of time.

- Turn down money requests accompanied by high-pressure warnings like "Tomorrow will be too late: or "Act now because there will soon be long waiting lists of others who want to take advantage of this golden opportunity."

- Always demand written information about the organization behind the investment plan and its past track record. But bear in mind that even printed documents can easily be created, forged, or falsified.

- Be suspicious of "inside information," hot tips, and rumors that supposedly will give you a big advantage over other, less knowledgeable investors.

- Ask for a prospectus, offering circular, financial statement, or other similar document before you even consider investing. Then read the small print carefully and make sure you understand the terms thoroughly before signing any kind of commitment.

- Before making a commitment, get a professional opinion from your attorney, stockbroker, accountant, or other reliable consultant.

- When in doubt, make no promises or commitments, no matter how tentative. It is far better to wait and lose an opportunity than to take the plunge and lose everything.

- When hounded on the phone by a promoter, don't be afraid to hang up without explanation. You do not owe the caller anything—in fact, this kind of solicitation is an invasion of your privacy.

Part Seven

If You Need More Information

Chapter 32

Websites About Saving And Investing Money

Financial Information And Education

AmSouth Bank
http://www.amsouth.com
Personal Finance Library: http://www.amsouth.com/pfrc/library

CCH Financial Planning
http://www.finance.cch.com

Citigroup Financial
http://www.citigroup.com
Education Program: http://financialeducation.citigroup.com/citigroup/financialeducation

CNN Money
http://money.cnn.com

New York Federal Reserve Bank
http://www.newyorkfed.org
Education: http://www.newyorkfed.org/education

Managing Your Money
Public Broadcasting Service (PBS)
http://www.pbs.org/newshour/on2/budget.html

About This Chapter: Websites are listed in this chapter alphabetically by topic. Information in this chapter was compiled from many sources deemed reliable. The list is not all-inclusive, and inclusion does not constitute endorsement. All website addresses were verified in May 2005.

MotleyFool.com

http://www.fool.com
Teens and Their Money: http://
www.fool.com/teens

National Council on Economic Education (NCEE)

http://www.ncee.net

U.S. Securities and Exchange Commission (SEC)

http://www.sec.gov
Online Publications for Investors:
http://www.sec.gov/investor/
pubs.shtml
Test Your Money $marts: http://
www.sec.gov/investor/tools/
quiz.htm

Investment Advice And Education

Alliance for Investor Education

Investor's Clearinghouse: http://
www.investoreducation.org

American Association of Individual Investors

http://www.aaii.com

Bloomberg.com

http://www.bloomberg.com

Bond Market Association

http://www.bondmarkets.com
Investing in Bonds: http://
www.investinginbonds.com

Columbia Funds: Young Investor

http://www.younginvestor.com

A.G. Edwards, Inc.

http://www.agedwards.com

Fidelity Investments

http://www.fidelity.com

Foundation for Investor Education (FIE)

http://www.foundationforinvestor
education.org

Future Investors Club of America, Inc.

http://www.futureinvestorsclub.com

Financial Planning Association

http://www.fpanet.org
National Financial Planning
Support Center: http://
www.fpanet.org/public

Investment Company Institute (ICI)

http://www.ici.org

Investopedia.com

http://www.investopedia.com

Investorguide.com
http://www.investorguide.com
Investor Basics: http://
www.investorguide.com/basics.html

Investor Protection Trust
http://www.investorprotection.org

Investor Words
http://www.investorwords.com

Kiplinger
http://www.kiplinger.com

Merrill Lynch
http://www.ml.com

Morgan Stanley
Individual Investors: http://
www.morganstanleyindividual.com

National Association of Investors Corporation (NAIC)
http://www.better-investing.org

National Association of Securities Dealers
http://www.nasd.com

North American Securities Administrators Association
Investor Education: http://
www.nasaa.org/investor_education
Investing Online Resource Center:
http://www.investingonline.org

T. Rowe Price, Inc.
http://www.troweprice.com

Salomon Smith Barney
http://www.smithbarney.com
Young Investors Network: http://
www.smithbarney.com/yin

Charles Schwab
http://www.schwab.com

SmartMoney
http://www.smartmoney.com

U.S. Department of Labor, Bureau of Labor Statistics
Statistical updates on the U.S.
economy: http://www.bls.gov/eag/
eag.us.htm

U.S. Treasury Direct
Savings bonds: http://
www.treasurydirect.gov

Washington Mutual
http://www.wamu.com
Planning and Education: http://
www.wamu.com/wmfinancial/
planningeducation/
planningeducation.asp

YoungBiz
http://www.YoungBiz.com

YoungInvestor.com
(Columbia Funds)
http://www.younginvestor.com

Online Investment Games

Investopedia Simulator
http://simulator.investopedia.com

It All Adds Up
http://www.italladdsup.org

nVe$tor
The League of American Investors
http://investorsleague.com/index.html

Planet Orange
http://www.orangekids.com

Stock Market Game
Foundation for Investor Education
http://www.smg2000.org

Stock-Trak
http://www.stocktrak3.com

Money

Federal Reserve Education
http://www.federalreserve
education.org

Know Your Money
U.S. Secret Service
http://www.secretservice.gov/
know_your_money.shtml

Online Calculators

Alliance for Investor Education (AIE)
Savings Calculator: http://
www.investoreducation.org/
cindex2.cfm

American Savings Education Council (ASEC)
Savings Calculator: http://
www.asec.org/tools/ycalcs.htm

Bankrate.com
Savings Calculator: http://
www.bankrate.com/brm/calc/
savecalc.asp

Bureau of the Public Debt
Various Calculators:
www.publicdebt.treas.gov/sav/
savcalc2.htm

CCH Financial Planning
Various Calculators: http://
www.finance.cch.com/tools/
calcs.asp

U.S. Securities and Exchange Commission
Mutual Fund Cost Calculator:
http://www.sec.gov/answers/
mfcal.htm

Online Financial Publications

Barron's Online
http://online.barrons.com

Business Week
http://www.businessweek.com

Entrepreneur
http://www.entrepreneur.com/mag

Forbes
http://www.forbes.com

Investor's Business Daily
http://www.investors.com

Kiplinger's Personal Finance
http://www.kiplinger.com/
magazine

SmartMoney
http://www.smartmoney.com/mag

Wall Street Journal
http://www.wsj.com

YoungMoney
http://www.youngmoney.com

Stock Exchanges

American Stock Exchange
http://www.amex.com

NASDAQ
http://www.nasdaq.com

New York Stock Exchange, Inc.
http://www.nyse.com

Philadelphia Stock Exchange
http://www.phlx.com

Toronto Stock Exchange (TSX)
http://www.tse.com

Chapter 33
Directory Of Investment Organizations

American Association of Individual Investors (AAII)
625 N. Michigan Avenue, Suite 1900
Chicago, IL 60611-3110
Toll-Free: 800-428-2244
Phone: 312-280-0170
Fax: 312-280-9883
Website: http://www.aaii.com
E-mail: members@aaii.com

American Financial Services Association (AFSA)
AFSA Education Foundation
919 Eighteenth St., NW, Suite 300
Washington, DC 20006
Phone: 202-296-5544
Fax: 202-223-0321
Website: http://www.afsaef.org
E-mail: info@afsaef.org

America Saves (Consumer Federation of America)
1424 16th Street, NW, Suite 604
Washington, DC 20036
Phone: 202-387-6121
Website: http://
www.americasaves.org
E-mail:
information@americasaves.org

American Savings Education Council
2121 K Street, NW, Suite 600
Washington, DC 20037-1896
Phone: 202-659-0670
Fax: 202-775-6322
Website: http://www.asec.org
E-mail: asecinfo@asec.org

American Stock Exchange

86 Trinity Place
New York, NY 10006
212-306-1000
Website: http://www.amex.com
E-mail: amexfeedback@amex.com

Bond Market Association

360 Madison Avenue
New York, NY 10017-7111
Phone: 646-637-9400
Fax: 646-637-9126
Website: http://
www.bondmarkets.com

Consumer Federation of America

1424 16th Street, NW, Suite 604
Washington, DC 20036
Phone: 203-387-6121
Website: http://
www.consumerfed.org

Federal Citizen Information Center

1800 F Street, NW, Room G-142, (XCC)
Washington, DC 20405
Toll-Free: 888-878-3256
Phone: 202-501-1794
Website: http://
www.pueblo.gsa.gov

Federal Trade Commission (FTC)

CRC-240
Washington, DC 20580
Toll-Free: 877-FTC-HELP (392-4357
Phone: 202-326-2222
Website: http://www.ftc.gov

Financial Planning Association

1615 L Street NW, Suite 650
Washington, DC 20036-5606
Toll-Free: 800-322-4237
Fax: 303-759-0749
Website: http://www.fpanet.org

Foundation for Investor Education

120 Broadway, 35th Floor
New York, NY 10271
Fax: 212-968-0742
Website: http://www.foundationfor
investoreducation.org
E-mail: foundation@
foundationforinvestoreducation.org

Future Investors Club of America

876 Sand Creek Circle
Weston, FL 33327
Phone: 954-217-1353
Fax: 954-384-2745
Website: http://
www.futureinvestorsclub.com
E-mail: ficaworld@aol.com

Investment Company Institute (ICI)
1401 H Street, NW
Washington, DC, 20005.
Phone: 202-326-5800
Website: http://www.ici.org

Investors Alliance, Inc.
P.O. Box 10136
Pompano Beach, FL 33061-9951
Toll-Free: 866-627-9090
Website: http://PowerInvestor.com
E-mail: info@powerinvestor.com

Investor Protection Trust
919 18th Street NW, Suite 300
Washington, DC 20006-5517
Phone: 202-775-2111 or
202-775-2113
Website: http://
www.investorprotection.org
E-mail:
iptinfo@investorprotection.org

Jump$tart Coalition
919 18th St., NW, 3d Floor
Washington, DC 20006
Toll-Free: 888-45-EDUCATE
Fax: 202-223-0321
Website: http://
www.jumpstartcoalition.org
E-mail:
info@jumpstartcoalition.org

The National Academy Foundation: Academy of Finance
39 Broadway, Suite 1640
New York, NY 10006
Phone: 212-635-2400
Fax: 212-635-2409
Website: http://www.naf.org

NASDAQ
One Liberty Plaza
165 Broadway
New York, NY 10006
Phone: 202-728-8333
Website: http://www.nasdaq.com

National Association of Investors Corp. (NAIC)
P.O. Box 220
Royal Oak, MI 48068
Phone: 248-583-6242
Fax: 248-583-4880
Website: http://www.better-invest
ing.org
E-mail: service@better-investing.org

National Association of Securities Dealers
list of district offices available on
website under "Contact Us"
Main NASD phone number:
301-590-6500
BrokerCheck Hotline:
800-289-9999
Website: http://www.nasd.com

National Council on Economic Education (NCEE)

1140 Avenue of the Americas
New York, NY 10036
Toll-Free: 800-338-1192
Phone: 212-730-7007
Fax: 212-730-1793
Website: http://www.ncee.net
E-mail: sales@ncee.net

National Endowment for Financial Education (NEFE)

5299 DTC Boulevard, Suite 1300
Greenwood Village, CO 80111
Phone: 303-741-6333
Website: http://www.nefe.org

New York Stock Exchange, Inc.

11 Wall Street.
New York, NY 10005
Phone: 212-656-3000
Website: http://www.nyse.com

North American Securities Administrators Association, Inc.

750 1ˢᵗ Street, NE, Suite 1140
Washington, DC 20002
Phone: 202-737-0900
Fax: 202-783-3571
Fax-on-Demand: 888-84-NASAA
Website: http://www.nasaa.org

Philadelphia Stock Exchange

1900 Market Street
Philadelphia, PA 19103-3584
Toll-Free: 800-THE-PHLX
Fax: 215-496-5460
Website: http://www.phlx.com

Social Security Administration (SSA)

6401 Security Boulevard
Baltimore, MD 21235
Toll-Free: 800-772-1213
TTY: 800-325-0778
Website: http://www.ssa.gov

Toronto Stock Exchange (TSX)

P.O. Box 450
3ʳᵈ Floor, 130 King Street W.
Toronto, ON M5X 1J2
Canada
Toll-Free: 888-873-8392
Phone: 416-947-4670
Website: http://www.tse.com

U.S. Department of Labor

Employee Benefits Security
Administration
200 Constitution Avenue, NW
Washington, DC 20210
Toll-Free: 800-998-7542
(publications)
Website: http://www.dol.gov/ebsa

U.S. Department of the Treasury

Bureau of the Public Debt
Frances Perkins Building
200 Constitution Avenue, N.W.
Washington, DC 20210
Toll-Free: 866-444-3273
TTY: 877-889-5627
Website: http://
www.publicdebt.treas.gov

U.S. Securities and Exchange Commission (SEC)

Office of Investor Education and
Assistance
450 5ᵗʰ Street, NW
Washington, DC 20549
Phone: 202-551-6551
Website: http://www.sec.gov
E-mail: help@sec.gov

Young Entrepreneur's Organization (YEO)

500 Montgomery Street, Suite 500
Alexandria, VA 22314
Phone: 703-519-6700
Fax: 703-519-1864
Website: http://www.yeo.org
E-mail: info@yeo.org

Chapter 34

Books, Magazines, And More About Saving And Investing

Books

To make topics easy to identify, books are listed alphabetically by title in the following format: *Title*, author (publisher, date)

50 Great Businesses for Teens, Sarah Riehm (Macmillan, 1997)

Banking on Our Future: : A Program For Teaching You and Your Kids About Money, John Bryant and Michael Levin (Beacon Press, 2002)

Becoming an Investor: Building Your Wealth by Investing in Stocks, Bonds, and Mutual Funds, Peter I. Hupalo (HCM Publishing, 2002)

Business Lessons for Young Entrepreneurs: 30 Things I Learned before the Age of Thirty, Mark Csordos (Customer Service Training Essentials, 2000)

Complete Idiot's Guide to Managing Your Money, 4th Edition, Robert K. Heady, Christy Heady, and Hugo Ottolenghi (Alpha Books, 2004)

Complete Idiot's Guide to Money for Teens, Susan Shelly (Alpha Books, 2001)

Dollars and Sense for Kids, Janet Bodnar (Dearborn Trade, 2004)

Early to Rise: A Young Adult's Guide to Investing...and Financial Decisions that Can, Michael Stahl (Silver Lake Publishing, 2005)

Everything Personal Finance: Manage, Budget, Save and Invest Your Money Wisely, Peter Sander (Adams Media, 2003)

Get a Financial Life: Personal Finance In Your Twenties And Thirties, Beth Kobliner (Simon and Schuster, 2000)

Investing 101, Kathy Kristof (Bloomberg Press, 2000)

Investing for Dummies, Eric Tyson (John Wiley, 2002)

Investing Online for Dummies, Kathleen Sindell (John Wiley, 2005)

Money Matters for Teens, Larry Burkett and Marine Wooding (Moody Press, 2001)

Motley Fool Investment Guide for Teens: 8 Steps to Having More Money Than Your Parents Ever Dreamed Of, David Gardner, Tom Gardner, and Selena Maranjian (Simon and Schuster, 2002)

Only Investment Guide You'll Ever Need, Andrew Tobias (Harcourt, 2005)

Organize Your Personal Finances ... In No Time, Debbie Stanley (Pearson Education, 2004)

Personal Finance for Dummies, Eric Tyson (John Wiley, 2003)

Secrets of Wealth: The Beginner's Guide to Financial Freedom, Fabio Marciano (Four Green Houses, 2003)

Stock Investing for Dummies, Paul Mladjenovic (John Wiley, 2002)

Street Wise: A Guide for Teen Investors, Janet Bamford (Bloomberg Press, 2000)

Teen Guide to Personal Financial Management, Marjolijn Bijlefeld and Sharon K. Zoumbaris (Greenwood Publishing, 2000)

Teenage Investor: How to Start Early, Invest Often, and Build Wealth, Timothy Olsen (McGraw-Hill, 2003)

Teenvestor: The Practical Investment Guide for Teens and Their Parents, Emmanuel Modu and Andrea Walker (Perigee, 2002)

Wall Street Journal Guide to Understanding Personal Finance, Kenneth M. Morris and Virginia B. Morris (Simon and Schuster, 2004)

Wall Street Wizard: Sound Ideas from a Savvy Teen Investor, Jay Liebowitz (Simon and Schuster, 2000)

Wealthy Barber: Everyone's Common-Sense Guide to Becoming Financially Independent, David Chilton (Crown Publishing, 1991)

Young Entrepreneur's Edge: Using Your Ambition, Independence, and Youth to Launch a Successful Business, Jennifer Kushell (Random House, 1999)

Young Entrepreneur's Guide to Starting and Running a Business, Steve Mariotti with Tony Towle and Debra Desalvo (Three Rivers Press, 1999)

Magazines (Print)

Bloomberg Personal Finance

Business Week

Entrepreneur

Fortune

Forbes

Kiplinger's Personal Finance

Money

SmartMoney

Worth

Young Money Magazine

Newspapers

Barron's

Investor's Business Daily

The Wall Street Journal

Television Shows About Finances

Wall Street Week (PBS)

The Money Wheel (CNBC)

Nightly Business Report (PBS)

See complete listings at:
http://dir.yahoo.com/Entertainment/Television_Shows/
Business_and_Economy

Index

Index

Page numbers that appear in *Italics* refer to illustrations. Page numbers that have a small 'n' after the page number refer to information shown as Notes at the beginning of each chapter. Page numbers that appear in **Bold** refer to information contained in boxes on that page (except Notes information at the beginning of each chapter).